MR. LYWARD'S ANSWER

By the same author

Novels
YES, FAREWELL
CHILDHOOD AT ORIOL
THE MIDNIGHT DIARY
THE TROUBLE WITH JAKE

Factual
FULL THROTTLE
WHEELS TAKE WINGS
ALAN PARSON'S SCRAPBOOK
THE LABYRINTH OF EUROPE
THE DEBATABLE LAND
THE AGE OF SLATE
TURNED TOWARDS THE SUN – AN AUTOBIOGRAPHY.
MARY & RICHARD

Poetry
POEMS AS ACCOMPANIMENT TO A LIFE
POEMS TO MARY
THE FLYING CASTLE
OUT ON A LIMB
OPEN DAY AND NIGHT

Plays
THE NIGHT OF THE BALL
THE DAY THE WELSH ROSE
THE MODERN EVERYMAN

Film
TURNED TOWARDS THE SUN

MICHAEL BURN

Mr. Lyward's Answer

From square pegs to well-rounded adolescents:
A proven answer for reshaping troubled lives

BADGER
MOON

BADGER MOON

First published in Great Britain in 1956 by Hamish Hamilton
This edition published in Great Britain in 2025 by Badger Moon

10 9 8 7 6 5 4 3 2 1

Copyright © 1956 Michael Burn
Copyright © 2025 Estate of Michael Burn

The moral right of the author has been asserted.

Photograph credits:
© Gabriel Kessler
© Peter Mould
© Estate of Alan Wendelken

Text design by Badger Moon

All rights reserved.

No part of this publication may be reproduced, stored in a retrieval system, or transmitted in any form or by any means, electronic, mechanical, photocopying, recording, or otherwise, without the prior written permission of the publisher.

A CIP catalogue record for this book is available from the British Library.

ISBN 978-1-0684162-0-0 (paperback)

Printed and bound by
CPI Group (UK) Ltd, Croydon, CR0 4YY

Papers used by Badger Moon are from well-managed forests and other sustainable forests

www.badgermoon.com

To an Adventure in Living!

Top: Michael Burn and Mr. Lyward
Middle: Finchden Manor
Bottom: A session with Mr. Lyward
                          circa 1955-1956

FOREWORD

When *Mr. Lyward's Answer* was first published in 1956 it brought George Lyward - and the community he founded at Finchden Manor - to public prominence both in the UK and in the United States. The community was described at the time as 'one of the most important educational experiments of the century'. Lyward's impact was recognised subsequently by the award of the O.B.E. and an invitation to give an address in Westminster Abbey.

Lyward hated labels, preferring everything to be as fluid as possible, but if we need a label for Finchden Manor, therapeutic community will do. Hundreds of troubled and troublesome boys and young men were referred to what Lyward liked to call 'a form of hospitality'. Some were there because everything else had been tried and those in charge of them turned to Lyward's unorthodox approach in desperation. Some were sent by a number of professionals who knew of Lyward's notable success in reaching out to, providing a sense of safety for, and achieving a deep understanding of those in his care.

Many familiar with Lyward's work had believed it would be impossible to describe it fully or accurately, given his genius for improvisation and operating without any one theoretical framework. Over some years he himself tried to produce a book setting out his methods and approach, but the task proved impossible even for him. In the end, he reluctantly invited the poet, writer and ex-commando Michael Burn to come for an extended stay at Finchden Manor as an adjunct member of the staff team, and this book is the result.

The consensus of those familiar with Finchden is that Burn did a remarkable job, and the book is a fascinating read, detailed, and full of insights. It contains descriptions of daily life in the community, portraits of Lyward, his staff and several of the boys, numerous accounts of Lyward in action, and many interviews with the man himself.

But, possibly because Lyward insisted on editorial approval of the manuscript, it would also be fair to say this book offers a somewhat romanticised, and partial, depiction of the work he undertook at Finchden Manor. Some have said that Lyward had the gift of transforming his own weaknesses into strengths. He seemed always to be on top of situations, yet harboured a deep sense of insecurity. He also could be deliberately fierce at times, even frightening. He called these interventions deciding to 'let fly', or the 'surgical' aspect of his work. A colleague reported Lyward telling him 'It is the fear of my anger that keeps Finchden going.' [1]

An exploration of these aspects of Lyward's approach would have been valuable - particularly because it is so at odds with current trends. One former Finchden boy, who returned as a staff member in later life, has since written an insightful memoir of his time there. This account describes Lyward's genius and also conveys some of the more problematical aspects of that genius in action. [2]

Nonetheless, *Mr. Lyward's Answer* is a vivid account of a community and the help it offered people who felt at the end of their tether. It is a landmark achievement, and a must-read for anyone interested in non-medical approaches to psychological disorders, therapeutic communities, the nature of community living, and the role of intuition in the work of an expert.

Norman Alm &
Tom Robinson

---

[1] Auster, Simon (1974) The anger of a therapist. The New Era, Vol 55, No 3, Special Issue on George Lyward. pp. 68-69. Available at finchden.com/auster
[2] Wendelken, Alan F. (2019) A Finchden Experience.
eBook. Lulu Enterprises Inc. Available at finchden.com/wendelken

Top: Finchden Manor in winter
Middle: The boys out with their go-kart
Bottom: Mr. Lyward

circa 1955-1956

PROSPERO ... The charm dissolves apace,
>   And as the morning steals upon the night,
>   Melting the darkness, so their rising senses
>   Begin to chase the ignorant fumes that mantle
>   Their clearer reason ...
>   Their understanding
>   Begins to swell, and the approaching tide
>   Will shortly fill the reasonable shores
>   That now lie foul and muddy.

THE TEMPEST *Act V, Scene 1*

PREFACE

Finchden Manor exists, and all the people in this book are or have been alive. Their names, except for those of Mr Lyward and his staff, are names I have imagined.

I am deeply grateful to Mr Lyward for his trust and candour in disclosing the story of his life's work to one who three years ago was a stranger. I am also grateful to Mrs Lyward, to his staff and to all the psychiatrists, teachers, social workers, old boys, and present boys of Finchden Manor, who have helped me with their advice and recollections, and must for obvious reasons remain anonymous; particularly to the old boy who in Chapter Nine goes under the name of Alastair Wilton, for permission to tell his story in full; most of all perhaps to Flynn, for his permission.

I have no expert knowledge of either education or psychiatry, and ask all educationists and doctors who may read this book to consider it as a narrative written by a respectful tourist in their land. Its chief purpose has been to serve as an introduction to Mr Lyward's work, about which no one can write thoroughly except himself.

M.B.

CHAPTER ONE

Finchden Manor was a timbered black-and-white caterpillar of a house, with a long lawn and a rose-garden, a mile from the demure country town of Tenterden.

The older part of the building was Jacobean, the rest a Victorian imitation tagged on. The bays overhung, and one was supported on huge struts, like an old tree. The house looked beloved; and at night enchanted. Till ten o'clock every window blazed. The voices were all young. Chopin came from one room, boogie-woogie from another, and there was nothing haunted; but later, after the lights were out, the house withdrew into itself, moonlight smoothed out bulges and slants, and tiers of zebras seemed to have left their stripes up and down the walls.

A hedge hid it from the road. You entered from the courtyard, and knew at once it could not be a private house. Even if no boy scampering like a monkey, or monkey scampering like a boy ran past, you knew; from the outbuildings, the field with its home-made goalposts, the pond that some boy always wanted to turn into a swimming bath, and the raggedness of the high cedars.

I think of it in two aspects, with which I associate two sides of what I witnessed there, and two sides of myself. The road skirting the townward side, though small and carrying little traffic, linked London directly with the sea. That way the boys walked to the cinema, the library, the shops, or to meet a girl; that way lay houses, newspapers, regular communications, and the postman came. The other way a lane slunk past the old brick pillars of the gateless drive, and after a few yards dropped rapidly to sea-level. You realized that the house was on a long ridge commanding a narrow valley. Very few houses were visible, and those few farms. Dense woods, from which flashed one white windmill, smothered the opposite slope, and southward the valley broadened in dyked pastures to the marshes. Sheep roamed them through spring and summer; in winter they were flooded and the floods would freeze.

I used to walk that way, sometimes at night, and the owl became its voice. The marshes had their legends, and were talked of as being strange and unlike other country. The sun sank boldly in front of the house, behind the four pinnacles of Tenterden Church, while here at the back the moon stole up, the air grew colder, the outlines less secure. A white mist rose out of the sodden ground, as if the sea that had covered it hundreds of years before had left a ghost. Evening after evening this mist rose, until it had breasted the ridge and islanded the four pinnacles and carved tower, which seemed to float. Bungalows, landladies, esplanades, were not far off, but here the land had not yet surrendered, and you could easily go out of sight of habitation and feel lost. The tower is a mark for miles; I imagined sailors straining their eyes in the old days, along a coast that has remained treacherous.

Thus, on the Tenterden side, things were as they are familiar to most of us from newspapers, the ground was built on and 'developed', life lived according to convention, nothing went too deep. The other side seemed still to be waiting; not for the builder and contractor, but explorers. It was open and exciting. The house stood fast between the two—tranquil, set apart, able to disarm violence, absorb tragedy and forget both; a place of occasional squalls, yet one of the gayest and most peaceful I have ever known, and the work done there among the noblest.

The enthusiasm of Dr Selwyn first took me there and introduced me to Mr Lyward. It was at the time of the notorious Craig-Bentley case. Two boys, of 'ordinary' family, living in a 'respectable' suburb, had gone out armed one night and, when pursued, one of them had killed a policeman. The whole country had become disturbed, not only by our responsibility for hanging one of the boys, but because crimes of this kind were being reported every day. Decent parents read the newspapers and wondered: 'If in that home, why not in mine? Do I know so little of my own child? Could mine be drawn or draw others into an act like that?' They became so eager to be offered cures for disorders hitherto unthinkable, that dozens of articles were published in the newspapers by those who had, or professed to have experience of juvenile delinquency. The answer, said Dr Selwyn, had been given for the past twenty-five years by Mr Lyward, although he had remained unknown to the public, and no newspaper had asked him for an article.

Dr Selwyn knew what he was talking about, since he had sent one of his patients to Mr Lyward; this boy had previously been asked to leave two world-famous schools, and his family had been at their wits' end what to do with him. He had at once taken to Mr Lyward and already been for some time under his care; with what Dr Selwyn called amazing results.

But Dr Selwyn was also a man given to enthusiasm, and I took everything he said rather guardedly. From what he claimed for Mr Lyward and had previously written to me, we were about to call on a St John the Baptist, and the Weald of Kent through which we were driving began to take on the aspect of the wilderness. In an hour or two we were evidently to see a man in whose establishment 'was no forced discipline and no corporal punishment—no limits of class or money—psychology is not talked, it is done—Christian behaviour is not preached, it is lived...'. I knew Dr Selwyn's enthusiasms of old, and enjoyed them; but the more he praised, the louder a voice within me protested, 'Be careful. Don't be carried away.'

He also quoted Mr Lyward as having said that anyone who wished to write about his work would need to be a poet. A strange comment. It held a challenge, and was not a label. Poetry is seldom dogmatic. It does not answer directly, or furnish solutions. It is oblique, may include anything, and thrives on the unexpected; a life's work, about all of life. I was curious about the poetry, and arrived in a mood half-cautious, half-excited.

We drew up in the courtyard outside a brick seventeenth century porch. A window opened from what seemed to be a kitchen; a boy looked out and stared, but said nothing. Another crossed the yard. He wore a brown leather belt, a faded leather jacket with tassels over the breast pockets, and a porter's cap set at a slouch. He was sharpening a peeled stick with a hunter's knife. He said politely, with a put-on American accent: "Do you want Mr Lyward? I think he's in. I'll ring.'

A girl came to the door and Dr Selwyn and I went in.

The hall was old oak, and the polished staircase gleamed. We were taken into a big sitting-room. Reproductions of old masters hung from the panelling, and Scarlatti stood open on a grand piano; downstairs somebody was playing Bach. We were not yet in the study, but the room where the house-master of a public school receives parents; I remembered rooms like it from my boyhood. I sat in a deep window-seat and looked out at the garden of a well-kept country house; at the long lawn, with an ancestral cedar of Lebanon in the middle, bushes clipped in the shape of gigantic cauldrons, an old brick archway climbed by roses, and through another archway in a hedge a glimpse of the rose-garden. Where were the tennis and the tea-party?

I heard shouting. Several boys had come out of another part of the house. I had to crane my neck, since they avoided the formal strip of garden under the window-seat. The sun shone. One was stripped to the waist; another wore a brilliant floral shirt like an American negro. Two were wrestling. These were not the guests for whom the atmosphere appeared to wait.

The Bach downstairs ended.

Later, I was to have a dozen contradictory impressions of Mr Lyward. But as he entered, I had a feeling of relief. He looked none of the types I had dreaded finding; not a professional crank or self-conscious eccentric; not the instructor of the young, complex, but hearty in manner, who is at pains to swear and 'be like everybody else'; not a Presence, or Grand Old Man, complete with half an acre of forehead, a prophet's hair, and the kind of majestic kindliness that leaves you admiring, but oppressed. He was of middle height and looked frail. He had a slightly abstracted air, and held his right hand over his heart, as if taking an oath or apologising for a hiccup.

'Do you play the piano?' he asked me.

'I'm afraid not.'

The boy who came in with him asked him to play the Scarlatti on the piano, which he did. A woman with a clear strong face and red-gold hair entered—Mrs Lyward. The boy went and we had tea. Dr Selwyn talked impulsively and brilliantly. Mr Lyward listened. I was hungrier for facts than for tea and wanted a hundred questions answered, but could not decide where to begin. I learnt that the boys had no set classes. Then what did they do all day? No set holidays either. Then did they never go home? How did they leave, and why, and after how long? Trying to ask something precise, which called for a precise reply, I said: 'How are you financed?'

'There is a balance sheet,' said Mr Lyward. 'You can see it if you like.'

I did not really want to see it. I asked, as dozens had asked before me, and have since: 'What is the curriculum?'

'There is none.'

'But... can you tell me what the boys are doing at this particular moment?'

'I have a rough idea. I can tell you that three are in London. Two, as you see, are playing croquet. One has just been given twenty pounds to start breeding budgerigars. Another is thinking of making a telescope, but won't get a penny till he shows that he means it. And one has run away.'

'Run away?'

'I think he'll come back. Oh—look—this is interesting!' He was at the window, and his voice became excited. 'How many of them? Eight—ten—twelve.'

The group of boys on the lawn were playing a game everybody knows. One stands in the middle of a circle, while the others throw a ball to one another and try to hit him. They looked healthy and happy. 'You wouldn't have thought, would you?' said Mr Lyward, 'that the ... County Council sent me that one'—he pointed—'with a note that he had the highest possible criminal potential. *That* one boasted when he came to us that he had beaten the educational authorities in ... shire single-handed, and would do the same with me. Oh, and that one—does he look as if he were all dirt and lies? That's what his father wrote about him.'

We went into Mr Lyward's room. Panelling again and reproductions on the wall; many books; Shakespeare and Shakespearian criticism, Keats and the letters of Keats, writings on education, writings on mysticism, writings on the origins of language, grammars in German. In one corner was an enormous filing cabinet, in another a bed. There were two clocks, neither of which was going. The alcove window looked out over the lawn and the boys playing there, and the afternoon sun poured in.

I asked why the boys had come to Finchden.

'Oh, some of them have been "deemed maladjusted",' Mr Lyward answered. I could hear the inverted commas. 'Some ... well, they just come. They're small, or they've been made to feel small, and they've wanted to feel big. They're really little boys, and here that's what they become.'

'Do you do a psychoanalysis of each boy?'

'No. But if by analysis you mean loosening, then I suppose we do analyse.' He got out the dictionary and established the original meaning of the word. One of his staff came in. 'What *do* we do here, David?' he asked. 'Are we a school? Are we a clinic? What are we?'

'Not a school.'

'I don't call this place a school. I never have, and I've always thought I never will. But perhaps after all, we are.' He went to the dictionary again, and read out—'School. From the Greek, *skola*. A place of leisure. But most people think that means just lounging. Lounging about in *their* way, whereas here it's lounging in *our* way.'

I began to feel bewildered. The telephone rang. Mr Lyward spoke firmly and at some length, and turned back to me.

'There you are!' he said. 'What am I to do with a father who comes to me with a boy in such a disturbed state, that he can scarcely even leave his room, and after he's been here only six months expects him to be fit for ordinary life.?'

'How long does it usually take?' I asked.

'I don't know. Can anybody ever know? I have an idea sometimes, but I never *know*, and I can't commit myself.' The telephone rang again. Two parents whose boy had been caught stealing wanted to see Mr Lyward 'urgently'. Mr Lyward had another long conversation, made an appointment, rang off, and began to talk about suicides in the Universities, and the relation of the Welfare State to the problem of emotionally disturbed adolescents. This reminded him of a quotation. The quotation led him to a file, out of which he fished an article he had written on this very subject years before the Welfare State came into existence or adolescent delinquency into the headlines. He told me suddenly of a boy in his care, whom no school had been able to hold, and who now seemed happy riding a bicycle dressed as a Chinaman.

'Why not let them have back their childhood?' he asked. 'Let them do all those things. If they don't do them now, they'll do much worse things later.'

A letter was lying on his bed. 'Look what the educational authorities in ......shire ask. They want to know what my methods are. Of course they do, but I've been at it twenty-five years, and surely someone would have had the time to come and find out. I beg them to come, even if they only spend one afternoon among the boys. The boys will tell them. The visitors needn't even see me, if they don't want to.'

It was obvious that if I were to form any idea of the place, let alone write about it, I must spend some time there, and Mr Lyward was willing, with that aim, to make me a temporary member of his staff.

'What shall I teach?' I asked.

'It depends what the boys will want you to teach.'

'I've no experience of teaching.'

'We'll see. The most important thing is that you should be on tap at any moment, including the early hours of the morning.'

It was agreed that I should settle in a few weeks later, and Dr Selwyn, his aim accomplished, drove me back to London. I said little, but what I was thinking was this: I had gone to Germany before the war because I had wished to find out for myself, and to the countries of Eastern Europe afterwards from the same motive. I had not the faintest idea what Finchden Manor would be like, but I did have two presentiments: one, that I was about to go back to an entirely new beginning, and that this had happened at the suitable moment of my life; the other, that this might turn out to be a happy story, of which the world had need.

CHAPTER TWO

It is easier to say what Finchden was not, than what it was. I soon ceased to think of it as a school, or clinic, or 'place for the delinquent'. It was not an experiment; the boys were nobody's guinea-pigs. It evaded categories. No one called it anything but its name.

At the time I went there, Mr Lyward had about forty boys in residence, between the ages of fifteen and twenty, with an occasional fourteen-year old. The average age was seventeen and a half, a time, as one visiting psychiatrist remarked, 'when many people used to this work think it's too late'. Roughly half were private 'patients', paid for by their families and sent from public schools; local authorities paid in part or entirely for most of the remainder. There were and always had been some half-dozen whom Mr Lyward kept for nothing. He had no money of his own. Financially Finchden had to support itself. For twenty-six years it had existed on a precarious margin, and looked like having to continue so. No one had endowed it. It received no State grant; as long as the boys remained there, Mr Lyward bore sole responsibility. His reputation as healer and teacher stood so high that most authorities and doctors were content to leave them to him; this, naturally enough, was not always quite true at once of parents.

He had a staff of six, most of them in the thirties. There were no fixed hours, except for meals, which the boys cooked and served themselves, and bed-time; no fixed term-times; and no fixed holidays. The local doctor, a wise and co-operative friend, looked after the boys' health. The staff had holidays, week-ends, days off, but could not be spared for the much longer vacations of an ordinary school. Although the house itself and the general sense of being immune and harboured reminded me of one of the old public schools, Finchden had no speech-days; no old boys' tie; no blazers; no chapel or school-hall; no Board of Governors, Visitor or Patron;

and no conventions, written or unwritten, of what was or was not correct behaviour. It did not publish a prospectus.

It was not Borstal nor an approved school. No boy, once there, could feel that he had been sent as a punishment and he found no punishments imposed. The rebel child of blue blood or a long purse lived for years alongside the black sheep of a suburban draper, the potential cosh boy, or some Hamlet of the slums. None seemed curious why any of the others had been sent. Once settled there, they had crossed a frontier from the past.

It was autumn when I joined. I spent my last night as Mr Lyward's guest in apprehension. For the last time I was still the visitor at a pleasant country house, without responsibilities, in the privileged aloofness of a sheltered onlooker. I felt as I did the day before I went to work in a factory. There I had been doubtful if I could put up with the routine; here I was doubtful about the lack. The work would be equally unfamiliar, and a lot probably equally monotonous.

For the first few days I was given time to find my feet. I had no duties yet. Changes, an occasional crisis, occurred all round me, situations and odd entanglements developed, of which I was only vaguely aware; some I did not know were happening at all.

I decided that I would try to understand Mr Lyward. I could understand him when he was talking to the boys; but when to me, I continued to feel as if I had walked into a labyrinth. First to the morning's mail, then to an article he had written during the war, then to a memory twenty years old and still fresh; and so to the New Testament, Shelley, Shakespeare, and back to some inquiry sent him from a County Council. (He spoke of local authorities as if they were the nobles in Shakespeare's historical plays: 'Kent wants to know', or 'Northumberland is now asking...'). I followed him, never fewer than two thoughts behind.

It became clear within a week that I had stumbled on something far more than rehabilitation. This indeed was achieved; but incidentally, as part of a much larger liberation. Some kind of secret or treasure lay ahead, which could only be pursued slowly and step by step; not like a hunt, but like a pilgrimage. For a long time it evaded me, and so did Mr Lyward. He reminded me of Proteus.

> 'A Greek Sea-daimon,' says the Encyclopaedia Britannica, 'shepherd of the flocks of the sea, (seals, etc.), and a great prophet. Like most sea-fairies, he could change his appearance at will. Those who would consult him had first to surprise and bind him during his noon-day slumber. Even when caught, he would try to escape by assuming all sorts of shapes; but if his captor held him fast, the god at last returned to his proper shape, gave the wished-for-answer, and then plunged into the sea.'

I decided on my own method. I would move like a detective, clinging to the words he used most frequently and taking my own time to discover where they led. These would be my clues, and at the end, I hoped, all would be unravelled.

My first clue became the small word 'respite'. 'Ponder over this word,' Mr Lyward suggested in a lecture to a learned society. 'I say it as one who loved teaching subjects, but has not officially taught them for twenty-one years; not since I decided that some young people needed complete respite from lessons as such, in schools as such, so that they could be shepherded back from the ways ... by which they have escaped for a while their real challenge ...'

I resolved to investigate what he meant. Over many months I therefore ascertained sufficient to clarify, in general, why and how the boys had come, and what happened on their arrival.

Mostly, the parents, guardians or responsible authorities arrived at Finchden hot-foot, after a boy had either done something that had got him into trouble, or begun to behave in a disquieting manner that might. This was the immediate reason; behind lay the deeper causes.

The immediate reason was brought to Mr Lyward's attention

in a variety of ways. A boy might be preceded by a letter from a mother who described the hours he would spend sewing laces and buckles and jewels, and duelling with imaginary foes who had sullied his good name, all with much bowing and kissing of hands. But that, she wrote, was an interlude compared with his passion for dressing up in a magnificent and flowing robe, sitting on a dais hours on end until he had definitely become the son of a great king. She added that the boy lived so intensely in each character that he did not leave the house for days, and she did not receive the same courtesy from one imaginary character as from another. She had tried everything to interest him in ordinary life, but it was hopeless. Or this:

> 'He told me it would be a good thing for him to come home and have it out with his father. He said he would like to have a row with him. I asked if he felt that if we were both dead he would then progress, and he said yes.'

The correspondence might be prolonged over weeks or even months, before Mr Lyward decided to accept or the parents to send the boy, or before the boy himself decided to come. It often happened that the parents, unwilling or unable to agree that there could be anything seriously amiss, would state that their son 'has been much better during the past few days', and change their minds; but hope proved illusion, and the request, on a more urgent note, would be renewed. The disturbance might be part of a steadily mounting crisis: One boy, the only son of highly respectable parents, had been in rebellion against family discipline for the past ten years. He had now begun to steal valuable jewellery from his mother, which had ended in his being bound over for two years. Or it might burst out of an apparently blue sky, as when Mr Lyward was one day faced with a hitherto quiet obedient boy, who suddenly broke into his own home, smashed all the glass, then disappeared for four days and was found sleeping in a field; to which the parents added that he 'has always had a happy temperament, then suddenly did not know what to do with himself, and we did not know what to do with him.'

Most of the boys had been interviewed by at least one psychiatrist, some by three or four, and arrived complete with past history and analysis. Interpretation of course varied according to the character and training of the psychiatrist; some terse, yet giving a picture of an individual human being, others pedantic and technical, signing, sealing and delivering him as a case. The diagnoses of the great old physician who had been one of Mr Lyward's first champions were brilliant and ruthless. Here and there a phrase escaped the technical vocabulary and shone; the doctor struck me as more than a doctor, who said of a boy that 'he feels like a bomb and is inclined to judge morally that the virtues of the bomb are preferable to those of the seed ...'

The story might start with a letter from a headmaster:

> 'I found out that he had been stealing, smoking, breaking bounds, and instructing other boys in the art of masturbation. It is quite impossible to get him to tell the truth. I and other masters had to persecute him fairly systematically for laziness, and I had to beat him twice or maybe three times.'

Or—(also from a famous public school):

> 'You will see that I have dealt very mercifully with him. Maybe my charity was misplaced, because the doctor regards the case as one of common theft, and not of mental defect.'

If the boy came of poor family and had been charged in a police court, his 'record' arrived with him, either stated verbally by the Probation Officer who brought him, or else typed out on an official form, with details of his heredity, his family life or lack of it, his environment and education.

> 'There are eight previous offences, and he has been treated by

four psychiatrists. In-patient treatment at the ...... Hospital has been suggested, but would serve no useful purpose; and as for out-patient treatment, it is doubtful if he could avoid serious trouble during the period required.'

Sometimes the story was given by a social or psychiatric social worker:

'The boy's mother has left her husband. The father is now secretary to a country club, and the boy, who boards fairly near, has had to leave seven schools because of bed-wetting and running away.'

One boy had left seventeen schools by the age of sixteen. Another:

'Step-father finishes work at seven each evening, and takes little or no notice of the boy. The mother then reports for duty and works until late at night. The boy spends most of the time by himself and masturbates every night.'

Another social worker asked help for a boy whose mother, said not to have wanted him, 'deserted him after ten months when he was in hospital with congestion of the lungs through her neglect. He has been brought up and petted by his grandmother. He knows all about his mother's desertion, and once attacked her violently for it, though only in words.'

The trouble was not always specific. 'It is difficult to say what the matter is, but he produces a general sense of uneasiness, is a bit light-fingered and has a certain amount of sex-trouble.'

Of one boy nothing more startling could be found than that 'his main defects are extraordinary unsociability and preference for his own company, so that (at a public school) it has always been a great bother to find anyone to share a study with him.' It would give a very false impression to suggest that all the boys had suffered from a lurid or desperate youth, until they came to Finchden. Some had been no more, outwardly, than what is called difficult and done no more harm to themselves or others than many who have not been 'deemed maladjusted'. They had stolen, lied, lost their tempers, or 'indulged in sexual practices' which most people, one would have thought, consider normal symptoms at their age, but many, to judge from Mr Lyward's experience, still treat as crimes. The people responsible for some boys had tried hard, often too hard, and failed.

How many boys had stories of the sensational cruelty and neglect that make headlines? A minority. Yet their number was large enough to deserve notice. After he had been at Finchden a while, a boy wrote his own story:

> 'My father liked to tease me. He used to shake a walking stick at me, and say he wouldn't defile it by touching me. My younger brother was cheeky and my father shielded him. I was often punished for bad manners at the table. My father asked me if I masturbated. I knew nothing about it and was mystified. When I left one of my schools' (where he had enjoyed himself) 'the head gave me a talk on sex, which I only half understood. Once I called my brother a damnable nuisance. My father heard me and kicked me down a flight of stairs. My father always lost his temper first, so it was hopeless to try reasonable argument. I was compelled to attend church twice on Sundays, and used to empty the alms-boxes.'

The parents of one boy had tried to get rid of him, because he wet his bed. In a family of six children, he was the deprived and rejected one, bearing with him a 'deep depression, resentment and reserve'. His parents had tried to saddle him with a false name. Treatment at three child guidance clinics had not helped, the reason given being that the people in charge were women, 'and his hostility is rooted in the feeling that his mother cast him out. He steals large sums of money, since hard cash has come to be the only thing on which he feels he can depend. He has lived in many billets and hostels and found no abiding place. He puts on a tough exterior, which cracks from time to time, and shows the intensely unhappy and lonely child within.'

Many boys were described as coming from respectable homes. Many did come from wealthy homes. The boaster arrived with the timorous, the furtive with the buccaneer. I often met their parents, and liked most. Most were living together, on the surface contentedly. The past of a boy called Martin Ferrers was typical of only a few. Abandoned in infancy by a mother who drank too much, he was adopted by foster-parents, who later separated. He returned home, but continually ran away. His father bullied his mother and sister, made the boy call him 'sir', compelled him to stand still for hours, and often beat him. His mother held him to the electric switch as punishment, got the children to do all the housework, and went away during the blitz, leaving them alone. They had no beds for two years and slept on newspapers and coats. This family were described as having an income of £1,000 a year. The boy had run away just before he came to Finchden, lived for a week in an old car, and been found sleeping in the fields.

The mother of this boy had been described as genuinely fond of him, but herself mentally disturbed, and unable to look after him for any length of time. Some of the boys who lived in homes as orderly as this was disorderly, had not experienced even spasmodic affection; or else too much, and of the wrong sort. Several had suffered from bad school-masters. One told of a house-master quarrelling with his wife in front of the boys and the wife leaving the room in tears. Another revealed, after it was too late, that the head-master of his preparatory school had been a drunkard. This man (the mother wrote) 'used to subject my son to all kinds of indignities. He put drawing pins inside his shirt and tied his hands behind his back to stop him fidgeting. Several times he was compelled to eat until he was sick, and then not allowed to change his soiled clothes for days.'

Another boy wrote himself of his preparatory school:

'I was beaten for breaking a glass pane. I was beaten for

putting a crust of bread in my pocket. I thought this unjust. I pissed in my trousers in moments of tension and was reprimanded. I sometimes wetted my bed and though not punished for it was made to feel it was a disgrace. I stole and told many lies. I was often punished and sometimes for things done by others ...'

A very great number of the boys had stolen, and more often than not from their parents; sometimes from both their parents and others. These boys had usually told lies as well. Many had been bed-wetters. Some had been violent. Many were afraid of the dark. Dozens had run away. Some were merely called backward and unable to pass examinations. One had been sending anonymous insults to his head-master. Two or three had threatened suicide, and one had written: 'I give myself up for mad.' Several were described as psychopathic. Four or five had some form of religious mania, and one, on the other hand, had set fire to churches. One was called 'the most complete case of Satanic sadism I have ever known.' Several had 'had illusions' and two or three worn women's clothes.

Such were a few of the labels with which the boys at Finchden arrived or were heralded, and some of the immediate reasons why they came. Concerning the deeper causes, it was not possible, with one most important exception, to detach any and claim that this predominated. I worked for some time at the statistics. I formulated elaborate tables of causes and results, hoping that some generalisation might appear, from which anyone who read this book, and had children, might take either warning or encouragement. But I found I could not simplify so easily, or do more than notice certain features and say that they tended to recur.

For example, a number of boys had parents living abroad. The father was in business in a far country, or in the Colonial or Diplomatic Service, or the Army abroad, or at sea. The children had been entrusted to guardians, grandmothers, aunts, who might not have been interested, who tyrannised over them or spoilt them; and they had been sent off to school thousands of miles from their father and mother. 'We are astonished,' wrote two such absentee parents, 'to hear of his lying, stealing, and blackmail, after two years at what we thought good schools'—the postmark Burma.

A large number, through death or absence, had no father (over forty out of two-hundred-and-forty); fewer than ten were motherless. An insignificant number were either illegitimate or adopted. I had often read that 'broken homes are the chief cause of maladjustment', yet, of those same two-hundred-and-forty, not thirty had divorced or separated parents. The parents of at least a hundred-and-fifty were living together. Among these homes were some which could never have been broken, because they had never been made, and the parents were absentee although they returned to the house each night. There were divorces and separations of the heart, more destructive perhaps than any sanctioned by law.

A good many boys were described as spoilt and pampered; often those without a father. Many had been dominated by their mothers, or overshadowed by older brothers and (more frequently) older sisters, whom the parents had favoured or held up as examples. The picture on the whole was individual, contradictory, and defied classification. For each category given, one would have to give its opposite. There were fathers as well as mothers who had spoilt their sons, and mothers who had never wanted them, as well as mothers terrified of losing them; the possessive, as well as the neglectful. A boy might be happy with his step-father, or hate him and be hated by him. Several, taken back by their parents, ran away to rejoin their foster-parents. There were only sons, and boys dislodged from their position as only sons; sons of aged fathers and sons of the young and immature; boys stultified by obedience, or exhausted by revolt; so many possible 'reasons', in fact, that anyone who assumed any single thing to be a likely cause of maladjustment would probably decide never to have children at all.

Yet one characteristic the majority of these stories did seem to have in common; that whoever had looked after the boy before he reached Finchden, father or mother or both or someone else, had tried to make him lead a life that was not his own. His own life had been 'usurped'.

Each boy could have expected to come into his own life as into an inheritance, a throne; yet when he sought to claim it, he found the grown-ups entrenched there. This word of Mr Lyward's, 'usurp', became my second clue.

It was not true of all, and many parents would be rightly angered at the suggestion. There were degrees, and usurpation ('unjust encroachment on the rights of others') had been perpetrated in many ways; frequently with the most upright benevolent intention, with that 'best will in the world' which is so often disastrous. A children's officer who had sent a boy to Finchden said: 'Parents are trustees for their children; yet so many think of themselves as owners.' The most complete usurpers were these owner-parents; owner-drivers, too, of whom some drove the child openly, some subtly; knowing what they were doing or unconsciously; in fear of him, or with what passed for love. What I read and saw makes inevitable the repetition, that a great number of fathers and mothers had done their best; and their best had been too much as often as too little.

Parents had their own experiences, difficulties, standards to keep up. 'The boy expects a miracle of Mr Lyward. It would indeed be one, if he could come to realise how hard a place the world is, and how difficult for those trying to swim, merely to keep their head above water.' Adults knew this and wished the child to know ... before the child was ready. He must hurry, he must get on. 'Our boy has no ambition to be top of the class. He is third from the bottom, but *he must go up.*' I had a picture of other parents, whose boys were two from bottom, one from bottom, bottom, and perhaps turned to the same expedient: 'He has had a coach these holidays'—against the same advice—'although the doctor says a coach is useless.' Sometimes an older brother was held up as the standard. A doctor wrote: 'This boy's mother is abroad, but in all her letters she is sure to be telling him to work hard and be like big brother, who *does* things and does them well.' Examinations were not passed, and failure interpreted reproachfully as ingratitude: 'It is disappointing to have done one's best and get no results or reward. Parents had their own pleasures to think of, their own level to maintain; 'If only he could become self-supporting, I could continue to run a small car by economising in other ways and living in a working-class street. But if he has to be kept indefinitely, the motor will have to go.'

Careers: 'He must write by return. My husband is in the West Indies and wants Jim to start work in the City as soon as possible.' The molehill the parents had struggled to establish was elevated into the mountain which the son must hold; 'We have quite a good business, built up by myself, and it would be a great pity if he, the only son, should prove unfit to carry on.'

Tradition: a father addressed his son: 'Your head-master says that never in all his thirty years' experience has he had to tell a boy so often to do or not to do things.' The boy was now asking to go into the Army, where, his father reminded him, he would be carefully watched, and those thought chronically slack or untidy or lacking in the power of leadership are returned to their proud parents with a polite note 'Removed as unlikely ever to become an officer'. The father added that 'The British Empire has plenty of tombstones up to men who halted at the wrong place, and failed to put out sentries and scouts.'

Sometimes the standards held before the boy were not material, but no less worrying and premature. 'By a simple receiving of the Lord Jesus into your heart, the whole outlook of your life can be changed,' a mother wrote to her fifteen-year-old. 'He is waiting to bring you joy and self-control and happiness and every other blessing. Remember that now is the accepted time, now is the day of salvation.'

Over and over again some moral judgment was either implicit or expressed. Words were used which meant different things to different parents, and had only this in common, that they meant nothing, except a pressure upon him, to the boy. 'He upsets the whole house, yet has all he wants. Nothing will make him see things *in the right way*, and friends drop us as soon as he gets to know their children.' That mother did not mean the same by 'right' as another who asked 'every chance for him to turn into a good upright man, with a *right outlook on life*, which after all is transitory, and just a preparation for the life beyond.'

Love might have been given, not as a calm continual light, but rather as a ferocious glare, setting a knife-edge between good and evil, shade and shine. 'I am intolerant,' wrote a father, 'and especially of laziness, funk, lack of keenness, and impertinence. I have not hesitated in my letters to the boy to try to prevent these, but have not failed to praise and encourage on every occasion. I have probably been too heavy with it all.' And a doctor depicted another father as 'well-meaning, but deeply unable to break with his ingrained idea on how a boy should be treated. He is obsessionally conscientious about his son's upbringing. He finds it hard to relinquish direction, pushing him and urging him, and feeling that things are sure to go wrong if he does not keep the control over them.'

The law defines those who steal, and are found out, as criminals. This is a definition, not a judgment. The parents of many a boy who later went to Finchden had delivered judgment. He had not 'lived up to something' and failure was represented as an offence. For one mother, her son was not someone who had been left short of love, but of pocket-money, and therefore 'stole, and was immoral'. A father was surprised when his moralising talk— 'I thought that one would be enough'—had no effect. 'I have spoken to him again, and do not think it will happen again.' But it did. A cadet of sixteen got into trouble for 'messing about' with other cadets. 'I gave him strict orders that it must cease,' wrote the officer-headmaster. But it did not. 'So I punished him severely.' But it happened again, and his father, *en poste* on the other side of the world, withdrew him. In a valedictory letter to the mother, the head-master still adhered to his opinion that the boy was not *morally* sound. He had gone in disgrace, but not quite as if he had been expelled. If a testimonial was sought, 'I would not refuse, as would have been the result of expulsion. I hope that this very severe lesson will enable him to get over his trouble.' So the boy went to Finchden, and got over it.

Judgments; moral tape-measures; duties called 'elementary'; responsibilities 'as our son'; images to live up to installed all round the boy, before he had had the time or chance merely to live. Sometimes only his hand-writing, set against that of his adult counsellor, was enough to indicate the gulf between them. A friendly guardian begged his ward, aged fifteen and exceptionally childish, to 'go very slow and above all be dignified. You may find things very exciting and want to enjoy them to the full. We want you to do that, but for some time, keep your enjoyment comparatively quiet, and prevent yourself from becoming hysterical with enjoyment. Avoid being a buffoon. That will do you no good.' And the boy, arrived at last at Finchden, wrote back in a round unpunctuated scrawl: 'I have been into the woods here and I thought that they were lovely I have been in the fields collecting acorns and the fields are lovely ones.'

But the answer was not always mild and passive. The boy could become desperate, like a wild animal tethered to a stake.

A mother wrote a postcard to her son, which the son annotated, scratching his words wildly across hers. (The annotations are in brackets):

> 'The least you can do,' she wrote, 'in view of all we are trying to do for you is to write home regularly. (Does it help?) True, I have had an occasional letter, but there has been no attempt on your part at the systematic performance of an obvious duty. (System kills all enjoyment. Tell me what you get from my letters and I'll write regularly if they give you pleasure which I doubt).'

And answering at length later the boy exclaimed, 'When I got your card, I went raving mad. Must I crawl about with my head downcast, saying I am a miserable sinner, when I think no such thing? More than once I have contemplated doing away with the black sheep. It would be a great relief to you to have no abnormal son to pay for, only *I can't stand being cursed*, and so I've had to resort to prep. school tricks for the sake of doing something, and that's why I've destroyed your property.'

Examples such as these furnished me with some idea of the deeper causes. They gave an unforgettable meaning to the word 'usurp'. Not all the boys had been nagged; but in the great majority of stories there had come a gap (to say the least) between the boy's capability of response and the parent's demands. As the gap became more obvious, the parents, faced with the other difficulties of life, became more impatient and the boy more lonely, more confused. The rift widened fastest where moral judgments were brandished most; sometimes the unsettling effect seemed almost to be relished. 'For some months he could not look his father and myself straight in the face. The fact that we found him telling deliberate falsehoods, and he realised we had lost confidence in him, must have hurt his feelings.' Often the boy came to think of himself as someone guilty, no good, one who had let down the two who had done most for him; until guilt, becoming the companion of his loneliness, drove him to fresh actions which accentuated both loneliness and guilt.

The words used to stigmatise clung to his thoughts and grew like a cancer. Exhorted to become 'normal', he assumed that he must really be 'abnormal'; badgered for being unable to do 'the right thing', he took it that he was heading for a life of crime. Some, in a kind of sullen glee, took over the character ascribed to them; they became a disreputable somebody they in fact were not, instead of the respectable somebody their parents wished them to become.

There were many such beginnings. One has remained in my memory as an exceptionally vivid example of the attempt to 'usurp'. A boy had just arrived at Finchden. After a few days he received a letter, six pages long, from a brother several years older than himself. The brother began by telling him to live to a time-table. Not one moment must be wasted, every minute being used 'for you to take up your rightful position in the world'. He must pin a fresh time-table to the wall each day, and stick to it, forcing himself to obey it to the minute. He must learn a list of words from books his brother would send to him, and spend one afternoon a week writing an essay to be sent to his brother for correction. His 'principal' (Mr Lyward) was to be asked to coach him in algebra, arithmetic, geometry, history, English, chemistry, geography, and French; and he was to get a book on physics and another on anatomy, read the preface first, then read each page slowly, listing the words he did not understand, and then read all of them a second time.

'You say you are happy,' the letter went on, 'but I doubt if you are. You can kid your mother, so as to keep her free from worry, but you can't pull the wool over my eyes. So never lie to me.' This warning was followed by a fresh table of instructions, each of them numbered. The boy is (1) to send home a list of everything received, (2) save all boxes and paper and string and send them home, sticking two labels on each parcel, one on either side, (3) always to lock his room before going out, (4) 'Don't do other people any favours. Don't mend their clothes. Don't lend them anything, you'll be the mug in the long run. Become a professional scrounger. Make a book-case, or better still find one among the furniture and take it for your own use. Make threats, bully, cajole, so long as you get what you want, and remember you are strong enough, if you choose, to fell an ox.'

The boy is on no account to let anyone sleep in the same room. 'If your privacy is threatened, write to me, and I shall act. Don't be surprised if one day you find me walking through the gate, because I shall be visiting you when you least expect it. And if I find you are unclean, with an untidy room, or unhappy or ill-fed, I shall give you a good hiding. Never lie to me, because I trust you implicitly, if necessary with my own life, and I expect you to trust and confide in me. Nothing could shock me so much, as to find that you are lying to me.' Admonition at an end, big brother changes the subject. 'Now let us talk of lighter things. For instance, air-raids.' Having exhausted this gay topic, he passes on to remind the boy that a questionnaire is enclosed, which is to be returned with answers. The boy is not to make his own letters too short, but 'not as long as this one, which took me three days to write and is to be studied *in privacy*.' Finally he is to look after himself, 'and don't overdo anything.'

The younger brother to whom this letter was written had arrived at Finchden, diagnosed as being in an agitated and depressed condition, with ideas suggestive of schizophrenia. After observing him in a home, the doctors had come to the conclusion that he was suffering from 'a severe anxiety condition'.

No wonder. The letter is, of course, an extreme example; but extremes can illustrate the mean, and the letter contained much which appeared in modified forms in many stories. Whatever may be thought of the advice itself, the boy was in no fit state to listen, let alone attempt to follow. It brought pressure likely even further to disturb. Big brother offered schedules and programmes, and presented life, not as an adventure, but as a straitjacket. He had written without a trace of casualness or lightness, to a child already near breaking point. Everything was in dead earnest, and behind stood a grim Jehovah, liable to swoop at any moment and give him a good hiding. The older confronted the younger with a legion of immediate aims and goals, whose inappropriateness consisted first of all in their frightening untimeliness. Lastly, the writer had never heard of the wind that bloweth where it listeth, or the life that flowers of its own; big brother had spoken, and little brother, 'whom I trust if necessary with my own life', had only to obey.

Taken out of their context, many of the exhortations sent by parents to their sons might have hung nobly in any parliament or town hall. Even the letter quoted—it might be excellent to have a time-table, and it is often unwise to lend. As for 'never waste a moment'—every anniversary of a great industrialist's death someone publishes these two lines in the In Memoriam column of *The Times*:

> But he, while other people slept,
> Was toiling upward through the night.

It was true that 'the world is a hard place'; true, that the British

Empire has many tomb-stones to men who 'failed to put out scouts'; it is sensible to 'avoid being a buffoon'; desirable to write letters home; unlucky, if the only son turns out 'unfit to carry on the business built up by myself'; an interesting belief that 'this life is only a preparation for the next'. But these and the whole multitude of other well-meaning precepts had the defect of being transmitted without any real reference to the receiver, like packages shoved through a letter box, whether or not anyone was in the house to open them. 'I would like to feel,' Mr Lyward once wrote, 'that no boy comes to school with any great ambition. I am appalled at the monotonous regularity with which they are urged to work for this or that reason or end. Over and over again I have seen a big boy near to tears at the thought that "father doesn't care for me apart from wanting me to succeed"'.

And so, by seeking to possess their child, some parents temporarily—or for ever—lost him; struggling to make him 'normal', they drove him into 'abnormalities' of which they had never dreamed; their moralizing and judging made him a moralizer himself, and a judge of them. They could not leave well alone, till love and due season might bring about some awakening, some spontaneous revelation. The symbol of their lack of insight may, for the moment, be taken as the uncle who insisted that his left-handed ward should write only with his right hand.

From all these censures and pressures, from all the noble or ignoble ideals within which other people had tried to stockade them, Finchden released its boys, and accepted them as they were.

Often the first interview with Mr Lyward decided them to come. I witnessed several. Tense and unable to communicate while his parents were still in the room, the boy unfolded as soon as he was alone with Mr Lyward; he became easier, responded, began to laugh. 'I like you,' Mr Lyward said to a new candidate. 'I like you, too,' squeaked the boy, described as unresponsive, and compelled to wear a deaf aid which he never used again. Parents wrote that their son now waited every morning for the letter with the Tenterden postmark, announcing that he could come. Martin Dunn, diagnosed as a possible schizophrenic, met Mr Lyward and emerged from the room into which he had shut himself for three weeks, refusing to speak to anyone. Hugh Andrewes, a boy dangerous to himself and others, said after the first encounter: 'I've never met a man who gave me such a feeling of strength.'

And yet Mr Lyward did not look at all strong. What he conveyed was immediate friendliness and warmth, which made these first meetings more like a reunion. Several of the boys told me they had known, after the first few minutes, that here was the man they had been looking for. They had felt deprived of something, and had taken their revenge in many ways; yet all were in search of someone. 'If only I could find someone who would tell me what's the matter with me,' said one unhappy twenty-year-old, who had fallen for bright lights and run his parents into hundreds of pounds of debt; there were no night-clubs at Finchden, yet after meeting Mr Lyward he came. Another boy, now over thirty, told me how he had been a thief, and had been given the chance of either taking a good job or going to Finchden. He met Mr Lyward and decided upon Finchden, feeling intuitively that it would give him something he might never find again. Mr Lyward made no attempt to force the boys to come; he might only talk a little and leave the decision to them. Yet some voice within them told them he could help. Finchden was that 'somewhere' in the world which they had always known to exist; they had only not known the address.

And so they turned up, often with visible idiosyncracies. Henry Collingwood, wearing a schoolboy's cap, also brought four dozen butterfly collars and a hundred ties. Tom Salford had on five vests. One boy, introduced by a lawyer and a doctor, arrived in a Rolls Royce; he wore dark glasses, a floral shirt, and a sombrero, spoke French, German and Italian, and at once taught baseball. Harry Nevin, having been put on the train by the police and told it was either Finchden or an approved school, refused to speak, eat or look at anyone; he ran away after three weeks, returned on a stolen bicycle, and put himself completely in Mr Lyward's hands. John Parsons could not sleep unless someone sat beside him. Norman Ferguson wore a paste sapphire on one finger and a jewelled chain round his neck. For a boy called Robin Marks, Mr Lyward engaged a special member of the staff, who slept by him and never left him day or night for six months. Bill Noble said he would come if his mother could come too. Mr Lyward made an exception (which remained an exception), and invited her. He had two rooms prepared for her in the annexe, paying for the alterations and charging her no rent. She stayed several months, and when Finchden moved into Wales, during the war, came too and took a cottage. Paul Nevill arrived with a loaded revolver. Arthur Grove, from Whitechapel, arrived for his rendezvous in Harley Street with several large volumes on psychology. On Jack Stormonth's first day at Finchden, a tile fell on his head, and he assumed it was part of every new boy's treatment. Edwin Mills fasted his first two days in penance for stealing a potato. Sam Woodhill fasted the whole of his first week. Fitzy came for three weeks, stayed seventeen years, and later started a place of his own; his own first pupil wore a sword and brought him his meals on roller-skates.

And after they had come, what happened?

They found security, emotional security from exterior pressures; from the mother who had badgered them with her griefs and the father with his ambition; security from ideals and from immediate goals. No one judged them.

They lost their labels, and were offered their lives.

I asked a man who had been a boy at Finchden twenty-three years ago and is now happy and successful, what had been his first impression. 'Intense relief.'

'Relief from what?'

'From school.'

What he needed when he first went there was respite from classes; he came to classes later. 'My boy hates games,' one parent said. The boy did not have to play games at Finchden; after a time, freed from the compulsion, he grew to like games and emerged an athlete.

The rambling house, with its black and white timbers and warm brick, the garden and the lawn, the sheep-cropped marshes below and the encircling woods, breathed an English tranquillity. To the boys from rich homes and public schools, this was something they knew; to the boys from suburbs something they sought on bicycles or on foot; to the boys from slums something they had never known. Day or night, no door in their part of the house—inside or out—was locked, except the larder. The staff seemed friendly, without being either painfully understanding or hearty. They did not coax you into corners and get you to tell them things. Neville might seem to be in a dozen places at once, and David might be equally elusive, but Sid–Sid was a rock. He walked across the courtyard, leaning on his stick; at one time, to please the boy who had given it to him, he wore a fez. He made jokes. If you died and were met by Sid, you would feel that all was well; if all was not well, at least you had the right companion. Mr D. was a brilliant teacher of mathematics. He kept himself to himself, was sometimes taciturn and gruff, and pretended not to like people, although he did. Peter Goddard was six foot three, a skilled carpenter and engineer, who had worked out his own method of teaching. It was he, chiefly, apart from the building firm, who had saved the house. I believe, given time, he could have repaired Westminster Abbey single-handed. He was the sort of man who seems to have an intuitive relationship with engines. Neither Mr D. nor Peter took any part in the 'psychological treatment', and at times made a point of talking jokingly as if they thought it waste of time. The boys enjoyed the dry asperity of Mr D. and Peter's rough directness, and respected both of them.

And the animals! Hamsters, rabbits, guinea-pigs, a hawk, an owl, pigeons, a tortoise, budgerigars, dogs, a monkey. Perhaps on your first day, you went into Sid's room, where you found a skeleton piano, a printing press, a hand-made television set, and the atmosphere of an alchemist's den. You might be allowed to make a tape-recording of your voice. You saw the things that other boys had made. You heard stories about old boys. No one, staff or boy, was inquisitive or censorious. You could cry if you wanted, and nobody would sneer. It was all unusual and intriguing and you felt you wanted to see more, that you might be happy there. Sandy Morton, brought by a Probation Officer from Lancashire, took to the place so much at first glance, that he went straight home for his baggage, without even waiting for an interview.

Sometimes I would be working in Mr Lyward's oak-room, collecting reasons why the boys there (and elsewhere) had 'gone adrift. Upstairs Mr Lyward and one of them were singing and playing the piano. I went to the boys' concerts. Two might be playing the guitar, one a year ago a 'thief and gangster', the other described six months before as morose and full of hatred for himself and the world. Now they were easy, carefree, and young. I went into the yard. A boy looking like the dormouse at the Mad Hatter's tea-party was sitting under a tree playing happily with a dog. His mother had pampered him, his father despised him, and he had been wretched at home and school; already, after two weeks, he looked relaxed.

It seemed to me that if all those who asked, as I had asked: 'But what on earth do they do?' could only know the boys' stories even as little as I, then see them now, they would need no further answer. If the visitor could only have known a boy's face when he came, taut and hostile, and have seen it again a little later, that would be enough. Finchden had given emotional security and a last long holiday before the stress of life. If Mr Lyward had done no more than afford this blessed pause, he would have done much. I recalled his account of a first interview. 'The boy wept for joy and my other assistant almost wept to see it. The only explanation the boy could give of his tears was: "I can do as I want here". Before that he had been telling me: "I think I ought to work", but soon he was laughing at the idea that it was Daddy talking and not himself. It was one of those interviews I shall never forget.'

'Respite' was my first clue; 'usurp' my second. Something else became clear to me as I followed them.

I saw that I should never be able to convey even half the story of Mr Lyward's adventure. Nearly three hundred boys and young men had now been in his care, (apart from women and girl patients) and each was a novel in himself. Each tale contained all the elements of comedy and tragedy; outside, and in every room in the house, the story was continuing, so that to turn from the past to the house was like moving among scenes still developing upon a living stage. The story of dreams alone (not 'collected', but accumulated casually) could have been presented to half-a-dozen poets and provided each with a new mythology. I wondered if anywhere in the country there could be found such fabulous richness of material for a writer, as had come to that straggly hall. Was it not equally priceless to the psychiatrist, the teacher, the social worker—and even to the historian?

It straddled the twenty-five years between mass unemployment and the building of the Welfare State and penetrated the most intimate difficulties of all classes. Rumours of war at the beginning; the explosion in the middle; and in the aftermath, the children of war's victims. Through the experience of Finchden one could see that the rich were now less rich, and more worried for the futures of their children; while the children of the poor, less now from poverty than from monotony, sought distraction in the cinema and the gang. The good and brave impulses of parents strove desperately with the Laocoon of rising costs; the dangerous injunction to 'get on' at any price received the sanction of what was called 'realism'.

I saw, in the post-war legislation which enabled local authorities to pay for a boy's keep, the makings of a wiser approach to troubled children than England had ever known before. The efforts of so many probation officers and social workers, the meetings I had with them, showed me how much dedication still went unknown. Finchden raised the contemporary issue between security and cosseting. It began at the beginning, and put the question: 'What is education for?'; and when Mr Lyward recalled, day after day, that 'education' means 'a nourishing', many kinds of educational effort elsewhere seemed to have been misconceived. People seemed never to have time, or to leave their children time, to grow gradually into fulness. Did they even desire it?

The term 'maladjusted' itself begged so many questions. Maladjusted to what?

To their families? Was it not sometimes the parents who were maladjusted? Was adjustment to the examples set in some of their homes a state to be commended?

To society? If everyone were to be adjusted to society, would society ever be improved?

To the world? Should one admire adjustment to war, fear, and the hydrogen bomb?

If adjustment implied acquiescence, surely the maladjusted were to be encouraged, and psychological treatment ought to be reserved for the adjusted.

I preferred the phrase 'emotionally disturbed'. It stated a plain fact without reference to any doubtful standard. It related the boys to the universal issues which have troubled mankind since Cain murdered Abel, or Orestes Clytemnestra. Inevitably, Mr Lyward's work laid bare nearly all the deeper human relationships. The liberation of the child led often to a reconciliation of the parents, and the parents' failure with their children exposed their own inadequacy to one another. Here surely are the everlasting situations; the clinging of a mother to her son, the awkwardness of a boy with his father, the love-hates within a family, will remain long after Yalta and Potsdam are no more than a legend.

Living at Finchden, I could not help recognising a dozen different aspects of my own experience, and of the experience of friends. I wondered if any parents reading this book might acknowledge any resemblance to their own treatment of their child. I doubted it. We all forget what we have been. We read what we ourselves have done, and do not recognise ourselves. Hamlet, to prove his uncle's guilt, put on a play, and the King betrayed himself. Would it not have been just as true to life, if he had not betrayed himself?

It seemed to me that all I could attempt was the missing prospectus; and writing now, two years after my first visit, I am still in agreement with myself about the limitations I decided on at the beginning. They do not trouble me, although I should like to have written much more than I have. One anxiety has remained in my mind, not concerning what I have omitted, but what I have included; a risk of a false emphasis, a wrong proportion. If this were not avoided, the whole picture might be rendered distorted and untrue.

It was natural that the colourful and spectacular should attract me, both as journalist and writer. It was inevitable that the superficially more 'dramatic' boys should come to my notice first. Both these things did happen. Two such boys—Flynn and Peter Storey—were my first two visitors; although it was not long before Peter Storey left, I continued to see a good deal of Flynn, and have described him in some detail.

Since chronologically he comes on the scene almost at once, I must at once say that neither he, nor Peter Storey, nor any particularly 'spectacular' person or thing was 'typical" of Finchden. On the contrary, the spectacular was the exception. Out of over two hundred and ninety boys who have lived there since the beginning, twenty may have been comparable to Flynn, if as many. While I lived there, at least thirty-five boys not less disturbed than he was, some of them far more disturbed, were behaving in a far less showy and, in the long run, less rebellious and perhaps less futile way. They provided the true atmosphere; Flynn contributed the atmospherics. They did not even provide the atmosphere, being themselves the successors of scores of others, who had accepted the love offered them wholeheartedly and gradually built up a surprisingly carefree community. Each newcomer found the community already there; many merged as easily as a sigh—and many did sigh with relief when they arrived—merges into a light breeze.

It is unfortunate that articles should have been written, films produced, which cause people to believe that any story about 'maladjustment' is bound to be violent and sensational. Finchden was neither. One boy said as he left: 'You are the most wholesome people I have ever met.' It was the world outside which seemed troubled, and Finchden that was at rest; whenever I left to return to London, I seemed to be leaving an oasis. I had this feeling long before reading the letters in which former members, from city and battlefield and many corners of the world, had written of all that Finchden had meant to them, and continued to mean. I felt in the same way still, long after I had grown used to the general sense of relaxation, and the calm humour Mr Lyward and his staff never lost, at moments which would have driven other people distracted.

The thought that such an atmosphere can accumulate among boys of whom families and schools had despaired becomes less surprising, when one remembers the pressures from which they had been set free. But release from pressure alone would not have rendered the comparative tranquillity so positive, so creative. Several men, motivated by a vague goodwill, or trusting to their 'way with boys', have started communities, and either had to give up or limit their aims to cramming for exams, providing billiard tables, and being kind. The boys at Finchden did go later into the same kinds of job as everyone else, or passed examinations and went into professions, several becoming eminent. They did become good citizens and good husbands and good fathers. But that was not all.

Their liberation was a major operation. It came about by a freeing of the whole personality from the deepest level, so that those 'immediate reasons', for which they had been sent to Finchden Manor, did not so much 'undergo cure' as fall away. Finchden's influence remained with them long after they had left; how deep it was, many did not understand for years. Adults too, including men and women experienced in the world and in no special trouble, found a haven there. One of Mr. Lyward's oldest and dearest friends, the late Canon Harold Anson, Master of the Temple, wrote five years ago: 'I feel I owe you so much for your splendid witness to the saving power of God in healing broken and seemingly hopeless lives, and I am thankful that you have been able to demonstrate God's power as you have.'

Were I writing a novel, words like the above would find their natural place at the end rather than the beginning. Since this is a documentary account of somewhere that exists and of people who have been and are very much alive, certain effects have to be sacrificed. One has not the same freedom to leave things to the reader. Certain truths have to be emphasised, which could be incorporated in a more leisurely way into a work of art. I should be more than sorry for my own sake, if a false emphasis were to give a wrong picture. I should have travestied my own feelings, if readers were to close this book believing that Finchden Manor was 'just another of those experiments'; or thinking of Flynn as representative; or mistaking a limb for the heart; or treating as nothing more than 'psychology' what was really a way of life.

CHAPTER THREE

My room in the boys' part of Finchden held a bed, a desk, an aladdin stove, and a sofa without springs, and until my arrival had been used as a class-room for two or three boys who had reached the stage of taking classes. It was on the opposite side of the house from the lawn, looking over the playing fields, and on a half-landing. Above, along a low dark corridor, lived David, Neville, Mr D. and a ghost; below, down a few stairs and through an immense oak door, the boys' rooms began, so that mine was a kind of half-way house.

The first morning I got up early and went down to the dining-room. One wall was almost all window. An old boy, lost at sea during the war, had painted robust murals of ships in full sail across another wall. Half-a-dozen boys were drinking tea out of taxi-drivers' mugs and eating bread and jam off trestle tables. A boy was stirring porridge in the kitchen. I ate some, and not being able to think of anything else to do retreated to my room and made the bed. Soon there was a knock at the door, and a boy came in who looked exactly like the Cruickshank drawings of the Artful Dodger. He was skinny. His hair at the back disappeared under his jacket, and in front a long black lock hung down like a question mark and obscured half his face, which was dead white. He had thick black eyebrows, and looked out from under them with an air of perpetually suspicious but amused reconnaissance, as if he were about to inveigle people into conspiracies that would surprise them. Imagine a poet and a squirrel and a jockey, put the mixture into blue jeans and a leather jacket with a bedraggled fur collar, and this was my first visitor.

'Have you really come on the staff?' he said pityingly.

'I have.'

'How long for?'

'I don't know. Anything may happen.'

'Well, as long as you've got that clear. It's the hell of a place, you know. We're all mad. Including the staff.'

'Mr Lyward doesn't strike me as mad.'

'He's the maddest of the lot. He's a ruddy genius.' The boy took out a tin box and began to roll a cigarette from tobacco dust. Suddenly, as if it had just struck him, he asked: 'By the way, do you smoke?'

'Yes.'

'Can you spare a fag?'

I gave him one from the packet visible on the desk. 'You'll have to look out,' he said. 'Everyone'll be cadging fags off you. By the way, you don't need to come down to breakfast. I'll bring you some tea up here. Unless ...' he ruminated, watching me under the lock of hair, 'unless you have coffee for breakfast?' There 'happened' also to be a tin of coffee on my desk. 'I'll make it for you if you like,' he said.

Another knock at the door. The Artful Dodger put his fist swiftly round the handle.

'Wait a moment! I'll tell you who it is. I bet you a dollar it's Fred.'

It was. Others followed. Each time the Artful Dodger, whose real name was Flynn, guessed who it would be, each time was right. They wanted to know why I had come there, where I had travelled, what I had done; a new member of the staff was unusual. Their reconnaissance was oblique and conversational.

'I'm staying here till next spring and then I'm going to get a job,' said one of them.

'God help your boss!' said another.

They began to argue amongst themselves, conscious of me, but not noticeably 'showing off'. I detected in one a genuine and open, in another a grudging respect for the place and staff, and in a third the hostility of someone who feels himself to have been challenged and does not like It. They used the word 'cured' jokingly. This particular group, whether in Cockney or public school accents and language, seemed fairly fluent at expressing themselves; now and then, but not regularly, they became staccato.

'Hey, what shall we call him?' said one, jerking a thumb at me.
'Got a nickname?'
'No.'
'I bet you have. You don't like it, or you'd tell us. Well, I've got one for you. Singe!'
'Why Singe?'
'Burn—Singe. See? Captain Singe. He was a smuggler round about here. No, not Captain. You're on the staff. Professor ... Doctor.'

All the staff were called either by their Christian names or nicknames, except Mr Lyward; he remained 'Sir', and when the boys were not addressing him direct, 'Mr Lyward' or 'The Chief'. I became Dr Singe.

Since I had no specific duties, I spent the morning wandering about the house and grounds. About eighteen of the boys had specific duties, such as cleaning, washing-up, or cooking. David and Neville taught a small group in the mornings. Two boys were with Mr D., studying mathematics. One was building his budgerigars a cage. Another, who had already built a tennis court, was starting on a canoe. Others were rehearsing a revue; others drawing, modelling, playing the piano or the trumpet, lying on their beds reading, chasing one another, making a dug-out, gardening, arguing. There was not one desk in the whole building, and perhaps one blackboard. The ordinary terms do not apply, but I suppose recreation room is the nearest description of the large and lofty hall, in which were the stage, a ping-pong table, a piano, and a dozen different activities going on at once.

The boys slept five or six to a room, although three had rooms to themselves, and huts on the edge of the playing field housed a couple each. The bedrooms reminded me of my time as a prisoner of war. Each boy had a small space which was his own and expressed his own personality, his own inscription and diminutive reclamation from the void; with the difference that in prisoner-of-war camps the personality had found its more or less fixed mould, but here was still in flux. What one saw might only represent a temporary protest against having hitherto been no one, a stage, a self-assertion, a fantasy of character through which the true character had not yet emerged.

One bed might be unmade and the clothes all over the place, and another as tidy as a barrack-room. I saw at various times above, near or beneath the beds a wireless set the boy himself had made; a model aeroplane or theatre; drawings of Finchden, portraits, abstracts; three hamsters in a cage; a kitten; and a puppy. One boy had collected several hundred second-hand books, another had taken a passing fancy to pieces of cheap glass, bought at the local auction; another had rigged up a telephone exchange, through which he spoke to different parts of the house; another had a selection of several hundred admirable photographs, taken and developed by himself; and another a fox, though this was stuffed.

At lunch everybody found knives, forks, and a place. A scrap developed on the floor; no one paid much attention, and after a few minutes the boys got up, shook themselves, and resumed eating. Peter and usually some other member of the staff came to this and to the evening meal, but they did not 'supervise'. The servers plonked the food down, returned, and shouted: 'Seconds!' and people went when they felt like going. The food was sufficient, what is called wholesome, and better or worse according to the boy who was cooking. All except one or two who sat morose and silent, taking no part, were talking; apart from shouting and slanging matches, there were also conversations, and their range and intelligence began to surprise me.

Later, unobtrusively, Mr Lyward appeared, wearing a brown trilby, and an overcoat and muffler. Arguments continued, but the boys were aware of him, and it was not long before somebody appealed.

'What do you think, sir?'

'What about?'

'What Jimmy's been saying!'

'What have you been saying, James?'

'I've been thinking we ought to have a grace before each meal,' the boy answered gravely. 'Why don't we?'

Everybody groaned. A picture came to my mind of an oppressive dining room, where the family stood demurely round the mahogany, while Father intoned a benediction. I thought of great public schools, and the neat scholars, the silver cups on the mantelpiece, the chaplain, and the long tradition. I could imagine nothing less suitable to Finchden, or the boys there, than grace before meals. But Mr Lyward took the question seriously. He did not answer yes or no. He enlarged it and put it on a different level.

'Doesn't it depend how much importance we attach to an outward expression?' he asked. 'How much do we need these forms? Is it enough if we feel things, and don't express them in any form at all?'

Jimmy answered: 'If I say my own grace, I suppose it doesn't matter what the others say.'

And so there began one of those discussions for which I shall always remember Finchden. I remember one after a concert, in a corridor, when they talked about children's theatres and ways of keeping the attention of children. Or it might be in a bedroom, or on the playing field, or in the courtyard leaning over the grocer's van; or like this discussion about ritual, in the dining room, with the cooks and servers devouring the spoils of the kitchen, and the wrestling and shouting and chasing continuing all round, until some boy, unable to waste his chance a moment longer, burst out with:

'Please sir, may I go to London on Tuesday?'

'To London?' Mr Lyward turned to the others. 'What does anyone think about Paul going to London?'

'No,' in a chorus.

One boy said: 'Yes, and stay there.'

'I want to see a show,' said Paul.

'A show? I thought you saw a show a fortnight ago. What sort of show? The Lord Mayor's Show? That's not till November.'

'A musical.'

'The Messiah? Henry Evans is going to hear the Messiah next week. You can go to that.'

'No. An American musical.'

'Ah,' said Mr Lyward, as if he had not known, and as if the boy had not known that he had known.

'It's very good. And I've got a friend who knows one of the actors.'

'Well, all the world's a stage. We're as good as a play here. Why do you want to see plays in London, before you've seen here?'—and Mr Lyward put emphasis on 'seen'. 'You have to pay for a play. It's free here.'

A boy called John Wirrall interrupted. '*We* ought to do a play. Take it round the country.'

'Fitzy did one,' said another. 'And he did a film too. I was the blushing maiden. He shot it on the marshes. The play he produced did go all over the country.'

'It ended up in London. John Mills came to see it.'

'I mean a play about this place,' said Wirrall. 'A play about *us*.'

'Impossible!' from someone. 'Nobody'd believe it. And they'd take all the guts out of it.'

And so they began to talk about bad language and why they used it, and those who used the worst found themselves discussing their own reasons; and so they passed to recollections of a fabulous yet once real Mr Knox, formerly on the staff, who had worn a white beard, and been a classical scholar and a scientist and a linguist and a big journalist before he came to Finchden, and a horseman and a maker of soap and by all accounts one of the last great eccentrics, and had sworn Homerically. And Mr Lyward told the story of the parents who came to interview him and found only Mr Knox, whom they mistook for the gardener; and how, when the mother apologised, Mr Knox replied: 'Dear Lady, I am not the first person to have been mistaken for the gardener.' And when some of them did not understand the allusion, he explained.

During these conversations, Mr Lyward would be standing in the thick of the group, in his apparently withdrawn mood, his hat well down over his brow, his head well down into his collar-bone, his right hand thrust under his left lapel, looking up occasionally to drop in some casual ferment. Or he would be fully involved, disputing, laughing, making jokes. Round him hung, and hungered, these to whom those terrifying epithets had been given— 'possibly schizophrenic', 'psychopathic', 'schizoid'—talking now of anything under the sun, listening avidly, seeking, feeling outwards. The adventure showed in their faces and voices. Those epithets, necessary and helpful to doctors, seemed out of place. Mr Lyward seldom used them, and I felt I needed simpler terms.

The subjects the boys discussed might have astonished those who had known them a little while ago and still only knew them outside Finchden. The talk moved on many planes and was fed from many experiences. At one moment the football pools; next, someone had asked the meaning of the word 'philosophy' and if there was any point in it, and so someone else had been reminded of a boy who had wanted the whole universe systematised and could not bear a clock to stop. Once they had begun to be reminded, there was no end.

On the outskirts of the group would always be a boy who could not yet join in. He might have just arrived, and was uncertain. Something held him. What was this place, where so much seemed to have happened, and yet nothing happened? Even against his will he wanted to know more.

'Well, James,' said Mr Lyward. 'We still haven't answered your question about grace.'

'No, sir,' the boy replied dourly.

'Come to think of it, we have very little ritual here. In fact, I can only think of one example.'

The answer came at once. 'Eight o'clock each evening.'

I asked what was meant.

'You're on the staff,' a boy said. 'You'll have to be there, same as everyone else.'

After tea some might go out. They had four shillings a week pocket-money and most of them went once weekly to the local cinema. They returned for the evening meal, and afterwards, until bed-time, came this 'ritual' hour, when they all collected in a room behind the stage called the 'Guildables', after the house where Mr

Lyward had started his adventure twenty-five years ago. In winter it was the warmest room in the house, except for the kitchen. As many boys as possible crowded round the stove. They read; they played chess or darts or cards; built models; argued. Some member of the staff was always there, joining in any of these activities, but never reading. Most evenings Mr Lyward came in and half the room would gather round him, some to listen and ask questions, others to scrounge. But I did not at first understand the reference to 'ritual'.

At ten o'clock the staff put out the boys' lights. For some reason or other I went downstairs into the dining-hall. Suddenly a boy entered with a mop of black hair and a red cheerful face.

'Hello,' I said, 'I thought you were supposed to be in bed.'

'I can't sleep. May I go home?' he asked.

'Now?'

'I must.' He was seventeen and his name Peter Storey. 'Now, or as early as possible in the morning. I can catch the first bus.' He put his head in his hands and groaned. 'I've got the most frightful headache. My temperature's 105°.'

'How do you know?'

'I just know it is. I feel as if I was going to burst. I wish I could burst. Are you going to bed?'

'I was thinking of writing a letter.'

'I ought to write a letter, but it'll be all right if I go. My father's a financier,' he added suddenly, and told me a number of his father's interests. 'Oh, my stomach!' he interrupted himself, groaning. But he did not look ill, and the more he talked about his pains the happier he seemed to become. He sat down at one of the trestle tables. 'You know what I expected you to look like,' he said. 'I was sure you'd be frightfully thin, and very well-dressed, with black hair and a wave—yes, definitely a wave. When I saw you first, I thought, 'Crikey, is that really him?' My dad's a genius. I'm going to make a terrific lot of money one of these days. I think I shall probably go on the staff and work here.'

I said he was unlikely to make a fortune that way.

'No, I suppose not. Some of the staff must be barmy to worry about us. I don't mean really barmy,' he tapped his forehead, 'but ... well ...'

'I know what you mean.'

'My dad hates this place. He says the best thing for me is to go out and get a job. I say, I shan't till I'm cured.'

'What of?'

'I don't know what it is. I know I'm dramatic and I'm very emotional and I'm a terrible talker,' he answered blithely. 'Mr Lyward says it's my hair. I used to look in the glass and watch the sun on it.' Then, between slightly morose pauses: 'You seem to know a lot of quotations. I was listening to you at supper. Do you learn them?'

'I think I've just remembered them.'

'It must be lovely to bring them in. My mother understands me. She wants me to stay here. I have to be careful not to run up big bills. Mr Lyward paid one. I nearly stole Riff's gold watch the other day, but I didn't. Besides I couldn't steal from Riff. He and I are great friends, you know.' Forgetting about his pains and his decision to go home, he embarked on a soliloquy about breeding, asking himself questions about the kind of woman he ought to marry. It was difficult to follow his chamois-like digressions. He talked with a kind of desperate fecklessness, and beyond there seemed to be somebody utterly adrift. He grew excited as he described 'his' psychiatrist, and acted him in pantomime.

'He was a great big fellow with whacking great arms and great podgy wrists, with a watch, and he sat there like a great bulldog. He said to my mother to take me and give me a good hiding. Well, she didn't, and when I went back he said, did I get that good hiding? So I said no, and what's more there's more wrong with you than there is with me, and I don't want to listen to any more of your blasted babble. And I just ——— off.'

He described the feats of strength of one of the staff with deep envy, and the strong man at the town fair who had lifted a fifteen-stone man sitting in a chair. It must have been nearly midnight when he said: 'I suppose I've exhausted you, but I like to talk to you. Is it true you're going away next week?'

'For a night, perhaps.'

'I wish you wouldn't. I used to depend entirely on Mr Lyward.'

I did not know what to say, and he went on: 'It's awful to think you can depend on a man who might go away next week. Still, I can depend on Riff. He's going to play Jelly Roll Morton for me. I'd better go now.'

'How's your pain?'

'Well, I shan't sleep to-night. It doesn't matter. I can stay in bed till lunch.'

He asked me to accompany him to his hut, and said on the way: 'Do you know what I think would be the most wonderful thing in the world? I think there's nothing more wonderful than a high note when you're singing. It just carries me away. I'd just like to get on to a concert platform and take top C or something, and hold it and hold it ...'

I put out his light and walked about a little. He had been surprising, but somehow not funny. He needed help. Later I heard his history, and how he had collapsed at his first interview, and knew how badly he needed help. I wished to do something, but did not know what to do. I supposed that sooner or later I should learn something, or that somebody would tell me. A curious swishing noise distracted me. It came from the front of the house, and I went there, wondering if Storey had come out again. The moon had gone behind clouds, so that I could only just see the figure of a boy pushing something up and down the lawn. He was mowing the grass, as if in daylight. I knew nothing about this boy, except that his name was Richard, and he was blind.

My first day turned out to have been rather an exceptional day, with exceptional encounters. For I soon realised that perhaps only one other of the forty boys resembled Peter Storey, and perhaps not even one resembled Flynn. What was it the remainder or most of them, had in common? They seemed quieter, not in behaviour, but quieter at heart. I wanted some clue round which to assemble this impression, as the word 'usurp' had served to illumine the causes that they had come.

Meanwhile I continued my reconnaissance in bewilderment and a rather fatuous goodwill. Somewhere about the building, boys who had never been able to study elsewhere were studying. All over the place things were happening in which I took no part. Apart from putting out the lights and giving people lifts, I was quite useless.

A few boys did make a perfunctory reconnaissance of my credentials.

'Hey, can you teach me French?' I was asked.

I said I could try.

'O.K. When do we start?'

'The day after tomorrow.'

'O.K. Mind, don't let me down.'

I bought a French grammar. I tried hurriedly to devise some stimulating and original method of instruction. The day after tomorrow came, but brought no pupil. It seemed out of place to send for him or go in search. I walked about, trying not to look like a tipster touting for a client, and came on him with a bow and arrow in the rose-garden. He said nothing about French either then or later, nor did I. The same happened with German and English literature. Russian I did teach for a week, swotting up a page ahead of my pupil. We advanced as far as writing out the names of every one in the house in the Kyrillic alphabet; then he acquired some other interest.

I complained jokingly that there was no demand for me. 'Why don't you advertise?' said a boy called Nigs Walker. He was fifteen, came from North London, and had a face like a leprechaun. I suggested that he might undertake my publicity, and next day he arrived with a large placard exquisitely drawn in coloured inks. Round the edge ran a classical key design. Two cypresses in the middle suspended a banner on which he had inscribed:

M. BURN

Teaches Greek, Latin, Mathmatics. (*sic*)

And Many Other Subjects.
Offers Gratefully Received.

We hung it on my door. Then we remembered that Mr Lyward did not care for public notices, so we hung it on my wall. It remained there as a decoration, but still no custom came.

Apart then from the few boys doing regular studies, were the rest learning nothing at all? If they were learning anything, what was it? One of them gave me a hint. His name was Carpenter, and he had sudden outbursts of rage which troubled himself and frightened some of the others. He had had no home life and suffered exceptionally in childhood; locked under the seals of resentment were intelligence and a profound sensitivity. I had taken him with some others to a famous house in the neighbourhood, belonging to a friend of mine called General Percival. General Percival showed us round. He was charming and avuncular.

'And what's the matter with you all?' he asked. 'You all look perfectly fit and healthy to me. What do they make you do? What do you learn, eh?'

No one answered. Then Carpenter said: 'We learn to live.'

It must have been about that time I began to see something.

What were these boys, really, after all the labels of 'delinquency', 'maladjustment', 'misfit', had been removed?

Physically they were adolescent. The recent report on maladjusted children, although concerned principally with boys younger than those at Finchden, remarks that 'adolescence is often thought of as an unsettled period between two relatively settled ones'. Mr Lyward once likened it to January, the month of the god Janus, who faces both forwards and backwards. Childhood is the dying year, manhood the coming. Adolescents are at the age where they still feel weak in relation to grown-ups, yet are passing through the physical changes of puberty, which makes them feel themselves grown-up.

The pull forward to adulthood and backward to childhood induces strain. They ease the strain 'by behaving in certain unexpected ways towards parents, themselves still getting over the shock of discovering that their sons and daughters are no longer children'.* Secretly uneasy with the grown-ups whom he is beginning to resemble, the adolescent can quickly become first difficult, then frightened, then start to feel guilty, unless understood and treated with understanding. A boy who had been made to feel frightened and guilty since early childhood would already have built a shell around himself; his transition from childhood to adult life would not be 'normal', or, to use a less ambiguous word, 'easy'. Such were the boys who came to Finchden.

In *Home & School*, the magazine he edited for thirteen years, Mr Lyward had more leisure than in his letters to illumine his outlook on the community at Finchden. 'Any careful observer will know that a fifteen, sixteen or seventeen year old may suddenly jib in the most unexpected manner. When this happens—whether the jibbing takes the form of silence, moodiness, sudden hilarity, or stupidity or evasion—the red light is out and the person is telling you: "When I was young, I was moved to fear, or a sense of guilt, or humiliation, or undue excitement, or tightening up, about this or something closely related to it. I'm helpless at this point. I become a child and no longer aspire to adulthood. You can say or do what you will. Nothing will come of your battering. I have slipped away into another world".' The boy did not say it in words, and did not know that he was saying it at all. Many parents and teachers had failed to sense this mood, noticing only the outward assertions by which their sons and pupils struggled to secure a foothold in the adult world. Such were many of the parents and teachers of boys who subsequently came to Finchden Manor.

'There is a child's world, and an adult world, but there is not an adolescent's world. He belongs everywhere and nowhere.' Many in whom the transition had been anything but gently eased, or not successfully ramparted behind an adult mask became, like Peter Storey, a leaf in the wind. 'My mother thinks I should stay ... my

---
* The quotations in this chapter and throughout the book are taken, where not otherwise acknowledged, from Mr. Lyward's articles and correspondence.

father hates this place... my psychiatrist said... but what I should like to do is take that top note and hold it ...', and he was blown away.

With the growing body came the growing mind, a dangerous ally, though not to boys like Peter Storey, to others who had not made a happy shift from one stage to the next. 'Nearly all, in vain, attempt, by thinking, to avoid the pain of growing through adolescence into adulthood.' The mind was invoked to furnish weapons and defences. As babies, the young had not known their own insecurity, because they were still identified with their mothers. Now, 'the boy is once again a baby in the adult world', and knows that he is insecure. 'His mind is at work, trying to help him to forget his individual challenge ... and he identifies himself (actually or by rebellion) with group or tradition or 'school of thought' to avoid the pain of difference. A boy may refuse to recognise the opposite sex and remain emotionally attracted towards his own sex, or a girl toward her own. If a boy goes to extremes of swearing or smoking or talking big, that is because he is more backward drawn than the others.' There were many such who came to Finchden. Nearly all that they did, at early stages, proved them to be just the opposite of what they wished to prove. One boy, for example, told by his doctor that he was—not incurable, but something like it—said, 'I wasn't going to have that, so to prove he was wrong, I went and spat in his letter-box.'

Parents and teachers had ignored the over-lapping of the two phases, and treated the child either angrily or proudly, as if he were already arrived in the second stage. 'If a child is forced by threat or praise or blame to behave as if he is established in the second phase, while he still needs to go back sometimes to the first, then he will not be able to say "I am sorry to have failed in this or that, will you help me?" He will not say "I am sorry" at all. He will feel "I am sorry for myself", and the emotion which would have been positively helpful, so long as it was attached merely to his inability, becomes negatively paralysing by being attached to the person as a whole. "I am weak" takes the place of "I am too weak as yet to do this or that".' From this kind of feeling it was not a long step to self-pity, and nearly all the boys at Finchden at one time pitied themselves.

The ideals, and the pictures of something or someone to 'live up to' with which so many of them had been presented had done them serious harm. While they were swaying through the delicate and dangerous transition, and needed to be left fluid, well-meant efforts had been made to fix them in a mould. Boys who brought off—to their way of thinking—a successful imitation of the ideal had been praised, then encouraged to continue. Boys were rebuked or punished when they, literally, slipped back, the slipping back being regarded as a 'moral lapse' by critics who should instead, in the hope that it might be only a natural swing back, have withheld their criticisms. By not withholding, they had introduced a judge into the boys' lives, and home began to take on the stifling atmosphere of a court-room.

It will go without saying that it was over words such as 'ideals' and 'morality', that Mr Lyward had many of his toughest bouts with parents. Some could never have given approval to a remark by Miss Gladys Bushell in *Home & School*, with which Mr Lyward sympathised in his editorial, that 'all ideals, however fine, are an imposition upon life itself'. Parents found it hard to believe that the ideals they presented or represented, whether or not the parents managed to live up to them, had been too much and come too soon for their children. 'The older discipline,' wrote Mr Lyward (although no supporter of the newer 'Do as you like' discipline) 'often went wrong by forgetting that the child is not something simple, but someone complex, to whom fixed standards are not applicable. ... Discipline is false whenever it brings about premature crystallization.' Most of the boys who came to him had begun to crystallize.

Sometimes, to illustrate a point, Mr Lyward invented cross-examinations of himself. Here is an appropriate one:—

EXAMINER: You are chiefly concerned with young men in need of psychological treatment and re-education?

G. L.: Yes. In other words, people who were once 'junior' and never lived as such.

EXAMINER: What do you mean?

G. L.: I mean that they were treated too often the wrong way when they were young and had to live unnaturally in consequence.

EXAMINER: But how did that help them?

G. L.: It enabled them to carry on after they were sick and tired. Suppose a mother nags her little boy and makes him feel more and more 'I'm bad, I'm insignificant, I'm frightened', then he may get the kind of illness that causes mother to send for the doctor, or he may start stealing or becoming very good or noisy or bullying. That sly cunning creature, or that unfeeling bully, who seems so unrooted, is not the original boy at all, but a part he is playing. It saves him from being quite so consciously sick and tired and starved at his roots.

The boys who became members of the family at Finchden had begun to live this kind of lie about themselves. How many hundreds and thousands, who did not come there, would go on living it and, almost without knowing, make their children live it too?

And it had worked. For a time, it had worked; until one day the model son, the supposedly contented one, had been discovered stealing or lying or bullying, and the parents discovered themselves, overnight, living with someone they did not recognise—and could not recognise, because they and the boy had never really met. 'He always had a happy temperament, and then suddenly did not know what to do with himself.' One boy came to be interviewed who had got away with it for a long time. He had looks and charm and had been good at games and prominent at school. Suddenly he was in grave trouble. Ashamed, afraid to face his parents, he disappeared. And there he sat in Mr Lyward's oak room, to all appearances a confident young man of the world, but really a small boy, saying in words: 'If only somebody would tell me what makes me tick', and with his eyes: 'Help me to find myself.'

Mr and Mrs Ashmore arrived. Mr was a solicitor, still quite young, not yet successful. They had denied themselves much, in order to send the boy to a good school, and now he had been expelled for a 'sexual misdemeanour'. They remained downstairs, while Mr Lyward spent some time with the boy alone.

Charlie Ashmore was fresh, energetic, and well-mannered—too well-mannered—with a good deal of poise and assurance, that made it hard to see what he was really like. He was very ashamed of what he had done, he said, and wanted to get over it. Mr Lyward, after making clear that he was not going to say much about the particular 'offence', asked Charlie if he was trying to forget it, to which Charlie replied that he had been told to remember and be sorry. For about half-an-hour all his answers appeared to suggest that he had an entirely happy relationship with both parents, especially with his father; that he felt he had brought discredit on his family, and was wicked, but would be all right again soon.

Mr Lyward asked: 'Do you think you've always had everything you want? Would you say you were a spoilt boy?'

'Oh, no, sir. Not at all spoilt.'

Something about this remark and the too rapid tone in which it was delivered caused Mr Lyward to ask another question, then wait. Suddenly the boy was talking quite differently. It became clear that a strong underlying antagonism existed between him and his father. His father, he said, 'would not let him do things' and gave no reasons. Neighbours in their Birmingham suburb had refused to let their sons associate with Charlie, and the stigma had been rubbed in. As he spoke of all this, he became far more communicative and less correct, banging the arm of the chair and throwing his hand out in expressive gestures, instead of sitting upright and not apparently ill at ease, with his arms submissive to his side.

When he arrived, he had been the kind of boy who caused Mr Lyward to write: 'I have no hesitation in describing the delinquent for the most part as over-moral ... one who does not so much feel guilty because he has committed an offence as commit 'crimes' because he feels guilty—about what he doesn't quite know ...' Charlie now became more like a real self. He did not complain or attack. He retained his good manners and lack of overt resentment. He merely said what he wanted to say himself. Denied achievement, he had turned to sensation. The withholding of reasons for refusals had, he said, made him want to be deceitful. He had asked to go on a walking tour, and been forbidden. 'I nearly ran away,' he added, 'but I didn't, because I thought I had worried my parents enough already.' He talked chiefly about his father, and said of his mother only 'Of course she's scared of him."

It seemed with him, as with so many others, that he had needed to be released from all this, and that the truth about the family relationship lay in his sudden outburst, rather than in his first 'correct' attitude. As the three Ashmores were about to drive away, Charlie put on a rough but not disreputable tweed cap. His mother said: 'What on earth have you got on your head?', and his father leant forward and took it off. I drove them to the bus-stop and the boy, who had been so talkative and ebullient a little while ago, did not say a word. He had withdrawn.

He had been nagged, nagging had tired him, and to avoid over-exhaustion he had played the part of a son who was sorry for what he had been told was a disgrace. This had been easier and less tiring than to argue and rebel. All that he had said when alone showed that he wished to rebel, and might at some later date. That too would only have been another role. Rebel and good little boy— two sides of the same false coin.

I often read or heard something at Finchden, which seemed a particularly vivid symbol of a recurrent situation. I remember a boy telling me of a father who drove him about the countryside, insisting that he should admire views and buildings. In order to escape the ever-increasing fatigue of feeling the response expected of him, he invented a little man, who sat on his knee and answered automatically: 'Yes, father, it's lovely.' He himself remained free—for what? Fantasies, perhaps; broodings, perhaps; certainly not for the natural spontaneous development of his whole personality, but for the fabrication, very likely, behind the bulwark of that little man, of the person whom one day his father might not have recognised ... had the boy not come to Finchden.

Finchden Manor existed to smooth the boys' transition out of childhood into adult life, to reduce the tensions which had made adolescence almost unbearable to them and render it as easy as possible 'at an age when most people used to this kind of work think it is too late.'

It was not a work of patching-up and makeshift repairs, carried out, as it were, on the boy as he had become by the time he arrived at Finchden; but a gradual and infinitely thorough re-creation, a return in life, not merely in analysis, to the stage at which things had begun to go wrong and a new beginning of his whole life from there.

In other words, the boys at Finchden were weaned. This was the word I had been waiting for. I am inclined to think it was my most important clue. It recurred so often that I asked three people closely connected with Finchden what exactly they meant by weaning. Their answers provide a general answer to all who ask what it was that happened there. One said that weaning meant the gradual detachment of a child from a stage where it is dependent for nourishment on someone else, until it either wishes or can be safely left to take its own nourishment. The second said that weaning meant a movement to and fro between the more advanced 'independent' stage and the dependent stage that was being left behind. Everything possible was done during this process to make the child ready for the more advanced stage before passing into it; preparation included freedom at will to return into the less advanced stage. The third person added that weaning involved a personal relationship between two people, one of whom knew what he (in the weaning of an infant, she) was doing, the other of whom did not.

All these characteristics were present in the re-weaning or re-education ('nourishment') of the boys at Finchden. Most of the following chapters contain a description of the way in which a process usually thought of as belonging to infancy was adapted and applied to boys with an average age of seventeen and a half. Their trouble was that they had only been half-weaned; at the slightest strain they returned, or 'slipped back' into the period at which they had been most satisfied. For many this was an extremely early age—according to Mr Lyward, between four or earlier and seven. 'They have come,' he said, 'because they failed to become seven-year-olds. However they may look, and however big or cleverly they may talk, they may in truth be no more than seven-year-olds with an L sign.'

It needed a good deal of daring and even more patience to attempt so fundamental a re-education, of which nothing could be foretold with complete certainty except that it would take time. The 'treatment' of the boys at Finchden made possible a natural development of head and heart together which they might have been thought past all hope of recovering. I had had my presentiment, as I drove there with Dr Selwyn, that I was about to take part in a new beginning. I had not expected to go back so far.

Yet on the whole the boys themselves seemed to take it all quite naturally. I have said that they lost those labels which made them sound so dangerous. It was not long before something even more important happened. Most of them actually ceased to be dangerous. They were disarmed, or at least piled their arms. This was a fact. I thought, in my first draft of this book, that I had made it sufficiently clear; but people who knew Finchden well said that I had not. At the same time other people, who did not know Finchden but had long experience of maladjustment in other places, doubted that boys diagnosed as the boys at Finchden had been diagnosed could possibly become as harmless as I had represented them. A psychiatrist, for example, familiar with the conduct of similar boys at Borstal and approved schools, asked me if I had not suppressed a good many stories of violence. Had not there been more window-smashing? Had not more boys done physical harm to themselves and others? Yet one of two boys permitted to read my first typescript exclaimed 'Does he think we're all thugs?'

How was it that so many became harmless? How was it that so many fretful porcupines could be so soon de-quilled?

The majority, Mr Lyward wrote, 'had assumed some kind of camouflage before they arrived, and slowly but surely had been labelled as this or that species of delinquent or maladjusted adolescent'. At our first meeting, looking out of the window at the group playing on the lawn, he had remarked, 'They're really little boys'. On the same occasion he had added of one in particular, 'Why not let him have back his childhood?' That patient was one of the exceptions. He was not even a camouflaged boy, but a camouflaged baby; he caused all the more disquiet to anyone who really knew him because, possessing a quick brain and an unnatural neon-like awareness of himself, he could camouflage his babyhood all the more successfully and so appear, to a stranger, older than the majority.

That boy obstinately retained his camouflage. The remainder did not take long to surrender it and emerge from underneath as boys, with all the attractive qualities of boyhood and little worse than its usual obstreperousness. This was the extent of their disarmament. Once it had taken place, different words had to be used to describe their conduct. For example, the 'fights' to which some were prone before they arrived, at Finchden became merely 'scraps'; the alarming 'crises' of others became, at Finchden, a series of much quieter 'changes'; their taut emotional 'knots', their exhausting 'conflicts' tended, at Finchden, to dwindle to 'tangles' and 'puzzles', which were far less harrowing and could be solved gradually. They remained passionate, wilful, wanton, but in an entirely different way; not with the ruinous passion, wilfulness and wantonness of frustration, but of boyishness, mischief, innocence. The game on the lawn had been a boyish game. The ragged clothes the boys wore were not the mark of those who have escaped from inhibitions into a self-conscious uninhibitedness, but the unaffected looseness and untidiness of boys. Their harmlessness was boyish.

Thus small episodes, which it might seem sentimental to record concerning other boys, become significant concerning the boys at Finchden; for example, that one of them, usually silent and withdrawn, gave Sid a flower on Sid's birthday, or that Henry Gore, a 'tough guy', picked Mrs Lyward a bouquet he was too timid to present. One Christmas Eve the boys hung outside Mr D's bedroom door rows of socks and pillow-cases, into which Mr D. put handfuls of coppers in the morning. One group built a miniature trolley car, painted it with inscriptions in foreign languages—Tenterden to Vladivostok etc.—pushed it into the town and parked it outside the Town Hall among the limousines. Two boys were discussing whether Mrs Lyward dyed her hair. Mr Lyward passed, and they referred it to him. 'Why not ask her?' he suggested; so they went upstairs and asked. In the year the Olympic games were held at Helsinki, the Lywards had a Finnish maid. Her birthday celebrations lasted all day. She found a banner in her honour hung across the drive, a boy ran round the grounds bringing her an Olympic torch, and she was presented with flowers. The impulses behind these actions were boyish impulses, which the boys had hidden and camouflaged before they came to Finchden but, once there, eagerly disclosed.

When a discerning psychiatrist did spend any length of time at Finchden, this harmlessness astonished him. One, an eminent man, with a great deal of experience, could scarcely believe that boys with such a history could sit round a fire together arguing or discussing, or play games together, or come down to breakfast together, without any supervision from the staff, and nothing happen. He saw for himself that they did not go in fear of one another, with extremely rare exceptions; that the disarming began quickly and was continuous; and he was amazed at the absence of explosive situations.

I had not been amazed, because I had nothing with which to compare Finchden. I accepted what I found, and did not at first go out of my way to record this harmlessness. Yet all stories of effective disarmament, of whatever kind, deserve to be recorded, and I came gradually to realise, partly from the comments of trained visitors, that this was one of the most important characteristics of the whole place; it was a part of that 'going back to the beginning'. Influences which contributed to it will be mentioned throughout this narrative, and enough of the general background has already been given to mention one now.

The boys needed Finchden. Therefore, apart from the exceptions, they did not indulge in constant plots or outbursts to destroy it. They did little physical damage to themselves or to the staff or one another, or to the building and its contents. During the whole history of Finchden only one boy tried to kill himself; another saved his life, and the rest never knew about it. Tales of real violence, as contrasted with 'loss of temper' or 'tantrums' will be found in a later chapter, in the proportion I consider they deserve. No boy deliberately smashed windows while I was there, although one did so after I had left. Furniture was not chopped up for firewood, and the garden was well cared for. All the boys, save the few, seemed, whatever they had lost or missed elsewhere, to have kept their instinct for self-preservation; and this was one reason that they, and the community, remained comparatively quiet and secure.

The boys' disarming came about before the weaning started, and continued throughout. It made possible the long processes of weaning, and was vital to them. Without it they could never have been attempted. Those processes had method and technique, which could be learnt; I shall discuss later whether the disarming was not part of some special 'gift' of Mr Lyward's, which was far more difficult to impart.

The majority of the boys were weaned from an attitude of 'I will never accept or co-operate with anything that interferes with me, if it comes to me as a person'. Gradually they came to accept an easy personal relationship with Mr Lyward, one or all of the staff, and finally with the community. In order that they should begin fairly regularly to make this acceptance, they needed to be met ninety-nine per cent of the way. In general, the process of weaning consisted in meeting them thus and in gradually modifying relationship with them in favour of a greater interdependence.

The exceptionally difficult ones, the camouflaged 'babies', as Mr Lyward called them, rather than 'boys', needed to be met a hundred per cent of the way. They too could be disarmed, but only spasmodically, and this incomplete disarming left them more resistant to the process of weaning. Mr Lyward took them with his eyes open, often after urgent requests, knowing that their resistance would be greater and more prolonged, but in the hope that it might prove possible to wean even them. Sometimes it did prove possible. Even when it did not, they kept in touch 'and retained their memory of Finchden Manor as a kind of unique reference concerning a love which was stern and undemanding in a way they had not previously known it.'

Did the boys realise that they were being weaned? Were they conscious of their need for Finchden? Mr Lyward thought most of them only dimly aware, until they had been there some time. We once spent a whole afternoon discussing this question. It was left to the dear scholar to whom I am infinitely indebted for his help with this book to give the answer words. 'Desire is always blind.' he said. 'Desire waits for something to illumine it. That something the boys find when they arrive at Finchden Manor. Once they have understood this, their desire is realised, and that is what keeps the place together.' The feeling for it which nearly all shared was an extension and strengthening of the feeling, at their first interview, that here at last was the place they had always known existed.

CHAPTER FOUR

Relaxed, disarmed, returned to boyhood, weaned anew, learning to live—none of these words answer the question, 'What did the boys do?' They were without everything they had thought they disliked, and belonged to themselves. Nobody told them not to do things, but nobody was certain to give them anything to do. With nothing to fight against and no one in whom to hide, sooner or later they were bound to take some action by themselves. Self-disclosings and re-discovery began from that.

Movement started. They became in play. Mr Lyward used the simile of the pendulum, swaying forward to the new stage, and back to the stage that was being left behind. I often saw them as live sculptures emerging limb by limb from rock, and suddenly, in fear, recoiling into the inanimate. But once the play had begun, all that they did and said was eloquent; even, maybe particularly, the boy who complained: 'I wish there were something to do, but I don't want to do it.'

Early on, they attached themselves to some 'thing', to another boy, or to a member of the staff. The 'things' had been numberless, and usually chosen with the aim of showing what big men they were. If they could become an expert or authority, then they might be turned to and looked up to, and mastery of the outward 'thing' could take the place of an inward development they did not want to go through. It did not occur to them that the former was part of the latter, until they had failed in it; failure became another citadel of the false self gone, another clearing for the true. Dozens of boys asked Sid to teach them wireless. He was the one who usually kept a supply of spare parts; they were the ones who thought grandly of the finished set. One boy knew how to make it, but never finished. Another built it by himself, made a mistake, and would not show anyone, unable to admit the mistake. Another knew how to get someone else to make it for him, and then sold it for a packet of fags. Most of them soon gave up, and either relaxed for a while with the new-found awareness of their own short-comings, or felt about for something else.

One boy kept a record of all the games of chess that anyone at Finchden ever played. Many of them made books their 'thing', and one was in a fever for weeks whether he should lock up his 'library' or send it home. One got up every morning and dug the garden furiously all day, where Mr Lyward could see him. He stopped, after a neighbour complained that flowers had been stolen to fill up the beds, and took over a passage inside the house instead, laying a carpet, locking the doors at either end, and announcing it was now his room. Many boys went through the phase of building dug-outs underground and Wendy houses in the trees. One annexed a little shed, where he gave tea-parties; if he had to go out, even for a moment, he locked his guests in to stop them leaving.

One boy attached himself to science. He rarely opened a sentence without the words 'scientifically speaking', and insisted that everyone not only should, but did function according to 'scientific rules'. Another made a 'thing' for himself of cricket matches. He liked to behave as if he was the only one who knew how to organise and preside; if he was bowled, or other people on the field took the game less seriously, he lost his temper and bats and stumps went flying over the ground. Many boys started furiously banging away at the piano, 'but they always,' said Sid, who taught them, 'go sweet and mellow later'. Some boys attached themselves to an animal. One passed through music and Plato to astronomy, which involved him in a study of logic and appalling mental knots. He talked of building a telescope, but never finished grinding the lenses.

Sometimes two boys attached themselves to one another. This was known as 'pairing-off'. Writing of ordinary schools, Mr Lyward noticed 'more than a few pairs who, like Rosencrantz and Guildenstern, are rarely apart, and are engrossed in and unwisely praised for their escape-absorption in, say, aeroplanes or birdwatching'. When this happened at Finchden, it was, gently if possible, stopped. Twice a boy was sent away because of it. The rule against pairing-off was the only rule.

The reason was that boys who paired-off formed, at a tangent to or completely outside the community, a closed circle within which their development came to a standstill. They had 'a mother-and-child relationship both ways'. Their influence on one another, if influence it can be called, became repetitive and sterile, and neither took any part in the growth of those who shared the ordinary life of the community. They were bores, drilling away at one another, and never striking oil.

At first it seemed strange that so many boys should have this ague for attachment, of whatever kind. By coming to Finchden, they had enabled themselves to be detached from the impositions they had resented and rebelled against. Mother was no longer at their shoulders saying: 'Change your underclothes', or Father: 'Get to the top of the class', or teacher: 'Play games, and you'll stop playing with yourself'. They were no longer typed as 'immoral' or 'disobedient' or 'ungrateful', or any of the hundred-and-one epithets parents and schools had fixed to them. Yet here they were, looking for new labels and fresh ties.

The immature clutch what they claim to hate as well as what they claim to love. Many of these boys had suffered from a mistaken discipline and an inhuman authority. Freed from both at Finchden, they were nonplussed. Had they been fully grown men they might have exulted, but they were not. Unable even to feel their own legs, let alone stand on them, they exchanged their chains for crutches.

I recalled the boy of whom the social worker had written, that he stole because hard cash had come to be the only thing he could depend on. Others had other makeshifts and substitutes for their own strength, and did not alter overnight. Mr Lyward wrote to one father that his son's manner when he came to Finchden 'was so strained and obviously "put-on" that it scarcely needed the diagnosis of a psychologist to determine that his anti-social behaviour was ... one of many symptoms connected with a totally false attitude to himself and life. ... Beneath a super-grown-up exterior manufactured over many years (thanks to intellectual capacity above the average) there was a very scared and puzzled little boy. ... He had managed to push it all away by clever cynical repartee, or by being a successful scholar. He was not even able to admit that he was a sham and bluffing. The bluff had become almost the facts.'

Seen in this pellucid light by others first, and later by themselves, some boys formed, temporarily, an opposite impression of Finchden from their first. They could not deny that it continued to give them security from all that had disturbed them. Mr Lyward stood square between them and those parents who persisted, as some inevitably did, in requiring that they should write home regularly, pass their G.C.E., and flex themselves for their careers. But within this lovingly protected terrain they were now thrown back upon themselves, and in another aspect found Finchden like a shadow. If they fell into a rage and tried to hit it, it slid away, leaving them to beat their fists against air, against thin air, with nobody bruised except themselves; though sometimes they were 'hit back', if they looked like being too scared by the absence of reaction.

And so, having previously hated lessons, they began to clamour for them, and having previously refused to do anything, demanded instruction in a craft, only to find when their wish was met that they could not absorb the lessons or persevere in the craft. Their pretensions to be grown up collapsed at every point. Many boys attached themselves to the staff. A staff is something to lean upon; they turned the staff at Finchden into their crutches. David, Sid, Neville, had the added advantage over a 'thing' like wireless, that they could be imagined as representing 'authority', and therefore blamed as well as clung to. That was what they were there for. It was no grief to the staff, since behind the blaming and clinging of the boys were smallness, fear and hungering for love; and if by clinging and blaming for a while they could be weaned, a day might come when they would neither cling nor blame.

All the members of Mr Lyward's staff except Mr D. and Mr Hannen had once been boys themselves at Finchden and knew what it had done for them; since then, they had themselves learnt how to do the same for others.

Mr Hannen, who would evidently be dealing with literature and the arts, was new, and away when I arrived. His room was next to mine. It had an excellent library and two comfortable armchairs. I looked forward to his return. Flynn referred to him as 'Old Hannen', and I had an impression of somebody rather cosy.

Mr D., as I have said, was occupied chiefly with teaching mathematics, and also with finance, Peter, among many other things, with the physical repairs of Finchden. The 'psychological side' or the 'treatment', were left principally—again apart from Mr Lyward—to David, Sid, and Neville.

I had a hunch, after I had first met these five men, that I should like them and get on with them—and I did.

One by no means trusting boy remarked of Sid, that 'you could not like him, you could only love him'. He came from East of Aldgate and had been a research chemist by profession. Heftily built, formerly an athlete, his feats of strength had become a legend; he had been able to lift two boys and hold them from the ground, one on either arm. An accident to his spine some years ago had made it impossible for him to walk without a stick, and he was seldom out of pain. His massive and still young face had a nobility which put me in mind of a Cockney Samson. He played the piano, the accordion, and other instruments. He was in remote or immediate control, as the occasion demanded, of the cooking. It was he who helped the boys who wanted to 'do wireless' and, if asked, taught or examined them in chemistry and physics. His true bent was philosophic, and had I been a sculptor I should not have hesitated to take him as my model for a Thinker.

The loss of his physical vigour may have deepened the resources of a spiritual and speculative nature already deep. The role into which he had moved at Finchden seemed to be that of one who reassured. The slowness of his movements seemed now to be in character. He took things quietly, humorously, and without hurry; and to many of the boys, especially the younger and more excitable, his mere appearance had the effect of a caress. He, like all the other members of the staff, knew himself thoroughly, and knew therefore how to prevent exploitation of his own particular strength, which lay in gentleness. He said of Mr Hannen: 'It is fine that he gives the boys cups of coffee. But can he also throw the coffee in their faces?' Sid could; Mr Hannen, as I later learnt, could not.

I did not at first have so vivid an impression of David Hobbs and Neville Guille, partly because they moved about much more. An account of all the boys did at Finchden would also be an account of what David and Neville had to observe, cope with and respond to. David worked unobtrusively, and since he was about to be married I did not see much of him in such spare time as he had. He had an exceptionally sensitive and happy face. He deputised for Mr Lyward, when Mr Lyward went away, and appeared to have the same kind of intuition, which gave the illusion of being effortless. Neville was younger and more obviously keen, and his insight seemed to me to be more in the formative state, and less completely absorbed into the whole character. He was more visibly on the move. He got things going. He chivvied and organised the details of chores and cleaning-up, but not because he liked them. He relaxed by making models of celebrated buildings, playing Chopin, and defeating me at chess, and is accompanied through my memories by a trail of half-emptied coffee cups.

Sid belonged to Finchden; I could not have imagined him anywhere else. David and Neville also belonged, but it was possible to picture either of them as highly successful in another profession. I say 'another', although their work at Finchden was not a profession, but a vocation. No vision glimmered ahead of headmasterships at more famous places, or of fellowships in cloisters, or lecture tours abroad. Although Mr Lyward knew at least as much about the problems of adolescence as anyone else in the country, and had solved scores, he had never been invited to broadcast, and was unknown on television. None of the present staff had money of his own, and since there was no pension scheme, I did not see how they could ever afford to retire.

I was struck by their openness and candour. The sense of mutual trust and happiness, which was among my lasting recollections of the whole place, expressed itself in their faces. They seemed to have come to some kind of inward peace, which I could only feel to be there and was never put into words. The motives behind their work were unexpressed and taken for granted, permitting an easy humour in ordinary relations, which made working with them enjoyable, although it might have been tense. They had no secrets from one another, admitting mistakes frankly and hoarding no private triumphs.

Apart from having something of Mr Lyward's intuitive gift, David and Neville were also, under his influence rather than direct tuition, becoming highly trained in what may be called his method. In two particular respects, they contributed to the boys' 'disarmament'. First, if a boy did something objectionable, they did not automatically insist, as many other people might have insisted, on discussing it with him and trying to 'get at his reasons' for doing it. This does not mean that they ignored it. They might come back to it in their own time, or, in other words, the time which in their opinion was most suitable for him. That time might not appear for weeks. It might possibly be immediate, but on the whole, if something disagreeable happened, they avoided 'having it out' with the boy concerned before passing on to anything else.

Secondly, they had somehow acquired the art of not provoking the boys, unless it had been decided that a boy needed to be provoked. The governor of a big prison, discussing his problems with one of Mr Lyward's staff, declared that many explosive situations could have been prevented from exploding had his warders been more highly trained in dealing with difficult people. Often good men, and in other ways efficient at their job, they failed in personal relationship because they lacked not humanity, but instruction. Insight can be taught, and they had not been taught. Slow to recognise the less obviously inflammable situations, they set them alight through ignorance and provoked without meaning to provoke. The staff at Finchden had learnt to discern the danger point of each boy in relation to themselves and to other boys, and managed not to set a match to it. Some innate gift may have helped them. Their own experience as boys certainly helped them. But the acute yet gentle insight to which gift and experience had been wrought came from training, in which observation of Mr Lyward played a principal part. Consequently the boys' feeling that they needed Finchden included a feeling that they needed the staff, which helped to keep all save the few exceptions harmless.

The temptation might have been great, in men without the staff at Finchden's training, to treat some boy, more difficult or more attractive than the rest, as their own special problem or case, work on him apart, and finally produce him, 'cured', as a feather in their own cap. But none of the staff had 'favourites'. The select tea-party, the long country walk between master and boy, which I remembered playing a large part in my education at a public school, played none at Finchden. Personal attachment there might be, and was bound to be at certain stages. A boy might demand it, and need it for a time, in order to help him to 'come in'; but never to the point where it could take precedence over the community. This kind of work, improvised from day to day, would have become disagreeable and hopelessly entangled, had one of the staff sought to keep someone or something jealously from the others.

I came only gradually to see what made up the staff's daily round. But I could at once recognise their patience. Often they had to take quick decisions and act at once; far more often, to wait and do nothing. It is true they were not dealing with the dull-witted, as are devoted people in other places. Mr Lyward preferred to accept no one with an I.Q. below 115, although he did sometimes make an exception. Thus intelligence, wit and quickness made for a good deal of comedy and diversity, but also at times for cunning and a remarkable power to exhaust. The boys were impulsive, merry, in need, robust, trusting, intelligent, reflective; they were also cantankerous, importunate, bitter, ingratiating, pretentious, sly.

Sometimes I would go to my room, assuming I could meditate, read, write letters, or do nothing. Within five minutes someone knocked at the door.

'Busy, Dr Singe?'

'No.'

'What are you doing then?'

'Nothing.'

'Your're a lazy ——.'

The boy stayed, or wanted something done, and my letter was not written. And I was only an auxiliary.

I had expected to find the staff room my one refuge. It would be, I had supposed, what a dons' common room is elsewhere. Here at least and surely at night, after the boys had all gone to bed, peace would float down and conversation become possible about worlds beyond the heaven and hell of adolescence. Usually it was so. Then would come bad spells, when the boys seldom were all in bed. Three, in mid-winter, decided to sleep out 'to see if we could stand it', and had to be brought in. One was sulking in the boiler room, another had planted himself on the stairs and would not go to his room until he had seen Mr Lyward. If a boy ran away, the headlights would wheel round the courtyard and off went David's car, or mine, or Neville's, down town, on to the London road, into highways and byways, until they caught or did not catch a figure with a rucksack, lurking for a last bus somewhere, or a lorry to hop, or merely waiting to be driven back to Finchden. And if no one was found, there were various people to be telephoned.

One hour and one hour only in the staffroom remained sacrosanct. From one o'clock until two in the afternoon Mr D. had his dinner. He ate it sitting with his back to the door, and his back proclaimed 'Keep Out'. If someone knocked, he did not answer. If someone came in, he did not look round. If someone dared to ask a question, he said, but less politely, 'Come back at two'. Had it been the Annunciation, he would have told the Angel to come back at two.

Only one boy occasionally kept late hours which made no one

anxious. This was Richard, the blind boy I had heard mowing the lawn on my first night. After the others had gone to bed, he would range the house and play sonatas in the unlit hall. He played quietly and quite well. I listened in the corridor. His playing sounded like a thread of reverie, as if he were musing to himself aloud, and his wakefulness was restful.

The suspending, within the community at Finchden, of moral judgments, and refusal to plant premature ideals and standards of Mr Lyward's own or anyone else's in the boys' paths, gave them the opportunity to feel their own way through unhindered. Respite came first, from the world in which they had been asked to lead the lives of others; then re-birth into their own.

EXAMINER: What about the words 'Train a child in the way he should go?'

G.L.: The proper translation of the original is not that at all, but 'Train a child in *his* way', and then he will not depart from it. How true we find that to be—those of us who set out to help people to be themselves once again, to abandon their poses and their dependence upon externals (their snobberies in other words), their straining after meaningless perfection, their mean clinging to ideals to which they have to hold, only in order to count.

EXAMINER: One moment. Do you discount ideals?

G.L.: Not at all. But we have to realise that (as someone has said) they should be 'like stars to mariners', and not something we hold on to possessively, while missing the real contacts in life.

The community at Finchden re-created these real contacts. To keep them real, two conditions had to be maintained.

One was a fairly ruthless quarantine. Mr Lyward had insight into the struggles of parents as well as of their children; he judged them as little, unless they themselves brandished standards of their own, under which he might think he had the right to judge them. But during the time their son was in his care he could not allow them to interfere with his methods, or warned them that, if they did, old wounds might be reopened.

Security from outside interference—although not outside contacts—was the first condition he insisted on; 'unfairnesses', within that security, the second. He used the word deliberately. 'Fixed reactions to their behaviour must fail, because that would render it automatic and compulsive.' And so Flynn, on behalf of another boy, was allowed to go in search of a bear, and someone else refused permission to go to the cinema. Three boys came to Mr Lyward with the same request at the same time; one was given a 'yes', the other two a 'no', one of which was later changed to 'yes' after he had taken the 'no', and all these answers being given in such a way that all three boys should feel, however vaguely, that there was something more important behind 'yes' and 'no'. The response was never allowed to harden into a rule or habit or tradition; never into the 'premature crystallization'.

At first a boy, having misinterpreted his new-found external liberty and taking Finchden to be one of those places where you 'did as you liked', might be astonished when something was refused. 'No', as a matter of fact, was not said often. It might be weeks or months before one boy was given his first 'no', but the first day for another. An intelligent receptive boy might be left on a loose rein, which could be shortened gradually; a different nature might have to be brought to a halt at once. It depended also on what they were asking for. One boy was told at once he could not stay out late; leave once given, it would have been much harder to withdraw from him than from others. Freedom of this kind nourished some; others were not ready. The 'treatment' consisted of a sensing and a prolonged study of each individual boy's need, in the long run and at a particular moment and related always to the needs of the community.

Far more often than not Mr Lyward 'went with them twain', spending twice as much time on them, giving them twice as much caring as they had asked; this was one reason that Christmas, for example, went on so long.

The money was spent as far as possible, and more continuously than anywhere I have been told of, on things the boys needed in the sense in which 'need' is interpreted throughout this book, rather than on things either parents or authorities thought they ought to need. Finchden was a place of 'fittings' rather than of 'fixtures'. The use of money was as 'fluid' as was almost everything else, and fitted to different boys and different stages of each boy. It might appear, to a stranger, to have been 'wasted', as when all the budgerigars, whose cage had cost so much, one after another died of cold, and the boy for whom they had been bought lamented 'It'll be my turn next'; yet that money, if considered in the whole long context of that boy's story, was not wasted. A stock of timber, a lens, a volume on birds or some animal, might be and were of far more importance to a boy than a new pair of shoes; and for boys at the later stage, who had come to study seriously and easily, the money would be spent, as elsewhere, on set books and, not as everywhere, on certain special books.

The boys came quickly to give up their calculating or 'accounting' mood, and to accept and value these 'unfairnesses'. After a while they ceased to clamour, 'Jim went to London to-day for the third time in a month. Why shouldn't I go once?' They accepted differences of need, and therefore differences of response to different boys (and to themselves at different stages), which elsewhere would have been labelled 'unfair' in its full derogatory sense and resulted in an outcry. 'A boy disobeys. Nothing may happen. Would our prestige suffer? No. We are felt already to be both reliable and unreliable. They have met with many pleasant shocks, such as having unexpected meals brought them when they return from the cinema. ... In this and similar ways, and by release from the idea of fairness (when, for example, the same boy received two or three times in succession more pocket money than another) ... and by the knowledge that we can hardly send them away lightly, they have been startled into asking: "I can't trust the staff's *reactions* to be meticulously fair, but can I trust *them*?"'

Sooner or later, the answer from the boys' own hearts told them 'Yes', and for the great majority sooner. From that 'sooner', that heartfelt belief in this new 'family', came the development of their lives, since 'unfairness' helped to awaken that personal relationship without which weaning would have been impossible. It rendered the boys curious, enquiring. What was at the back of it all? At the back of it all they became aware not of a 'what', a theory, but of a 'who', a human being. 'The real secret of living with children lies in knowing how to be creative in taking away and in being "unfair" and haphazard, so that the gift shall never deny the children increasing awareness of the giver. ... A gift by itself means nothing.' The boys at Finchden became aware of Mr Lyward and of the staff, and so, gradually, of themselves and one another. 'It was one of my great joys,' Mr Lyward wrote, 'when I discovered how quickly they each sensed the dignity "unfairness" gave them.'

They started to feel outwards, as they would have continued to do at a much earlier age, had not something stopped them and turned them inwards on themselves, or outwards in dangerous and unnatural ways. In this process of 'going back to the beginning', they seemed to have been forced back, from what parents and others had told them, to discover and declare what they wanted for themselves. Through their wants they disclosed their needs. Their tale might almost have been told in the re-arrangement of half-a-dozen elementary words. Parents said, 'You ought', until the boys came to say 'I think I ought', but not from their hearts, and conflicting—whether they said it aloud or kept silent—with 'I don't want'. After they had come to Finchden they might say, 'I think I want' or 'I must have', which was the expression of a blind instinctive want, altering later into an 'I want' uttered with joy and without involving hurt to other people; while the staff were saying to themselves, and perhaps at a certain moment to the boy, 'You need'.

The following conversation took place between Mr Lyward and a boy:

Boy:	May I go and lie on my bed after lunch?
G.L.:	Why?
Boy:	The doctor at home says I ought to.
G.L.:	Go and lie outside on some rugs.
Boy:	But my mother says I ought to lie on my bed.
G.L.:	You think you ought to?
Boy:	My mother ...
G.L.:	Well, you can't.
Boy:	Oh, but I want to.
G.L.:	You *want* to?
Boy:	Yes, I *do* so like lying on my bed.
G.L.:	And that's why you want to go?
Boy:	Yes.
G. L.:	Go and do what you want, this time anyhow.

Mr Lyward commented on this conversation, 'I wish to suggest that in thus pressing him back from "he thinks I ought" to "I want" I am preparing the way for a deeper appreciation of the truth in science, art and religion; that he is not ready for any teaching of "subjects", and that when he is, it will be necessary to use them with a constant eye to that boy's further release from his early indebtedness to an over-anxious moralizing mother.'

Beyond their wants all the boys needed love. They needed to show and yet to hide their loneliness, fear and eagerness, but could not say so. Their need was recognised, and love offered; but some, for a long time, could not continuously accept love. They would ask for things, when they really needed people, and questions, when they needed someone who would see and understand, beyond the questions, the boy asking. They could feel safe in asking. Sneering might be one of their own defences, but none of the staff would sneer. Some, especially the younger boys, had to be allowed to cling; and all kinds of self-pitying insistences had somehow to be gently heard. 'Mr Lyward,' said Freddie, one of the few fourteen year-olds and just arrived, 'your staff simply don't understand how badly I sleep. I *must have* a private room.'

The same day, he cried.

'It's difficult, isn't it?' said Sid.

'Do you really think so?' Freddie asked. 'I'm so happy I don't know what to do. Can I have a cigarette?' He asked why he had come to Finchden. 'Was it because Grandma was nasty? Is it because the staff are nice?' Particular trouble was taken to care for him and make him feel at home, but unluckily a mishap occurred. He built a nest for a lame bird. An exceptionally difficult boy rushed by and said he'd knock it down, and did. Freddie cried. Mr Lyward passed with visitors.

'How terrible to cry in front of Mr Lyward,' Freddie said. 'Did he think I was a baby? I bet you've never cried?'

'Oh, haven't I?' said Sid.

'I bet you never have in front of Mr Lyward?'

'I bet you I have.'

The staff had cried!—and were not ashamed of admitting it. How reassuring for one who, like Freddie, was nearer the child than most of the other boys. The security he had felt on his arrival, and for a moment lost, returned. Everything possible was done to fortify it. He followed Sid everywhere, and sat outside the lavatory door, waiting for him. He wanted to know everything. It was not really the answers he wanted, but someone to give answers he needed; someone just to be there.

All the boys asked questions.

'Euripides comes after Aeschylus, doesn't he?'

'If a woman is pregnant, and she'll die if she has a baby, ought she to have it?'

'Hey, who was Goering? Was he a Wop?'

Happy generation, that had to ask who Goering was.

'How do you become a ruddy journalist? I'd rather like to try it. That's if I don't go on the staff.'

And once, out of the blue: 'Dr Singe, can you tell me a cure for effeminacy?'

'I hope you didn't give him one,' said Mr Lyward.

I replied that I did not know one; not out of a bottle, anyhow. Instead the boy had begun to talk about his earlier years. 'At school I took up smoking and drinking,' he had told me. 'So they expelled me, and I came here. Do you remember, the other day, I ran away?'

I reminded him that I had stayed up past midnight looking for him.

'I was hiding in the garden the whole time,' he said. 'Do you know why I did it? I dared myself. I just wanted to prove to myself that I could. It made me feel more manly.'

And he talked of his childhood, explaining the need he had felt to get himself noticed, forgetting the supposed effeminacy. Often, in such conversations, a special immediate anxiety receded, giving place to deeper and more general things.

Late one evening Richard felt his way into my room, sat on the sofa and asked, in a voice that always seemed a little to mock his own words,

'I've come to ask you something about literature. I read somewhere lately about a man feeling as if veils had fallen from his eyes. Have you ever had that feeling?'

'Sometimes.'

'It seems rather peculiar,' he went on slowly and gravely. 'I just wondered if you knew what it meant.'

I recalled a passage in the Acts of the Apostles, about the conversion of Saint Paul. 'And as it were scales fell from his eyes.' I said that I had always taken it to mean a spiritual rather than a physical change, clearing the spiritual vision of passions and material things. Richard listened carefully.

'Yes, I thought it meant something like that,' he said, and felt his way out again.

Grave questions, funny questions, questions that disguised an anxiety or came straight out with it, all were met; often not with a straight answer, but always in such a way that the boy's first trust was left intact, he did not feel inferior or snubbed, and his exploring continued. Some questions seemed to have a kind of heart-ache, which no crudeness or casualness or jauntiness could hide. Sensing this, you could not go away. Even in the older boys, you would have a glimpse, if you were brusque at the wrong moment, of something that had once been deeply harmed and was still not healed; and the boy would become temporarily hostile—as his whole life might have become, through a continued brusqueness.

The staff went along with the boys, now leading, now leaving them to spurt on their own, picking them up, but most of all just waiting, and able to explain (to visitors or each other, not to the boys) why they were waiting. They had themselves run their own course at Finchden years before. Mr Lyward had stood and moved beside them, as they now moved by the side of the boys who had succeeded them. In their own day they had learnt the unwisdom of taking too much thought for the morrow, and the morrow had taken care of itself. 'A quickening of interest and an increased power of relaxed and effective concentration ... never fail to bring about an advance in educational standards'; and later, if those, who had hurried the boys before, did not start to hurry them again, examinations would be passed, jobs and openings would be found. The predecessors of boys now at Finchden, heading once for dead ends to be reached by the meanest means, had turned away to become doctors, architects, workmen, farmers, heads of businesses, probation officers, lawyers, artists, teachers; so would they. Meanwhile Finchden 'helped them at the stage each boy had reached and said in various ways: "Do not be endlessly preoccupied with what he will be later on. Give him his *now*".'

None of the staff had gone into this work for the sake of power —power over youth, the easiest of all—nor as a compensation for some weakness in himself. They saw into themselves as clearly as they had once been seen into, and thus became free to see and meet the needs of others, clear of prejudice or predilection. The boys' *needs* ... 'There must be thousands of people in this country, who know that if a boy fails to achieve a spontaneous relationship with his father, then he is likely, short of a proper subsequent release from his childish values, to remain maimed for life. ... But people are not moved. They pass by on the other side ...'

Or, writing of a judge who had advocated whipping: 'It is of course very likely that the eighteen-year old labourer to whom this was said might have *behaved* differently if he had had the whipping. But he would certainly have *been* different, if he had not remained lonely and hungry for want of a proper understanding of his *needs*.'

Or, 'When a child says "Mine" of its parents, or a parent "Mine" of a child, in the particular tone of voice which indicates security, we know that the emphasis placed upon "mine" is not a sign of possessiveness, but of something ineffable. ... I have recently been trying to help two young men who as children were not able to say that with any proper abandon. As far as they know, all they want now is "things", especially money. They dare not yet be called upon to discover their *real need* because, being unable to accept what is now available, they would suffer unbearably.'

For a time, the boys' suffering was done by others. But neither Mr Lyward nor the staff indulged in being 'hurt' or 'disappointed'. The first meaning of 'respite' is given as 'a putting-off of that which is appointed'. The staff could not be 'disappointed', if the boys grew into manhood slowly and erratically, since the staff were there not to force but help in the weaning of them. As long as sympathy was never lost, patience followed. Back-slidings were expected, some changes to a *temporary* unpleasantness and rebelliousness were welcomed, and anyhow, at all times,

> Love is not love,
> Which alters when it alteration finds.

What importance had it, whether the homes the boys came from were 'broken' legally, or not, if the boys had never dared ask questions (*not* intellectual questions) and disclose the need that lay behind, recognising no one at home who could understand them? Each boy who had lacked this someone was a waif, however many relations he might have; he had been in need, however large the family income. Each sooner or later stole, though it might not be money, but pity or power. Each had had nobody to turn to; those with nobody to turn to are likely to turn on somebody; this is what each had begun to do and might but for the community at Finchden have continued doing. Riff spoke for many when, after a few weeks, he said, 'I feel a person, not a pawn'.

Sometimes Mr Lyward invited me to be present at interviews. They were an exhilarating and often a moving experience. But they did not play a conspicuous part in the life of this community, and months might pass before he saw a boy alone. During the early thirties, while he was still feeling his way, deep analysis and individual examination had played a much larger part in his treatment. But it may already have suggested itself, that the conditions which had grown up at Finchden had advantages over the hospital or psychiatrist's consulting room. People who live the whole time with their 'patients', year in and year out, informally, are likely to learn at least as much about them as the man who only sees them once or twice a week—and all the more if the relationship is not thought of by either as one between doctor and patient. Relaxing drugs or stimulating injections, the couch, the drawn curtains, the skilled listener and evoker discreet in the background, can do a great deal to unseal the gnawing secrets. At Finchden they came out, or dissolved, more gradually, but without artificial excitement, and as part of an accompanying growth. The boy—and sometimes he was a young man—was seen whole and in the round, in the innumerable situations of life, which just happened and were not merely re-created. It was not necessary, although possible, to provoke a desired situation; it was almost certain to occur.

The psychiatrist aims at helping his patient to live with himself and others. He sees him by himself, but seldom amongst others. He hears the patient's personal version of the way others have behaved. The psychiatrist has not witnessed what is being described.

He cannot be sure that the patient is not talking to impress or to excite sympathy, and does not always know the others involved at all intimately. Some sick persons can put on a consummate act, and some act without knowing they are acting. Masquerade and camouflage may be revealing in themselves, but the psychiatrist has only limited time to penetrate them, and skill is not enough. 'The key to all deeper insight, as the analyst knows, is not technical proficiency, but love that knows something of the interpretation of one personality by another.'

At Finchden time seemed infinite. The lights which played upon the boys, and the mirrors of the rooms through which they moved, showed them in all planes and phases. It could not be otherwise. Gay, playing games, asking for money, talking big, laughing at each other for talking big, sulking, wanting or not wanting to go home, lonely, in need, they revealed themselves in relation to themselves, to their parents, to the staff, and to forty other boys, each quite unlike the other.

For example, when they were cooking. They took it in rotation as soon as Sid, who ordered the food, felt that it could be trusted to them. One boy said: 'I want to learn to cook, because I want to be a bachelor, not for anyone else. Of course, I will cook for others if I have to, but only here.' He squared his muscles and scrounged for recognition of himself. After a time he forgot his original reasons for cooking, and began to enjoy it; about the same time he announced that he had fallen in love.

Another boy could not allow a normal meal to emerge. It had to be Chilean or Chinese, anything but British. Expecting him always to be late, Sid got everything ready, so that the boy could administer a flourish at the end. Sometimes the boy arrived for the first part, and then went away, leaving Sid to finish and inventing an excuse later. After a while he reached a point where he could complete nearly the whole meal, and Sid no longer had to arrange the ingredients; this happened about the time when the same boy was ceasing to come in so late at night.

Nigs Walker liked to be the maitre d'hotel. He popped up behind visitors with a plate of bacon and eggs and a deep bow, and walked about with an air of 'This is what my men have done'. On the days he was to cook, older boys, who had passed that stage and no longer hungered for kudos, came to the kitchen and prepared the meal to a point at which Nigs could finish.

Mr Lyward once told a boy he could have a special menu for a week if he would take the trouble to write it out each day; but after two days the boy could not be bothered.

The kitchen was not a consulting room, nor Sid a psychiatrist. Yet all of this was revealing, and supplemented each day by other inactively observed activities. With no routine in which to take cover, each boy stood in the relentless open. Of this, at moments, they became sharply aware, but most of the time they did not bother. Their own rhythm slipped more or less easily into the rhythm of the community, and one soon saw where it jarred and where it harmonised.

Most just lived. The introspective boy was rare, although a few arrived introspective. One day, for example, Mr Lyward said: 'There's a boy in the staff room. You might like to go in and talk to him.'

I found a boy called Arthur Ney sitting on the sofa, with his arms folded. He raised his eyebrows slightly, and gave me a look as if to say: 'So here's someone else come to use me as a guinea pig.' He was tall, with dark hair, and a pale fine face which made me think of an Assyrian; intelligent, but closed-up and unyielding.

He said he was going to leave.

'Mr Lyward doesn't want me to, but I'm going to, whatever he does.'

'How long have you been here?'

'Over a year.'

'Hasn't it done you any good?'

'I don't know. It may not have. What proof is there? How do I know it's done me any good?'

He was electric with suspicion and hostility. Words poured from him.

'Mr Lyward says I'm pairing off with John Venning. Why

shouldn't I pair off? Mr Lyward says I should mix more. Well, perhaps I will gain something by being part of the community, but I may lose myself.' I was to hear this dread again. 'I'm *myself*, aren't I? I've got something that's *myself*. Why should I give it up, just because of the community? What proof do I have that I'll gain more than I lose?'

He said that he distrusted Mr Lyward. I asked him why.

'Because whatever I say, he's always got an answer.'

'He's had a good deal of experience. Perhaps he's right.'

'Perhaps he is. But how do I *know*? He's just got us all here, and he's tying us to Finchden, so that we can't go.'

'He can't stop you.'

'He says that, but he makes us think that we can't go against his advice.'

'Has he ever said that to you?'

At that the boy was silent, gnawing his knuckles.

'I thought that the object was for you to go, when you're ready,' I said.

'How does anyone know when I'm ready? *I* don't know. Do I?' He went on without waiting: 'It's all an experiment. We're watched the whole time. The staff never do or say anything without an ulterior motive. It's obvious that you came in here just now to get something out of me.'

'I was asked to come in ...' I began.

'Yes. To find something out.'

'To talk, if you wanted to talk. Or listen.'

'How do I know there isn't a microphone in that fireplace?' he interrupted. 'It'd be easy to put one in the bedrooms, wouldn't it? Anyone can fix up a microphone. John Venning and I reckon Mr Lyward's got a spy among the boys.'

I asked him if he really believed this.

'Why not? If I was Mr Lyward, I'd probably do the same.' He saw no point in mixing with the others. Except for one or two, they did not interest him. He was an intellectual snob, and I told him so. He looked surprised and slowed up for a moment.

'I thought there was only one kind of snob,' he said. 'I didn't know you could have an intellectual snob.'

'Well, now you do.'

'Was Chopin an intellectual snob?'

I said I doubted it.

Intellectual snobbery was a new conception. His mind was like a sandstorm in a glass ball; a new conception set it whirling. He had gifts, but people fond of him had told him this too often. He had been informed that to become a superior person he should mix with people of superior attainments. He did not find them, he said, at Finchden. That was why he kept apart.

He appeared to think that I was one.

'When you came,' he said, 'I thought you had the face of someone who would understand me. Besides, I'd heard you'd travelled and written and knew about Beethoven and Milton.'

I answered that these were not in themselves qualifications for understanding anyone, and that I expected to learn far more from Finchden than I should ever give.

'How can you say that?' he asked, amazed.

'Of course. Why not?'

'From Mr Lyward, you mean?'

'Not only from him. The whole place.'

Suddenly I had a strange illusion. I seemed to be talking to myself as I had once been, and to hundreds of other people who, at one time or another, had not learnt to live, but become imprisoned in a sterile treadmill of self-questionings, the brain turned tyrant. Here was pride in the possession, not of feelings, but of 'finer feelings'. Here was the determination, through an assumption of lofty mental ability, to be different from everybody else, without understanding that all people are different anyhow. Like the boy who had wished to live by 'scientific rules', Ney demanded ideas and catchwords which would solve everything, here, now. Beyond lay only his fear and insecurity. His feelings had craved outlets and found none. His eyes seemed red with unshed tears.

I said something about warmth of heart.

'Did Shakespeare have warmth of heart? Did Beethoven? Ought I to have it? How?'

'Try not to think at all. Just live. Take it easy. Enjoy things and people.'

'Did Shakespeare enjoy things and people?'

'Yes.'

I said that all the authors who gave me most pleasure had enjoyed things and people, by which I meant life. We talked about Dickens as well as Shakespeare; I suggested that both had found as much colour among ordinary folk, as among superior people he, Arthur Ney, had been encouraged to mingle with.

'Then is it possible,' he darted, 'that everything I've been told is wrong? Were my teachers at other places wrong? *Ought* I to learn something entirely different? Is it possible to learn something from everybody?'

I was going to say 'yes', but he didn't give me time. The hunted voice sped on, addressing itself not to me, but to some demon conjured in himself to be questioned and hurl questions back. Gradually he softened, and once he smiled. For an instant the tautness was dispelled, and I remembered that he was seventeen. I told him this, and the clever arrogant air returned.

'How do you know I didn't smile on purpose?' he said. 'How do you know I didn't do it just to show I could? Just to make you think something?'

'I don't believe you're as frightful as all that,' I answered, though at that moment he was insufferable.

'Perhaps I am. Perhaps I'm just doing things and saying things to see what you say. Perhaps I'll never be cured. How do I know? How does Mr Lyward know?'

We were back where I came in. Mr Lyward rejoined us. I am sure Ney believed that he had been listening at the keyhole, and he had communicated his suspicion so forcibly that I almost believed it myself. I told Mr Lyward we had been talking about Dickens. He looked annoyed, and asked: 'Is that all?' I guessed he thought we had been enjoying the kind of high-falutin' literary talk, of which Arthur Ney must elsewhere have had too many.

I tried to explain how we got on to Dickens, and he looked relieved. Ney declared that he felt happier, and that he was now going to stop worrying. Mr Lyward smiled and looked over his spectacles. 'Now we shall have you worrying about not worrying," he said. 'Go on, to bed, to bed! Who said that?'

'Macbeth. Or Lady Macbeth.'

'They didn't sleep, though. You will. To bed, Arthur Ney! To sleep! Perchance to dream! Are you a relation of the Marshal?'

'I don't know, sir.'

'Anyhow, to bed.'

I went too. Quarter-of-an-hour later Ney put his head round the door. 'Thank you for the talk,' he said, and vanished. I felt a glow of gratification. Perhaps I had said the right things after all. Perhaps I had 'got a transference'?

In the morning I informed Mr Lyward what Ney had done.

'Yes,' he replied, without offence. 'I told him to.'

I quote this interview with Arthur Ney, not because it was typical of the community, but because it was not typical. If the loosening of a boy's tongue came as a true release, it was welcomed. When this became mechanical rotation on the same theme, which appeared to him as his 'problem', it was discouraged. If it had been encouraged, those who most needed to move outwards and connect with others would have continued to revolve fruitlessly on themselves. The staff, seeing and sharing all day in living answers to the questions they might have asked in psychiatric wards, did not set the same store by formal interviews; and few of the boys ever had—or not for long—the feeling that they were part of a laboratory.

They had come in some way warped and been offered an adventure into life. They had expected school-masters and doctors, and found companions who had embarked on the same adventure before them, and now helped and beckoned them from a forward stage. In this new panorama, the 'crime' or 'offence' or 'maladjustment' became dwarfed; not because it was thought unimportant, but because it now stood in a bigger landscape. It was a symptom and even as that, for the most part, was forgotten. Groping their own slow way towards fresh hopes, fresh hazards, the boys could be aware of abrupt checks or a steadying hand and some, at certain crossroads, of anguish. But they did not feel themselves to be under clinical observation; that had happened before they came.

The tormentedness, which in Arthur Ney took the form of suggesting that Mr Lyward had a spy among the boys, or a microphone in the fireplace, was extremely rare. One other boy for a time believed that all their letters were steamed open. One County Council did ask Mr Lyward to read a boy's mail before giving it to him, because they wished to discover the names of his adult leaders-astray and hand them to the police. Mr Lyward refused. Had he consented even in this one instance, a fatal doubt would have been sown, an essential trust made suspect. Suspicion had thriven in Arthur Ney long before he came to Finchden Manor, and continued there, because he had not yet begun to take part in the adventure. Remaining static, or moving only in dry circles on the same point, he might indeed feel like a butterfly on a pin; the pin was held in position not by Finchden, but by himself. He could take it out. A year or so later, after he had left Finchden, he said: 'I suppose all those things I used to worry about must have sounded funny,' and laughed. The laughter sounded like a winged leap onward from that involuntary smile which he had been so swift, in his suspicious phase, to disavow.

He did not then know my role; the reporter-intruder, who had arrived to write a book. None of the boys knew. As far as they were concerned I was on the staff. Later I forgot the book, and thought of myself chiefly as on the staff. Now and then the pretence embarrassed me; once, in a particular vivid way.

The police had telephoned to say that a boy from Finchden was in the village of Appledore, four miles away, and 'people had been upset' because he was blind and had no one with him.

Richard had told us that he was going to walk to Appledore. This was nothing unusual. He had come to Finchden from one of the colleges for the blind, where the boys did or attempted all the things done by those who have their sight. He was merely continuing in the same way at Finchden. Earlier he had climbed the sixty-foot trees, and terrified everyone by swinging out exultantly from the summit on one foot. In November, I had taken him bathing in the English Channel. He struck out boldly for France, and I was half-frozen before he would come in. He often took these long walks by himself.

David asked me to drive out to see that he was all right. I was to follow, but not interrupt, unless I thought I must. Richard could recognise the engine of David's and Mr Lyward's car, but did not yet know mine.

He was two miles from Finchden on the way back when I saw him. A policeman was riding some way behind on a motorbike. He and I talked in a side road, while Richard stalked confidently on.

The policeman said: 'I know your methods up there. I know you want the boys to get to rely on themselves, but this lad was nearly going down the wrong road. And he was swerving about a bit at corners, like, so I just thought I'd keep an eye on him.' He had merely followed, showing great understanding, as did most of the police in the neighbourhood, and said nothing.

I took over. It was a secondary road. Lorries thundered along every few minutes, in both directions. Richard moved at about the pace of a State procession, lurching just enough to attract the attention of the observant, but otherwise unremarked. I followed about a hundred yards behind in bottom gear. Now and then he made a gesture with one arm, as if he were feeling the air, or touched a hedge to check his position. At a corner he had not memorised he swerved out, until he realised it was a corner. He never swerved when cars were coming; he waited, hearing them. It was a flat landscape, and he looked extraordinarily defiant and stubborn, out there by himself. One driver stopped me and said: 'If you've got anything to do with that fellow, I should watch out or he'll be in the Canal. He's as drunk as a lord!'

'He's blind,' I said. 'Really blind.'

'Good God! Why hasn't he got a stick?'

'He's thrown it away, I expect.'

'Good God!'

Richard went faster, as he came nearer home. He had walked this way often and knew all the turns. He rolled cheerfully in between the brick pillars, and I drove past and met him in the yard. He said he had had a fairly pleasant walk, but hadn't done what he had intended to do in Appledore, because a lot of sentimental old ladies had come round fussing him.

Suddenly he said gravely: 'I don't like this feeling that I'm watched.'

I wondered if, with that other sense which those develop who have not one of the five, he had guessed why I had come to Finchden. At that moment I did feel like a spy. I wished to tell him that I had been following him, and why, but did not. I believe, should he ever read this book, that he will understand, or at least be interested in, the sources of this wish. None of the regular staff could have felt the same kind of embarrassment. It arose from the double exception, that I was a writer, and he blind, although he saw some things which the others did not see.

The regular staff did not think of themselves as 'watching' the boys. They did not even write many notes, and once a boy had arrived seldom, if ever, looked at his file. They had little time for notes. Besides, whatever entered their memories seemed to pass under a spell which kept it there. Even at night their 'material' continued to accumulate. They did not have to ask the boys for dreams. The boys brought dreams of their own accord, at random.

'Hey, Neville, know what I dreamed the other night? I was in a room, and there was another room next door, and I had to get into it. And I couldn't. But there was a hole in the wall, see, and in the same room as me there was a man about the tenth as big as me. So I took the little —— to bits and shoved him through.'

Dreams were a part of the boys' stories, that emerged in poetry. They told something that was already known, but with a concise visual force few poets could have imagined, now lyrical, now funny, now frightening. A boy might every now and then bring a dream in writing, or one of the staff might write it down. Mr Lyward might interpret it as a kind of cartoon, or ask the boys to interpret it, and so a discussion might begin. Or else it was forgotten.

This casualness was far more typical of Finchden than my conversation piece with Arthur Ney. 'Casualness is almost my keyword,' Mr Lyward once wrote, and the word became another of my clues, with a note that I must later explain the 'almost'. Casual disclosings, casual counsellings, gradual casual growth, sometimes an inner crisis exploding casually, often a casual departure.

I began to see what Dr Selwyn had meant when he said that at Finchden the psychoanalysis was not done, but lived, and so the community became human, warm, alive. The healers went among the 'patients'. There were no barriers.

CHAPTER FIVE

I KEPT out of my room as much as possible and began to see rather less of Flynn and Peter Storey and the one or two others who, to start with, had converged upon me or insisted upon my eating at the same table. They were all intelligent and good company, but, at that time, hangers-on. Flynn might have some project for a compass march, or Riff wanted to tell me how he had met the Aga Khan; and I was quite ready to prove that I could also read a compass and had met the Aga Khan. This passed the time of day, but was not the reason I had come. I had felt I was allowing myself to be flattered into the most subtle conspiracy to form a clique, especially by Flynn, who more or less admitted it. I had given him a lift into the town one day, and we were alone in my car.

'I'm going to ask you something tricky,' he said. 'You don't have to answer.'

'What is it?'

'Suppose you went for a walk one night and went into the woods, and found Geoff and me there making a camp. What would you do?'

'Try to get you back, I suppose.'

'What else? Would you tell Mr Lyward?'

He watched me carefully. It became important to him, but much more to me, what I should answer.

'Yes,' I said, 'I should tell Mr Lyward.'

Flynn looked disappointed.

'H'm,' he said, 'I've lost a bet. You'll have to watch out, all the same. Or you'll get a group round you.'

I replied I would try to avoid it.

'Oh, *you* may not do it,' he went on. 'It's not *you* I'm thinking of! It's us.' He gave me a side-look under his eyebrows, and repeated with relish, rubbing his hands: 'So watch it!'

Flynn had a varied and entertaining technique for getting cigarettes. He started by asking for a puff, and worked up; or, after offering to pay, suggested a cigarette as a loan, promising to pay me back on Friday. Or:

'Dr Singe, do you want me to be cured?'

'I suppose so.'

'Then give me a fag.'

'How would that cure you?'

'It'd be psychologically good for me. I'm frustrated, see. Now if you give me a fag, that'll get rid of my frustrations.'

'And if I don't?'

'You will. You'll see.'

Once after long cajoling I gave in. He took the cigarette and added, 'Weak!'; it was some time before he got another.

He shared a shack on the edge of the football field with Geoff Miller, a boy whom he depended on while apparently succouring. They had been at the same place together before coming to Finchden. At Finchden they had been kept apart until, just before my arrival, Mr Lyward, with a definite purpose, had decided to try them together. (A similar plan had worked with another pair.)

Flynn was willing to agree that Finchden was a peaceful place but claimed, after he had left, that he had 'made a racket' out of it. Geoff Miller was his partner. Cigarettes mattered more to them, or at all events to Flynn, than to any other boy, and if something went wrong or they had had a row they would share their last to calm themselves down. They sold cigarettes to other boys; also empty jam-jars, which did not belong to them, for which they charged 1/6d.; also ideas, for which they charged sixpence each. They usually managed to collect three times as much tobacco a week as anyone else, and kept their capital hidden in the back of a book; at one time it was as much as five pounds.

I must admit that I liked Flynn greatly and, although I later saw his unpleasant side, I continued to like the rest of him. Hardly anyone else in the community liked him at all, partly because of that unpleasant side, partly because he did not enter their world, but remained a disturbing lone wolf and nuisance on its fringes.

Tolstoy begins Anna Karenina: 'All happy families are the same. Unhappy families are unhappy in different ways.' Finchden Manor had the characteristics of a happy family anywhere. It is convenient to use the word in order to illustrate those characteristics, but I do not wish to press the resemblance; fifty people, none of whom is related by blood to another or has shared any part of the other's childhood, are not a family.

But, like a happy family, this community did seem to have existed always, and to be unimaginable at an end. Finchden Manor was the old home. Only war drove the family away. Afterwards the natural thing was to return as soon as possible. 'We, the undersigned,' the boys wrote, in Shropshire, their second wartime migration, 'want to return to Finchden Manor, so long as we have light, water, and a roof, building licences or no building licences.' Finchden was empty only once again, on the night of June 1, 1951. when coming-of-age was celebrated in London.

At some schools, the older boys become prefects. In a nagging family, they may become 'big brothers' of an oppressive kind and upset the younger children. In a happy family they are friends to the younger, and may become, casually, guides.

A number of older boys at Finchden had been there several years. Some, still struggling with themselves, were unaware of others and of little help to the younger boys. Several, now at the stage of working for examinations, or about to take up jobs, were given a position almost on the staff, but not at all like prefects. They seemed about to cross a frontier; helped to this point, the next stage of their growth would come through a deeper sensing of relations between boys and staff. Mr Lyward would invite them to talk to a boy arrived for an interview, who might be the same age as themselves. By a word or two, he could indicate to them the new boy's particular need. They responded. They came not only to games, or to work, more easily than they had before, but also to people. It is nonsense, of course, to call intuition wholly a 'gift'. Intuition—and the understanding born of intuition—grows, or does not grow; it is more likely to grow in an atmosphere, as at Finchden, of relaxation, where neither intellect, nor physical prowess, nor will-power, has been forced at its expense. These older boys at Finchden Manor had a deeper understanding of people than most boys at their age elsewhere, some of whom might be more brilliant or more obviously dutiful; were likely, too, to feel especial understanding for younger boys at Finchden, now approaching or passing through the same stages as they had passed through. This humanity, renewed each year as boys growing up attained it and filled the places of others who had taken it with them into the world, was part of that unenshrined tradition; part of that 'strength of the community', which made quite impossible any organised bullying or forming of gangs.

Of course there were boys who did bully now and then, or tried to, and boys who stole from the others, and boys conspicuous for their crude language—as many at least of the latter coming from wealthy homes and public schools, as from poor homes and State schools. But they could not dominate the community, and could not impress or frighten any other boy for long. It was not only the staff who knew what these boys were doing, and knew the fear and need to appear grown up from which bullying or swearing might spring; the other boys knew too, and soon the bully himself. It might be necessary to stop bullying at once, by ordinary methods. It might, in one or two instances—which I shall give later in this chapter—be necessary to send an exceptionally disturbing boy away. But, in general, bullying, stealing, swearing, fell away as the need to bully, steal or swear, diminished.

Some boys tried to take Finchden Manor by storm at once. One of them was a boy deprived of love. He had wrenched attention to himself in the usual ways, and been found out. Sent to Finchden, he played for it again, and on his first evening succeeded in dominating a whole room by bravado. It shook him to find that the conquest did not last, and had not really been a conquest. He was not deliberately rebuffed, but the others did not respond.

At their different stages, the boys were aware of the deeper impulses behind the actions another, particularly a newcomer, flaunted on the surface. They sensed fear at the root of any kind of compulsion to 'show off'. Boasts and boastful deeds, intended to provoke awe, were met with emotions more like condolence, as if, at the end of a dictator's tirade, the audience were to rise silently, pat his hand, and murmur: 'We're sorry for you.' And it was in their hearts, not emotionally, or in their heads, that the audience at Finchden meant it. They did not need to be told how the new boy had suffered in the past. They only knew that he had. They all had. Otherwise they would not be there.

One day there was to be a dance. The boys had borrowed some trellises belonging to Nigs Walker, as a foundation for the décor. Someone annoyed him, and he demanded his trellises back, which meant—as he knew it meant—no décor. The dance was to start in a few hours. Sid came in, and found the boys helpless.

'Take the whole thing down,' he told them.

He thought he knew what would happen, and it did. Nigs broke the trellises to bits and refused to cook. Sid became extremely unpopular. The boys stood about accusing the staff of 'giving in again to Nigs'. Nigs stood outside sulking, isolated. After a while the boys came up to Sid, and one said: 'We thought you were hitting at us. Nigs is the one who's suffered.' They all looked at Nigs, until one went over and asked him to help them with the lights, and so, although the trellises were destroyed, he was brought in again to help with something different. The boys did this, not Sid. They seemed often to understand that when one of them, in sulks or rage, destroyed property, he might suffer, and certainly destroyed something, within himself. A few boys showed their 'independence' by running away. They were sent back from afar, or found in Tenterden. No penalties. No reproof. Nothing might be said at all, or the member of the staff who had driven the boy back, late at night, might get him a hot meal. It was not independence the boy had shown, but dependence.

Alastair Baker turned up at Finchden; his parents were in another country. Each day he made a point of announcing how much he hated the place and how soon it would see the last of him; even after he was clearly enjoying some of its aspects, he still clung to the idea of leaving. A friend telephoned. Mr Lyward took the call and told him what he thought of him for ringing up a 'patient'; a word he seldom used unless someone outside had to be reminded for some special reason. In Mr Lyward's hearing, Alastair then repeated what he thought of Finchden. He arranged to meet the friend and said: 'I'm off down-town.' Neville offered him a lift, and when the friend did not turn up invited Alastair to have coffee. The boy accepted grudgingly. Next time he was left to meet the bus alone, and on this occasion David happened to be shopping with his wife in Tenterden and saw him still waiting. They invited him to tea. Alastair came and, suddenly forgetting himself, unburdened. He talked and talked. The friend never turned up. David asked:

'Are you coming back to Finchden?'

'Yes. I'd like to.'

Next day he was as hostile as before. Yet for a moment the hating role had been abandoned. In his state of mind at present he wanted nothing to do with any families at all; and yet, gently, casually, he might be drawn into the family at Finchden, accept love, and remain.

It was not always by any means the staff who did this 'drawing in'. Often it just happened, as a beggar is drawn to a fire. Boys who agreed to stay, but with a blank and hostile condescension, which proclaimed 'Go ahead and cure us. *We*'re not going to help', were drawn into a game of cards, or suddenly had to smile— it might be at a concert, or at someone playing with the monkey, or during one of those discussions—and the game of cards, the smile, might be a beginning, though they went back afterwards to scowls. Some boys accepted Finchden from despair, saying to themselves that this was their last hope. Some revelled in it; one, now thirty, remembered sitting on his bed and thinking what a joy it was to wear a dirty shirt. The feeling that had come to these boys at their first interview— 'This is it'—never left them. They found there all that had been missing, and gave all that they had been unable to give, within their own family.

Finchden had the hospitality of a happy family. When you said goodbye you were asked to return. When you returned you were welcomed. A place was kept for you, and food appeared. Nothing seemed to have changed. A few new boys might have arrived; you did not notice them at first, because they were already behaving as if they had been there for months. You recognised a boy you had seen on your previous visit, at his first interview, strained and unhappy; already he looked relaxed and younger. Sometimes there would be a boy who sat by himself and could not yet join in. An old member of Finchden might be at supper. Perhaps he had brought his girl, or you would see him wandering about on his own, remembering places, incidents, people, Mr Knox. So it could be at any ordinary school. Here the memories were more poignant; memories not only of youth, but of thankfulness, transformation.

Visitors were sometimes nervous of coming to the boys' meals. They had no need to be. If a stranger wanted to ask questions, many of the boys could give at least as good an impression of Finchden as anyone else. They were direct and unpretentious, and talked about themselves easily, on the level of ordinary conversation. Naturally, they championed the place. If a visitor were skeptical, they suggested he should stay there for a few days and live among them. Once half-a-dozen young psychiatrists arrived and spent an hour or two in the dining-hall, each amongst a group of boys. The boy who praised Finchden most highly was one who was doing his utmost to leave. Another went home for a wedding and told his friends that everyone would benefit from a week at Finchden. Nearly all the boys understood they were learning something they would find in few other places. They no longer thought of themselves as odd or guilty or to be pitied, and wanted to describe Finchden because they thought it worth describing, and were proud of it; and by describing they revealed it.

They had visits from head-masters, social workers, doctors, probation officers, magistrates, men and women. The boys could quickly recognize whether strangers had or had not an open mind. Consequently, even in an hour or two, a visitor could often feel a touch of those intimate challenges to rigid attitudes which Finchden presented to the boys. It was sometimes the cleverest visitors who seemed to be the most closed, as if they felt the challenge and were saying: 'Oh, don't make us start all over again.' But the boys took to someone like the Educational Officer who asked 'Do you fellows ever cry?', and on being told 'Yes', said: 'You're lucky. It was a long time before I could.' They took less to a tough-looking but vain Australian, who lectured them on I.Qs. After they had begun to call him the Queen of Sheba, he came to Mr Lyward, said 'They don't like me,' and burst into tears. They liked an old lady called Mrs Hallam, grandmother of a boy who later came to Finchden for years. Her daughter, the boy's mother, had paid a brief visit and disapproved. Mrs Hallam, an intelligent dowager aged seventy, determined to see for herself. She tramped all over the place, had long talks, enjoyed and admired. 'I suppose she understood,' said one boy, 'because at her age she has no axes to grind.'

The kind of visitor they did not care for at all was the man who set out to impress them, or to analyse them. A person arrived, known ever afterwards as Educated Jones. He picked on two of the most intellectual boys and took them, without Mr Lyward's knowledge, to the local pub, where he bored and annoyed them with his views on complexes and inhibitions. Unwisely returning to interrogate the rest, he was all but thrown into the pond.

Children felt at their ease at Finchden. One boy taught a little girl visitor pottery. A boy of twelve came for a few weeks before going to public school, because his mother wanted him to experience

Finchden's depth and ease; he could hardly be persuaded to leave. A visiting head-master's child took off his clothes and bathed happily in the pond; but his parents stayed suspicious.

The boys had many friends in the neighbourhood, and no irreconcilable enemies. Any tradesman who saw them week in week out was bound to observe the alterations in them. Mr Bolton, who owned the sweetshop, would keep an eye on certain boys, perhaps for a long while: but a time came when—except with a few—he could take the eye away. Finchden had a good and much-loved neighbour in Colonel Cosens, who owned the adjoining orchard and took the swill from the kitchen for his hens. He and his daughter had long been friends of Mr and Mrs Lyward and the boys, and came to all their shows, pantomimes, concerts and parties. Now and then there would be big occasions, such as the play Fitzy produced and later took on tour. The hall would then be packed to the walls. The boys were hosts. They had good manners, worn as easily as their good suits, and completely without their tongues in their cheeks. This often surprised visitors. But why? It was 'the result of years of letting be, during which the boys have grown to feel that they could not buy approbation ... and that nobody will attempt to buy them either.'

They had also a kind of chivalry towards one another. Once Mr Lyward invited the local string quartet, although concerts given by people outside were rare. One or two guests sat in front in the home-made chairs, with the boys all round. The monkey perched in one boy's lap, a dog, a cat, a hamster in somebody else's, and the log-fire blazed. In an interval between Schubert and Schumann, Richard rose without a word, felt his way between the musicians to the piano and played Chopin. No one was embarrassed, no one thought it strange. When my wife went later to speak to Richard, two boys at once joined her, in case she did not know he was blind. Another night Fitzy was given a farewell present, in a hall crowded with old members of Finchden, parents, and friends from Tenterden. The presentation was made after a revue, which ended with a scene from *Hamlet*, and the boys chose Tubby John as their spokesman.

Aged nineteen, he was an amateur of heraldry, and weighed forty stone. They helped him on to the stage, where he made his speech surrounded by the Danish court in jewels and slashed hose. It is within a corner of this quiet picture that one should place the troubles—the burning of a barn, a theft, a dog, supposed to be tied up, left loose and killing chickens. Every so often something of this kind happened, just as every so often some boy ran away. These events were not the atmosphere; like Flynn, they were the atmospherics.

The police showed the understanding the constable had shown who followed Richard. Another of them became friendly with a boy who was a wireless fan, and turned up in uniform so often that Sid had to ask him to come in plain clothes. The constable was amazed. 'I didn't think it mattered,' he said. Police never came to the house without telephoning, and never came at all unless they had to. When they did I used to have an impression as if all the windows had been shut, or someone were walking over a grave. When the police had gone everything seemed to open up again. While I was at Finchden they only came about five times.

Ordinary people in the neighbourhood did not judge the boys. After the move into Shropshire Finchden's closest friends became two old folk employed by the new landlord. A Tenterden taxi-man driving me away gave a lift to another fellow, who said 'I hear one of the boys up at Finchden set fire to something', and added a derogatory remark.

'Don't be a damn fool, Jim,' said the taxi-man. 'You were a lad once—besides, what you don't understand is, the boy that's done it's ill.'

There was a commercial traveller who used to make frequent visits to Finchden, and struck up a friendship with Sid. One by one, he drove all his family over from the other side of the county. His father, eighty, became ill and was unconscious for three weeks; on recovering, he came to Finchden. 'I thought I'd be all right,' said the old man, taking both Sid's hands, 'I knew you were all thinking of me.'

The happiest families have sorrows; the most healing communities, those they cannot heal. No account of Finchden Manor or any other community could be a true account which left out those boys it either could not help or could only help a little. The reasons vary, that no more could be done for them. About a third could probably have been helped a great deal more had their parents been willing for them to remain. More than half the remainder needed medical treatment elsewhere. And what about the rebels? People said to me, 'It's all too good to be true. Surely there was somebody who loathed the place.'

Just under two hundred and seventy boys, including those who are at Finchden Manor now, have been in Mr Lyward's care since he began his adventure at Guildables in 1930. (This excludes girls, women, and about a score of men well into their twenties). Of this total about fifteen came for a brief treatment during the early days and went back to school immediately afterwards. Of the rest, just over two hundred and fifty, about thirty stayed only a few days, weeks, or at the most six months.

Ten of these thirty went away almost immediately to mental homes, hospitals or State institutions. During the short time they remained at Finchden, they demanded and were given all the attention of which Mr Lyward and his staff were capable, in the hope that their instability might possibly turn out not to be a sickness but a disturbance, curable outside a hospital.

How sick some were will become clear from the following extract. It is taken from a diary written by one of the staff concerning a boy called Peter Fell.

> 'On Wednesday afternoon I saw him in the hall, and he was crying. He said he was not unhappy. The reason for crying was that he was so happy to realise he was cured and could lead a normal life again. His chore for that day was washing

supper dishes. This job, which normally takes fifteen minutes, took him an hour and three-quarters. Throughout, and during the following days, he addressed himself with phrases like: "Peter, you must take a hold of yourself; Peter, you are wonderful"—referring to his ability to play the piano. Next day, after playing, he came to me and said: "Shake me by the hand." I did so. "You may now say," he continued, "that you have shaken hands with the second Mozart, the next genius." He burst into tears, and ran upstairs. ... Later he started singing. He sang all night ...'

One boy, who went into a mental home after a week or two, did damage to Finchden costing a large sum, and disturbed the others by talking about his experiences in mental hospitals. He had an obsession that he could cure everyone. Another was described as taking up the whole attention of the staff and making every meal a shambles. He set up an altar by his bed. Another of these boys too sick to remain at Finchden, sold tickets for a bogus raffle in the town, and stole from the Church and other places. He 'could not sustain an ordinary conversation'.

Another arrived with over thirty convictions. He committed two offences outside Finchden almost at once, which were quashed in the hope that he might remain there. He had an obsessive hatred of the police, stole a car, drove at seventy miles an hour, and tried to knife the policeman who arrested him. Extremely strong, he threw two policemen on the floor, and slipped several pairs of handcuffs. He gave no trouble as long as he remained within the grounds of Finchden, and the other boys were never frightened by him. He could only be persuaded to go to the police station on condition one of the staff went too. He had a warm affection for Neville, and has kept up a cheerful correspondence with Finchden from a State Institute.

Another boy stayed a few days, then went to prison, where he smashed all the furniture in his cell. He too was sent to an Institute.

Such boys—and the rest were similar—were unlikely even to have been considered at any other place without warders or resident doctors. They never injured the other boys. One, Michael Feldman, not sick in the strictest sense, proved so disturbing that after several exhausting months both staff and boys asked for his removal. He came in war-time, and Mr Lyward has never since taken anyone like him.

'When he walks in, all the laughs become forced, and nobody dares say anything. He teases people in a way that really hurts them, and says he has only just started. He was sent on a job in the lorry, and made one boy cry the whole way. If two boys are playing he has to spoil their game, and he terrifies the little boys. He threw one of them out of a car. He steals from shops, pushes people off the pavement, uses obscene language to girls in the town, and taunts the Jewish boys.' Every member of Finchden to whom I mentioned Michael Feldman, at once said that he was the most disturbing person they had ever met.

Of these thirty boys who remained at Finchden Manor less than six months, about eight ran away and for various reasons could not be brought back. A boy arrived called Marlow, during the Christmas fortnight—and Christmas at Finchden was a fortnight. 'Give it a chance,' his probation officer said.

'What do you think of it?' David asked him on his third day.

'Lousy. There's —— all to do,' he answered, although he had made no effort to find out what he might do.

'What do you want to do?'

'Go into the Secret Service. Can you teach German?'

David said he could start to-morrow. But the boy walked out. Later Mr Lyward received a postcard, postmarked from London, saying: 'I've only gone to get some money. You know you needn't worry about me.' Then—silence.

Jim Learoyd stayed two weeks of May, 1947. There was a dance in the hall. Mr and Mrs Lyward were going away next day. All the doors in their part of the house were left open for the guests from Tenterden. Mr Lyward went to welcome the girls and for once went straight through to the big hall to see that one boy was being brought into the party. He forgot to return. Jim Learoyd slipped into Mr Lyward's study, pocketed a large sum which for the only time ever was lying in an unlocked drawer, and vanished. He was found a fortnight later in London, with only a quarter of the money left. The law took its course, and he could not come back, though Mr Lyward would have taken him.

The remainder of these thirty boys (about fifteen) were taken away by parents or guardians before they had given or been allowed to give Finchden a fair trial. Three were removed on the instructions of fathers living abroad, who had never seen the place. The mother of one insisted on 'supreme control or nothing'. None was permitted to remain more than a few weeks.

There is no record what later became of the majority of these thirty, apart from the ten who were mentally sick. About five have since been in prison.

The remaining total of about two-hundred-and-twenty boys stayed at least six months. Some stayed only six months or perhaps a year, a few as long as six years.

About ten of this total were as sick as those who only remained a few days, and differed only in that their deterioration came about more slowly. The father of one could not bring himself to believe that his son was really beyond cure within the sane community of Finchden, and Mr Lyward had to insist on a second opinion. Another boy had done many pounds worth of damage, suffered a progressive deterioration over months, and had to be sent home. He begged to be allowed to return, and was described as waiting by the letter-box for Mr Lyward's answer; but it was impossible to take him back. All these eight went afterwards either to some kind of hospital or prison ward.

About seven boys not mentally sick had to be sent away, or asked to remain at home, because they were either too disquieting to the other boys or to the townsfolk and neighbours. It cost Mr Lyward an effort to send any boy away. One or two of these seven stories may be briefly mentioned here, since they illustrate the limits of 'maladjustment', as distinct from mental sickness in the strict sense, beyond which Finchden could not go, and may even cast light on the whole problem, 'What is maladjustment?'

Mat Harvey had spent his childhood in a Colonial territory and been sent back to England, away from his father, at the age of eight. He had been sexually assulted by the headmaster of his preparatory school. At Finchden, where he remained a year after the war, he would fly into rages over the most trivial things, yet when Mr Lyward told him in very simple language how unreasonable he had been, he could smile and reply: 'You win' quite cheerfully and make no more trouble till the next outburst. He had an angelic appearance. Sid and David took him out to tea. He made a terrible fuss over a shirt they had bought him, and Sid told me: 'Everyone in the tea-shop began looking at David and me, as if we were wicked uncles.' They went on to a cinema, where the boy made more scenes and ended by throwing the shirt over the balcony into the seats below, where Sid and David had to grope apologetically among the audience. Mat once attacked David with an iron bar. 'We could only keep him as long as we have,' Mr Lyward wrote, 'because a younger member of the staff was prepared to give him hours on end and to be perpetually at his beck and call.' But soon, even for this younger member of the staff, perpetuity was too long. Mat had to go away, and Mr Lyward wrote a letter many pages long, telling the story of the boy's life at Finchden and recommending the kind of treatment to which he seemed likely to respond.

Simon Parker was cruel to small animals. He refused to stop going for walks on a hill the Army used for training with live bombs; the other boys were afraid he would be killed, and begged Mr Lyward to send him home. It was also fairly common for Simon to avoid meals, having sources of income from home which enabled him to feed outside Finchden. Simon was also unique in that he used to insult boys of 'lower social status', which 'is resented,' Mr Lyward wrote, 'by boys who have been to public schools, on behalf of those who have not.' He boasted, went about repeating: 'I refuse to recognise the group', and provoked bigger boys by 'borrowing' their property and offering money in compensation.

'I fear violence beyond the ordinary school-boy scuffles,' Mr Lyward wrote, 'if Simon's insults and general behaviour lead the others to retort, and he then defends himself by kicking and biting.' The boy understood that he was to go 'into the world'. When informed that he was to go home, he became overwrought and burst into tears. Other boys consoled him and helped him to pack, and Mr Lyward's letter to the father said that Simon 'had left with everybody's good wishes. I hope that the memory of the boys' kindnesses will remain, in spite of what he may say, and that he will continue to look on me as a friend. Our best contribution is to write him a short friendly letter now and then, and let him know that he can visit us if he wants'. Mr Lyward was asked a year later to take Simon back, but could not.

Sandy Hollis identified himself completely with characters in books. He used to come into Mr and Mrs Lyward's sitting-room night after night and sit cross-legged on the hearth-rug, gazing queerly at the fire. Mr Lyward would have continued to put up with Sandy, had it not been for his effect on the other boys. One holiday, after he had been at Finchden nearly two years, it was agreed with his mother that he should not return.

Harry Meadows, not mentally sick in the strictest sense, was sent away as too dangerous to people in the neighbourhood. Another boy in this group was neither dangerous, disturbing, nor mentally ill. He had had a bad spinal injury and wore a steel corset. His behaviour had been described in the letter introducing him as 'perfectly normal in appearance, and exceptionally charming, but quite unstable. He has been turned out of twelve places and occupations in three years for lying, pilfering, disobedience, and brutality. He is irresponsible about money, has run up big debts, and disappeared.' Finchden did a great deal for him. He stayed two and a half years and was happy.

Unfortunately his parents decided to take a house in the town, thus bringing to the doors of Finchden the kind of influence from which he and the other boys needed to be temporarily withdrawn. Since the parents could not be asked to leave, Mr Lyward asked them to take the boy away. The boy wrote a year later, regretting that he had gone. In 1953, nine years afterwards, the father wrote that his son was now married, and appeared to have settled down.

Thus, of the total of boys who may be considered to have been, as it were, 'a part of Finchden', ten were sent away to receive medical treatment at once, either in hospital or prison. Of the seven not medically sick, but too disturbing for Finchden to keep, three since they left have been to prison. Mr Lyward has remained in correspondence with several of these boys, and one or two of their parents are his friends.

How did the mentally sick boys ever find their way to Finchden Manor? One Mr Lyward took to save from a remand home—'perhaps a mistake?' he noted. Of another he wrote that 'the hopes of those who recommend such boys to us are not always based on any very sound knowledge of their case'. In several instances it was through Finchden's efforts on a boy's behalf that room was found for him in hospital.

A social worker wrote to Mr Lyward: 'I have seen the boy's mother and think it extremely improbable, even if one could see her regularly, that she could have been helped towards an understanding of what is happening to him. However, she has agreed that he shall go to hospital for a period of observation and treatment. The fact that you suggested it helps enormously, since she so much admires all you have already done for him.' The boy (who now has a responsible job) had run away from Finchden; once in hospital, he ran back to Finchden.

That these boys were sent at all is a measure of the hopes placed in Mr Lyward, and of the extreme cases he has been ready to attempt, being sometimes misunderstood in consequence. Finchden has never suffered, and although the parts these boys played were sad and ephemeral, no one can say for certain that they were uncreative. Boys like Matthew Harvey spent evenings in the Guildables room among the others, joined in the same games, attended the same 'sessions'. The others were often reminded of them, and mimicked them. They said 'So-and-So was really bats', but their memories never sounded callous or their mimicry cruel. Mental sickness within a family affects not only its victims, but its witnesses too, awakening—as it did in many of the healthy Finchden boys—a responsibility towards their own fortunate sanity, and a compassion towards others, which many are unlikely to forget.

I was in the dining room one evening. Lights were out, and I meant to go to bed. David passed along the corridor with a boy I had never seen. I supposed it was a new arrival, except that he looked unusually ragged and furtive. Soon David returned, and told me that this had been a boy called Walter Finch. He came to Finchden the 'complete institution child'. Soon after his arrival neighbours had invited him into their home, thereby showing him something Mr Lyward was holding back. He had run away, then he had been in a hospital, and later in a job in London, from which he had suddenly disappeared. For weeks nothing had been heard of him. According to one rumour, he had stolen something; according to another, he had been living in the neighbourhood and been seen in Tenterden Church.

The truth was that he had not been living anywhere. There was a lorry parked in the drive which had been used to take the play on tour and now was used for collecting rations. It turned out that he had been sleeping there, creeping into it after lights out and leaving before anyone was awake. Unable to face any of his former companions, he had slept there for a week; during the day he wandered. David said the police would be coming for Finch in the morning. The boy's sister had charged him with stealing, and the charge could not be dropped. David had found him, fed him, and made him welcome; and while he was telling me the story, I felt for the first time something of the suffering David must go through himself on such occasions, and something of what Mr

Lyward had shouldered from the beginning. There were some who could be saved, others who perhaps could not. By now, in Finch's case, the law had been invoked, the machinery set in motion, and all that could come from Finchden was intercession. Mr Lyward would send David to court, where he would give evidence of the boy's sickness and plead for treatment rather than punishment. He would ask for one of the gentler remand homes, and the rest would lie with magistrates, wardens, police.

The boy slept in my room. He had my bed, and I pulled the couch across the door and lay awake. On David's instructions, I had removed everything with which Finch might have harmed himself, but he lay talking about his friends. He liked the piano. Was it still in tune? Did Riff still play the Boogie Woogies? Was there to be another concert? He came to breakfast in the morning, and the others treated him as if he had been on holiday. Whatever curiosity anyone may have felt, no one showed. Riff surrendered the piano, and Finch sat down and played the Moonlight Sonata. Neville came to the door while he was playing and beckoned to me. The police had come, and Finch went away with them. Riff went back to the piano and everything in the hall continued as before.

A little while later, David had a letter on yellow paper, from the boys' prison at Wormwood Scrubs.

'I know this is rather a sordid address,' Finch wrote, 'but there is nothing I can do about that. Well, I thank you and all the staff for all they have done for me.' He was sorry to have been so much trouble, and said that the short time he had spent at Finchden had been the happiest in his life.

We shall see later what damage a boy's own family could cause him when, having sent him into the family at Finchden, they subtly or openly maligned it, and tried to hurry him away. The family of Peter Storey—my first visitor—were not of this sort. They were good-natured but weak. Once he was home, they could not send him back; once he was back at Finchden, they could not leave him there. He was again asking to go home. Mr Lyward suggested that he be allowed to go for four days, and that I should fix the date. It was then the end of October.

'Will November 20 be convenient for you?' I asked Storey.

'Will you be here to see me come back?'

'Yes. On the 25th.'

'All right. And I swear I will. This time I really will. I know I exhaust everyone. I expect I exhausted you the other night, but I can't help it, and I'll be better after I've been home. November 25? Will you meet me at the bus-stop?'

'Yes.'

'And then soon after that there'll be Christmas, and after that my birthday in January.'

'Nobody said anything about your going then.'

'Oh, but I must. Anyhow, November 20 to 25 is settled. I like to get things settled,' he explained. 'I'm so unsettled myself that I like to know. And my family want me home. I expect you've heard about them.'

He told me more about them and about what he called the Bohemian habits of his family, leaping from fact to fantasy, with a kind of affectionate despair. He had run away four or five times already, and not always homeward. He had never yet come back on the promised day. Sure enough, as evening fell, the telephone would ring and Mr Lyward be asked to accept a reversed charge. The same the next evening, and the next. In hotel bills, reversed charges, and other 'extras', Peter Storey had cost a large sum.

He knew his weaknesses. He was terribly sorry, he said, but this time he was going to show that he had changed, and I felt sure he meant it. He did mean it when he said it. He seemed to have settled quite happily to go on November 20, but a few hours later he went to Mr Lyward and asked if he could go home at once. Mr Lyward was going away himself; hence the leaving of the date to me.

'But if you can't give me leave now, sir, couldn't you come back even for a minute or two, tomorrow or the day after, to give me leave then?'

Mr Lyward could not, and November 20 was again agreed, and November 25 for Storey's return. At that early stage in my experience it mattered to me personally that he should keep his promise. He had awakened my vanity, making me believe that where all the others, even Mr Lyward, had failed, I might succeed.

'It's all right,' Storey assured me. 'I just felt I must go to-day, but now I can't. Now I'll go when you said. If I have to drag myself on all fours, I'll be there at the bus-stop.'

He went. The day of return approached. It became one of my dear ambitions that he should be there; at least as much for my own satisfaction as his good. I longed to return with him and to present him modestly as my personal miracle. But he was not there; and when I returned from the bus-stop without him, the reversed telephone charges had already begun.

I remembered his excited manner as he told me that the most wonderful thing in life must be 'to take that top C and hold it.' I remembered seeing it happen. He had been singing Genevieve with four other boys, and when he came to that top note, he had really held it, the veins on his neck standing out and his cherub face turning bright purple. I had had a picture of the note sailing away into the sky, growing smaller and smaller in the distance, like a balloon, with Peter Storey clinging to it.

'A leaf in the wind,' Mr Lyward had said. Peter Storey had been deeply confused when he came to Finchden. There, at least, he had been secure. Now he was returning into the heart of those circumstances which had confused him.

Not many weeks had passed before he wanted to come back; but by then it was too late. However, he is still in touch.

It was nearly always the same. Peter Storey does not belong amongst those boys mentioned earlier in this chapter who were taken away after a few weeks or had to be sent away or walked out at once. He belongs to a small group who stayed well over a year, and either left 'on their own judgment' or were withdrawn by their parents strongly against Mr Lyward's advice. The great majority regretted it; I shall say more of them later. A few went to prison or to a mental home. Nearly all wrote or returned to ask for help. Some begged to come back; of these Mr Lyward was able to take back a few. One wrote, two years afterwards: 'I regret the chances I threw away by leaving you'; another: 'Finchden was a fountain of life. Now I give myself up for mad'; another, having lost or thrown up many jobs and been discharged from one of the Services, wrote: 'I have always thought I did not spend enough time with you.' The parents of another admitted they had been mistaken in removing him, but only after seven years of wretchedness and disaster. Another boy, taken away, sent back, then taken away again, wrote: 'It is no go ... I long to be at Finchden', and when he came on a visit, could not say good-bye. As I studied on in the oak-room, I heard many cries from the heart, while music came from upstairs and the boys shouted in the garden.

All those around me would remain but two or three. Arthur Ney appeared more tranquil. He assailed me frequently with 'Am I better? Am I still worrying?'; or, looking as if he was about to assail me, darted away, gnawing his knuckles. He now appeared, as Mr Lyward had foretold, to be worrying about not worrying. 'After our talk, should I give up everything I've been told before? Ought all my ideas to be quite different? *Ought* I to like jazz?'

He wanted the world and his path set out like a chess gambit. A week ago he had seen everything from the side of black, and that had given him headaches; now he supposed he should see it all from the side of white, and that also gave him headaches.

He wrote verses, some of them morbid and contemptuous. The others were influenced by the Romantics, particularly Keats and Wordsworth, and extolled the peace-giving solitude of Nature and the pastoral simplicity which does not exist. They were imitative, but here and there a true rhythm and some longing of his own came through. At Mr Lyward's suggestion he had begun to cook.

'I was a gibbering wreck after the first try-out,' said Sid, laughing. Arthur Ney showed willingness, but the basic things had not occurred to him. For example, that the oven had to be hot, or that a pan put into a hot oven to heat the fat for a batter pudding would be hot too. He took it out with his bare hands. He did not drop it, or appear to blister, but gazed at it in surprise, as if this were his first real contact with worldly things. Later he had to drain the potatoes. Sid heard a dull thud, and saw them all on the floor. Arthur had taken the boiling saucepan out bodily, instead of by the handles.

At the end of the day he said: 'I don't think I was so hot, but the food was,' and grinned. He continued sitting aloof, but now and then a smile broke through, making his morose face young. Small signs, and undramatic stories, not of the kind to headline an article about 'delinquency'; yet it was in these terms that the growing-up within this community all round me began to interpret itself.

Nigs Walker appeared to be biding his time. He was one of those boys of both potentially high intelligence and achievement, who deluded strangers that he was sophisticated. To anyone living at Finchden he certainly was not. He exacted constant attention. Night after night, he turned up in the staff room and refused to go to bed until he had seen Mr Lyward. If he could not see him, he remained downstairs, or put on his mackintosh to walk out. No other member of the staff would do; it was always the Chief he had to see. Although Mr Lyward wrote the following lines eight years before Nigs Walker came to Finchden, about another boy, they reminded me of Nigs:

'He finds excuse after excuse for leaving his fellows and invading me in my private sanctum. I can't allow this robbery on his part to continue unchecked. But I must recognise him, behind it, for the small lonely thing he is. I must watch, for instance, that he is not compelled by his feelings of guilt and his love-hunger, nor by anybody else's blindness, into undertaking a heavy or even average programme of schoolwork. Challenging has its place, but so has the feeding which should precede it.'

Nigs Walker was a voracious 'feeder'. At times one had happy glimpses of a child, unhampered by some inner compulsion to prove himself adult. I remember how he ran under Mr Lyward's window, tilting a long pole and wearing a biscuit tin for crusader's helmet. At a dance he was the child at a party, excitedly teaching Mr Lyward the St Bernard's Waltz and the Dashing White Sergeant. After a year something still kept him at Finchden, although he had 'beaten the ... County Council single-handed', and had never stayed anywhere else more than a few weeks. He might announce that he was going and still be there next morning, or put on his mackintosh and go; the same with Flynn, except that Flynn would have despised a mackintosh.

Flynn was Irish, but his people lived in North London. He was the youngest of a large family and at a very early age had been adopted by a well-to-do benevolent woman who lived in the country and had no family. When he first came to Finchden, a year before, he had been impossible. He boasted that he knew all the ropes and ran away repeatedly. He particularly baited Neville. All authority appeared to him as ponderous well-equipped enemies, bent on invading his patch of wilderness: he saw himself as the partisan behind a rock, sniping at them.

'Do you want to see my room?' he said to a visitor. 'It's the dirtiest in the whole house.'

It was. Flynn's and Miller's beds were never made, except after the general clean-up every Thursday. Their clothes carpeted the floor, entangled with stray acquisitions. I would say they reminded me of excessively Displaced Persons, if the Displaced Persons' Camps I had seen had not been so neat. But the room had a character apart from squalor. Abstracts done by Geoff papered the walls, and Flynn had hung up his collection of bits and snaffles. He knew all about them. 'This is Mexican,' he explained, taking them between his fingers. 'This is Spanish. I found this in a barn. You needn't ask where I got this one.'

'Why not?'

'I said you needn't ask.'

'Do you ride at all now?'

'I'm not allowed to get on a horse within a hundred-and-fifty-miles of here. I asked Mr Lyward to let me have a horse here, but he wouldn't.' (In fact Flynn had come on those terms). 'He said he couldn't cope with horses, but that wasn't the real reason.'

'What was?'

'I'd never have been in the house at all. I'd have spent the whole time outside or in a stable. Anyhow, I'm too heavy now. I'm eight stone. I was only six when I came.'

One of his ideas was to go to Austria and be schooled on the famous Lippizaner horses. He knew a certain amount about the theory of *haute école*, and had compiled from learned works an enormous genealogical chart, showing the family tree of the horse. He admired men who had made difficult journeys. One day he asked if 'authors ever answer letters'. Mr Lyward said—and I hope he was right—that it is an unwritten law among authors to answer letters from the young. Flynn asked if Mr Lyward would help him. Mr Lyward had a hunch and said, 'Is it to—?'

It was. Mr Lyward was able to introduce him to this man, a celebrated explorer, who became Flynn's hero and for whom he made a wallet. The explorer died before receiving the present, and Mr Lyward wondered if this had not had its effect on Flynn.

Flynn had read all the books of W. H. Hudson and dreamed of thumbing his way to South America. He was interested in stories about the Commandos and prisoner-of-war camps, and since I had been in both, this was one reason I got on well with him. He understood that the Commandos were not thugs, which is more than can be said for some who have written about them, and there had in fact been something in our training which Finchden recalled. I remembered how young soldiers, not much older than Mr Lyward's boys, had altered from dull to deft, from timid to daring, as each had been given rein to his initiative; and how the most unruly had come round to discipline.

'I'd have done well in that mob,' Flynn said.

I told him I saw him (with his hair cut), scaling cliffs, stealing past loutish sentries in the dark and pinching secret papers.

'And I can see you,' he added. 'Onward, men!' And he made the gesture of an officer urging his men on from the rear.

He made me climb a tall tree and jump from the top branches to another. He had built a canoe; although it now had thirty-four holes in it, I had to pilot it round the pond till it sank under me. One day he asked me to drive him to a point several miles from the house. We left the car there, and I followed him across the fields. He detected tracks of animals and stopped to show me a rabbit which, he said, was watching us a hundred yards away; I could not see it and as a matter of fact it was not there. Geoff emerged, with porter's cap and hunter's knife. They led me to their bivouac, boiled a canful of muddy water with tea filched from the kitchen, and told me about their one long absence. They had walked out while Mr Lyward was away and gone hiking. They had become so hungry once, they were reduced to catapulting crows, and after a week outside they telephoned Finchden (reversed charges), and asked to be fetched back. I wanted to know why.

'Because we were done in. At least Geoff was. We didn't want to be picked up, so we got old Fitzy to fetch us. We were near Winchester. We just gave him a map reference and stuck out a flag and went to sleep in a ditch until he found us.'

Flynn might, a few years later, have been useful to the Commandos and quite possibly a valuable companion on an escape. These are advantages of war-time; yet I did not see him as the adolescent to whom war brings release from failing to become a man. His love of horses and the open, and his not so foolish dreams of South America, seemed to express true adventure. And he had his romantic aspects, now the Artful Dodger, now Huckleberry Finn, and was Irish, with a sense of comedy about his own scrounging. But there was another side, of which I saw less.

He could not be depended on in dull duties. If he proposed a compass march, he would add: 'For me and Geoff and one or two others, not the whole lot of them.' He shirked routine chores.

He had an excess of self-pity, with days of blackest gloom, when he hated everyone; then there was no approaching him. There was something in himself he hated. He hated it particularly at Finchden, because there he was seen into, and because the place showed him that he was not ready to attempt all sorts of things. He still seemed to need the natural love of his own family and could not accept the love of the family at Finchden, although he respected Mr Lyward.

Flynn was one of those who provoked important questions. I asked myself—things which Mr Lyward claimed to *know*—why he should not pair off, sleep in the woods and ride horses if he wished; and then I wondered if all these desires were not defences against the real issue with himself, which engendered those sunken glooms, and asked myself if I should not pay more attention to that side of him which scrounged and slid away. I learnt slowly to be wary of superficially romantic boys; in the heart of each nearly always lay something deeply unresolved and not likeable. Flynn had, in his own mind, and in talks with me, a constant vendetta with Finchden, in which Finchden did not join. Yet he had stayed two years; and when Mr Lyward had allowed him to go on two hikes to distant counties, he had returned from both. But he still talked every day of leaving. 'The outdoor neurotics are often the most difficult,' Mr Lyward once said. 'You can't communicate with them, because they're simply not there.'

But none of those who ran or were sent away was ever thought of as an outcast, none in this family was 'disowned'; several returned on visits and remained in touch. They were a small number. Out of about two hundred boys (excluding the mentally sick, and all who remained less than six months), only about seven were asked to leave, and about ten more left—as Flynn and Nigs Walker were to leave—'on their own judgment'. Out of the forty boys at Finchden while I was there, only three or four were permanently restive. The remainder had put their trust almost unreservedly in Mr Lyward. What they had to work out of themselves, they lost in the security of Finchden, instead of in the unfeeling world. Those against whom they battered themselves—if now they did—were no longer parents who could not go along with them, or strangers who did not care, but the staff and Mr Lyward, and they were willing to leave the decision, when they should go, to him. They were the community, stable, ever altering, and light of heart.

They used technical terms as jokes. Mr Lyward once said that 'you can talk to them about themselves as a doctor talks to his students about his patients, and they don't think of the subject as themselves', but they did not get the technical terms from him. They did sketches like the following:

Enter a Boy disguised as Mr Lyward. To him enter a Boy to be interviewed.

G. L.:	And what can we do for you, my boy?
Boy:	Please ... I want to come to Finchden.
G. L.:	And what is the matter with you, my boy?
Boy:	I've got schizophrenia. (*Bursts into tears.*)
G. L.:	There, there, my boy. (*Pats Boy vaguely on head.*) You shall come to us.
Boy:	Oh, thank you, sir! What shall I bring?
G.L.:	Bring? Bring nothing.
Boy:	Nothing, sir?
G.L.:	Well—ah—my boy—bring a toothbrush. And ah—if—you have one, bring a dream.

That 'ritual' hour in the Guildables room was the time at which the boys were together. Only two or three were regularly missing for lengthy periods. Sooner or later the absent phase would end. Henry Carpenter gave up companions in the town and said: 'I can get all I want at Finchden, and much more.' Once he had either ignored or disliked the other boys; now, he told me, he had come to like most of them. He no longer resented the homelessness of his own childhood or thought the world 'owed him a living'. After having lived in adolescence within the community at Finchden, accepted it and shared it, he would be less likely to make a living at the expense and grief of others. The experience of his early life had not been lost. He kept the ruggedness and directness it had given him; he kept the knowledge that brutality exists, and that the outwardly charitable may really be warped hypocrites. Those livid years, followed by the years at Finchden, had made him, at nineteen, one who had deeply experienced mankind both at its most cruel and most loving; yet he felt no resultant strain, or gulf within himself.

Nobody will be surprised that in such a community the differences of social and financial status mattered little. The externals either of wealth or poverty appeared little, all the boys had the same basic pocket money, all wore alternately the same good or torn clothes. As their own lives developed, they became less hopelessly enslaved to externals, money included; a boy who boasted of his money was not only a boy with money, but a boy with some inadequacy in himself, which made him boast. I have no memory at all of social bitterness at Finchden, although one or two boys came from among the richest in the land, four or five from among the poorest. Each of course took into himself something he learnt from the others, including awareness of other social backgrounds than his own, their disadvantages no less than their gains; but the influence of one upon another went deeper than that.

The boys' awakening relationship with their fellows was of the utmost importance, and is difficult to describe. Part of the secret of Mr Lyward's psychotherapy was the contact of each one, not merely with Mr Lyward or with the staff, but with the group. One reason that he now undertook far less interviewing than before was because the group had shown him how great a healing effect it could produce of its own; the interviews themselves now turned often around current happenings at Finchden, and their significance in terms of general problems, rather than around the past of the boy being interviewed.

'A balance was struck between each boy's interests as an individual and as a member of the group'. This claim may possibly have been made by every community that has ever existed, and such a balance has certainly been advocated by innumerable writers, teachers and preachers. At Finchden it was neither imposed as a rule, nor advanced as a precept. It was achieved with a very special kind of group, and simply developed as part of the recommencing of a boy's whole life. One boy who had hurt himself said of another who helped him, 'Isn't he kind?' Before he came to Finchden the boy who gave help had had a reputation exactly the reverse of kind and had not altered at once. He was kind now, after three years, not because he had been told or taught, but because something had happened within himself and situations occurred in which, spontaneously, he expressed that something. Preparations for a dance, for a pantomime, or for Christmas, apart from all the daily co-operation involved in cooking or games or the evening hour in the Guildables Room, enabled boys, who hitherto had been unable to form a living relationship with even one person, almost effortlessly to achieve it with twenty or more, though it might be only for a short time and mark no more than a beginning.

This awakening was part of their rehabilitation, their 'cure'. On its other side, the educational—although the two are not really to be separated—the group worked equally as a casual and all-important agent. How much education was conveyed obliquely through those discussions of which my first day had at once offered me an example! They sprang up repeatedly, impromptu. One began in the middle of a pantomime rehearsal. Mr Lyward, stopping the actors, asked whether they preferred a play to be enacted all in one place or to range through several places. The cast gathered round, other boys joined in, and soon he was telling them about the dramatic unities, and Dr Johnson on Shakespeare, and Sir Philip Sidney. Another discussion started somehow at tea, during which Mr Lyward fetched two books and talked about the constitutional significance of the old forest laws. Once the boys were talking about the Bible. Six of them went to their rooms and brought down six different Bibles. Mr Lyward explained why the versions were different. The boys fell silent, listening. 'It's when they're quiet,' he said afterwards, 'that you feel that they're little.' Examinations are usually forgotten afterwards; so is the kind of work done merely to pass examinations. These group discussions, unorganised, at random, remembered, were followed up as links in a continuous story.

'This is a community with a personality,' Mr Lyward once wrote to a County Education officer. The boys became as Riff had said, 'persons not pawns'; and as another boy said to Mr Lyward, 'You treat us as if we were grown-up', meaning 'as persons'. They went back to the point at which personal relationships had failed them, and at Finchden discovered them anew; first it might be with Mr Lyward, then perhaps with one of the staff. As they became more widely and deeply aware, their living relationship with the community developed. Thus it was that they were weaned from their prolonged but camouflaged childhood, through adolescence, into readiness for adult life; and being themselves part of the community they became part-agents, almost unconsciously, of their own growth.

Finchden Manor was therefore something more and something less than a family. No family can prepare a child to take his way through the world without yielding him to some other group, whether it be community or school; and no other group can wholly take the place of a true family. The analogy with a family is best confined, as I said at the beginning of this chapter, to illustrating those characteristics—hospitality, cheerfulness, warmth, and sanity—which Finchden shared with happy families anywhere. The boys had the festivities one would expect, for example at Christmas, which were neither more nor less moving than they can be in hospitals, or orphanages, or other places, where love has been given to those who have suffered from the lack of love. Many boys went home at Christmas; some might not. Mrs Lyward sent about two hundred cards to former boys and friends of Finchden. At such a time the sense of family was more deeply felt, maybe, than at others; but once you had grown conscious of it, it was as likely to strike you unexpectedly—perhaps in something a boy said after he had left—as on a set occasion. It also seems true to say, since nearly all that had been missing in the homes of childhood had been re-created, that, returning to their own hearth, or going on to marriage, the boys took with them embers from the hearth at Finchden.

CHAPTER SIX

Mr Lyward was a man with certain exceptional gifts and a number of distinguished accomplishments. His uncommonly varied experience of teaching now extended over more than forty years. Although, for twenty-six of those years, diversity of both gift and experience had been applied chiefly to his work at Finchden Manor, he was also well-known as a lecturer, writer of pamphlets, and speaker at public conferences, and especially as Chairman of the Home and School Council and editor for thirteen years of its magazine. He is at present a vice-President of the English New Education Fellowship. In what may be called his other role he was, technically speaking, a lay psychotherapist, in the sense that he did not hold a medical degree. Most psychiatrists would, and the many who had sent boys to him certainly did consider him to be highly skilled, highly trained, and occupied in work as arduous and responsible as their own.

He had woven the work of teacher and healer so closely together that the two cannot really be separated. Education, in the sense in which he used the word, meant a marriage of both roles. If they are separated in this chapter, it is only for the purpose of a brief biography.

Mr Lyward came from London. 'I was born immediately after the eldest of my sisters (his twin), and towards her I was expected to behave like a little gentleman. Discouraged doubtless by my lack of success in this direction, I nearly died at the age of six, and took instead to being top of my class.' He suffered from ill-health, later discovered to be largely a physical injury, from domestic disturbances, and from poverty; and at eighteen began to teach for forty pounds a year, at a nondescript private school. Most evenings for five years he attended evening classes at King's College. He had a fine bass voice and won a choral studentship to St John's College,

Cambridge, where he took a second in History. He taught at various schools, at one commanded the O.T.C., ran an agricultural camp, and while still a young man was on the short list for the head-mastership of a large grammar school.

In his late twenties he went to Glenalmond, where he took charge of the sixth forms and was responsible for English and history throughout the school. He also coached the Rugger XV, produced and sometimes wrote plays, and was Librarian. Not long afterwards he was offered but declined the post of Organiser of Educational Studies at Durham University. The Warden of Glenalmond, Canon F. W. Matheson, wrote of him at that time as 'a born teacher. He came to me recommended by a friend, now Head of a College, as the ablest man my friend knew, certain to have won the first-class honours to which his abilities entitled him, had he not been handicapped by private circumstances which hindered his work'. He was invited, in addition to his sixth form work, to start and take charge of a house for junior boys. In much that he learnt and initiated among older and younger boys then (which does not belong to this book), he was preparing his way without knowing it for what he was later to do entirely independently and at greater depth at Finchden. After strenuous years at Glenalmond he had a breakdown and went away to recover.

'I had by that time an inside knowledge of a variety of elementary and secondary schools and fifteen years' teaching experience. ... But teaching can be a way of avoiding growing pains. I ... at last found myself sufficiently released from the fear of plunging out, to turn my back upon a too cloistered safety.' Chance had put him in touch with two or three doctors, now eminent. They were looking for someone to treat and coach the kind of public school boy who either could not or would not fit. These boys had nowhere to go and it was suggested that Mr Lyward might be able to help them.

He went to live at Guildables, a Kent farmhouse owned by a friend, and the first boys shared the farm-work. He began with two, and made a success of them. In a letter written early in 1931 he described his work: 'This place is the result of my determination, when a sixth form and house-master at a public school, that those boys who were sent away for delinquency, or for obvious mental sickness, should have a chance of being put right, instead of being left to the further mercy of their inward conflicts and compulsions. I have made a special study of many of the special problems of the schoolboy, and this work here has more than justified me in my contention, that the boy who was generally left to "go to seed" could, with the right help at the critical moment, turn into a very useful and happy member of society.

There is no difference in the emotional condition of any of them. They are all cases of arrested feeling development. The community life here is arranged so as to give them confidence in life and one another, the while they are severally going through analysis, or whatever I feel is likely to help them best towards a life in which their thoughts and feelings will diverge less widely than they did when the boy came to me. Before anybody has been here very long, he has come to accept without resentment the fact that, like many people who never come here, he has failed to grow up. The fact that the boys do all accept it makes life easier for each of them than before, where there was need for camouflage. I am, as it were, the house-master, but, while treating them all as grown-ups, I know them personally as small boys, who need encouragement and fatherliness and firmness in order to grow out of their frightened and therefore self loving state of mind ...'

Mr Lyward became more widely known in this new role, but other friends wished him to return to bigger responsibilities in orthodox education. An eminent scholar wrote to Lord Hewart, then Lord Chief Justice, asking him, 'in the cause of good learning and good teaching which we both revere', to support Mr Lyward's application for the vacant headmastership of Shrewsbury. The opinion psychiatrists had of Mr Lyward may be illustrated by what one of the most celebrated added in his favour at that time: 'I have seen him catch hold of and enthuse a boy who is a scholastic failure, in a way little short of miraculous. He has an insight into the adolescent mind which is unsurpassed in my experience of school-masters. He has a vision of educational improvements which in theory would satisfy some extremists, but which is subordinated to practical considerations on the one hand and a genuine reverence for public school tradition on the other ...'

The headmastership of Shrewsbury had been filled and Mr Lyward continued with his work at Guildables. His 'practice' came to include girls and women and grown men. The numbers of boys went up rapidly to twelve, then twenty. The farmhouse became too small and unsuitable, and in 1935 he and Mrs Lyward discovered Finchden. They passed through the wicket-gate on the Tenterden-Appledore road on a day in high summer. The grass, parched and brown with sun, was waving waist-high. Bees and dragon-flies swarmed everywhere, roses sprawled over the half-hidden brick, and the way to the house was thick with briars.

They bought it on mortgage and gradually reclaimed it from the wilderness. By the beginning of the war they had nearly forty boys. They lived through the summer of 1940 in a shored-up cellar, on the direct route of the German bombers, while the Battle of Britain was fought overhead. The house was not hit, but the Army took it over at three hours' notice for soldiers evacuated after the fall of France. Nine of the staff—which was larger then— and eight servants—there were servants then—were called up. Nearly all the boys were sent home for a fortnight. Had it not been for Mr Lyward's perseverance, for the encouragement of doctors, officials, and many parents, he would have been forced to close down. With large debts, little capital, and reduced numbers, he moved first to Hereford and a year later to a Hall on the Welsh marches.

When he returned Finchden Manor was again on its way to ruin. Grass had obliterated beds and paths, and was marching on the windows. Only one window had more than one pane of glass. Lighting and plumbing had been torn away. Compensation was far below the cost of the repairs. But Peter, Sid, David and Fitzy, together with one or two of the boys, set to work, builders were brought in, and life was resumed in the old home.

New conditions after the war gave Finchden wider importance.

Mr Lyward had begun by helping public school boys and undergraduates, but '... more and more news reaches us,' he had written in 1942, 'concerning the effect of the war and the years preceding it on all our young people. We cannot ignore the heightened awareness amongst group after group of the child's needs; but neither must we shut our eyes to the increase in juvenile crime, that is, to the number of people who are found out. And to listen, as I have done recently, to authentic stories illustrating the shifting standards of the many who are not found out (parents of the near future) is a painful experience. Must we face with more certainty the fact that the world we know is being smashed to pieces ... what must we do?'

The headlines were soon echoing him. Spivs, cosh boys, delinquency, terms that had scarcely been news before the war, became household words, and people looked round bewildered for an answer. Mr Lyward's work had become recognised as a national need. The first boy whose fees were paid from public funds arrived in 1944. At one period in 1946 education officers, probation officers and social workers were applying for vacancies at the rate of four a week. After the passing of the Education Act, 1944, and Children's Act, 1948, applications came in dozens, and by the time I went to Finchden, doctors far beyond Harley Street, Councils far removed from London, had begun to make use of Mr Lyward's gifts and experience. Yet lack of money, uncertainty about the future—his own and that of his staff—have never ceased to be anxieties. One might say that Finchden has given security to everyone who lived there, except to its founder and director.

Mr Lyward had a pale slender face. His hair lay flat across the top of his head, above a high forehead. I have a photograph of him at a Christmas party, with a lighted candle in front of him. Face and candle bear a resemblance to one another; were the candle to blow out, the table would still be lit.

I find with him, as with Finchden, that it is easier to say what he was not than what he was.

He was never cruel, mean, sneering, or disloyal. But when I begin to think of other characteristics and say 'he was this', the opposites occur at once and I have to say 'he was that too'. His moods and expressions ranged between the extreme of withdrawal and the extreme of participation. He had once had poliomyelitis, which had injured the muscles of his neck. This was the reason he often held his head so low, which made his withdrawn moods seem more withdrawn. With his spectacles well down his nose, and his eyes looking over the rims like scouts over a half-lowered drawbridge, Nigs Walker might well call him 'Old Tortoise'. But I felt that when 'withdrawn', among a crowd of boys or in private conversation, he was very much present, enjoying, listening between the words, absorbing. He seldom struck me as being absent-minded or preoccupied.

When he joined in, he chaffed and chivvied and laughed and seemed as young as the boys. He enjoyed looking on at people, and overhearing the conversations of complete strangers, and seldom came back from some visit outside Finchden without an account of a family playing on a beach, or people seen in a restaurant, who had been 'just like a Chekhov play'. He acted them. He acted boys and parents of ten or twenty years ago, gaily and without malice. These flash-backs were continually interrupting his answers to my questions. 'Oh, but surely I told you that story?'—and suddenly the lights seemed to go out and I to be watching a film of something that had happened in the 'thirties. I looked forward to the time we spent, going through the story told in Chapter Nine. He brought the characters of nearly twenty years ago to life.

He had no hobbies apart from occasionally making rugs. 'The only thing I can really do is sing,' he said, but he could also and almost daily did play the piano. Bach, Mozart, Scarlatti were his musicians. His heart was in music and I enjoyed listening, especially when I was working late and he was playing in the room above. He often led rollicking choruses on the hall piano, leaving the high notes to Peter Storey. There was always music in the house. Boys believed not to have a note in them learnt to play the piano, after a fashion. All this came from him.

He loved beautiful things and cherished good furniture without fuss. His house was seldom without guests. He was fastidious in personal taste and the boys' untidiness repelled him. When he gave a present he did it unexpectedly, after great trouble to select; he once gave me a rare medallion, and Neville an ivory chess set. He did not dun parents who owed him money—some still owed him hundreds of pounds. He once paid for a boy's operation out of his own money, and was always keeping several boys for nothing. He seldom bought anything but books for himself.

> Me, poor man,
> My library were dukedom large enough.

Mr Lyward reminded me of Prospero; but livelier, gayer, and without a beard.

The atmosphere of civilisation at Finchden came from him. Although he had rejected the forms and limits of a public-school education, he had felt at home in those surroundings. They were recalled by his way of speaking, unhurried and amused, by his books, his habit of quotation, even by the panelling in his room. No one would have been surprised to find him blue-pencilling Greek verse. Everyone knows that life at a public school can pamper and stunt those who are already too sheltered, rendering them fearful yet envious of the rough world outside, and perpetually homesick for their youth. But a public school can also offer the tranquillity and the respite from emotional disturbance, which elementary and secondary schools do not offer; and Mr Lyward, who knew both— as pupil and master—once wrote: 'Does the isolation of a public school protect its members from a too premature challenge? And if this is a psychological fact, would it be possible to provide similar security for those who cannot afford to buy it?'

It was the security of the public school he valued, not the

trademark, and the security he had recreated at Finchden, in a physical as well as emotional sense. True, he had only a few fields, a garden and a romantic manor house; but as he walked about and talked to the boys, he conveyed the leisure of meads and cloisters, and into a quiet setting had successfully gathered many who were raw and loud, much that was unorthodox and adventurous. The result resembled an Odyssey in a harbour. Gradually the boys absorbed rather than acquired a culture, growing tolerant and curious, ceasing to peer at life along the tram-lines of a job or career, and beginning to reconnoitre in width and depth.

This civilising enlarging influence is far from unique among teachers, but at Finchden humanism was not its only source. The boys had some opportunity, during years of relief from the pressures that had brought them to Finchden, to come naturally to a deeper wider truth than either humanism or science can reveal. Mr Lyward quoted the New Testament to them as often as he quoted Shakespeare, and moved between many planes with apparent naturalness and ease, as if a single and spiritual vision joined them.

Finchden may have had many characteristics of the 'rebel' school, but Mr Lyward was not a rebel. Not many of the boys, and he never, went about saying: 'Just look at us! Aren't we uninhibited?' He was both daring and original, but in ways too serious and profound to boast. He did not set out to shock, and if he did shock, it did not gratify; that was not the point. Should a visitor see a boy with a beard, or another with tattered trousers, or a third flashing a turquoise, a few words with Mr Lyward made it clear that this little world which had grown up about him went much deeper than its superficial surprises. But if a visitor appeared interested, Mr Lyward would take him round and make a point of showing him the beard, the tattered trousers, or the turquoise, and introduce the friendly boy wearing them. ...

There are orthodox rebels and orthodox diehards; one thrives on the other. Either has only to champion anything for the other automatically to oppose it. In education, one bellows 'Obey!', the other 'Do as you like'. One demands corporal punishment and blazers; the other wants no discipline and insists that children should go about with nothing on. The emphasis is on the word 'insists'. Both would like their opinions to be enforced; one in the names of law and order, the other for the sake of liberty and progress. Neither is capable of learning anything from the other, and in consequence neither grows up; often they act not out of concern for others, but some muddle in themselves.

Mr Lyward came to his conviction by life. Self-government, once so popular among reformist teachers, he described as an extra liable to be 'served out in parcels, and no solution for the boys' tautness, being only another kind of imprisoning formalism'. He thought little of any kind of teaching that was lifelessly added on for the sake of being called either conservative or progressive; or of any training 'divorced from the child's wishes, fantasies, and needs'. If he had got into the public eye, he might have been given a 'character', like a film or television star, and no public label or slogan can ever be subtle. A slogan repeats itself like a stencil, and no single phrase or expression could cover a treatment which was as varied and elusive as life. Finchden was neither explicitly 'for' nor explicitly 'against' the various attitudes for which various schools have become known. It might stand 'for' many of them in the long run, and 'against' any one at unpredictable times. There was discipline, but none you could see. Finchden was neither Left Wing nor Right; it had movement and flight, for which one needs two wings. Mr Lyward said that it was 'neither one thing nor the other, but the third'. Publicity has no time for such distinctions.

He did possess the gift of power, in the sense that many people trusted him and were willing to put themselves in his hands. He stood in awe of power, which made misuse difficult, and never stamped the boys at Finchden with his own image, nor bound them to him, nor insinuated his own theories. His life was spent trying, to erase the disaster of such errors.

Finchden had grown. The artist loves what has grown and distrusts what has been organised, and by temperament Mr Lyward was an artist. Finchden had begun without rules, charter, tradition; without even a freehold, it had matured like a work of art. Mr Lyward's lack of money and of influence led him to suppose that he might always remain an employee. After he had left Glenalmond and started his independent work, he still did not know what would become of it, nor what he wanted it to become. It had unfolded out of him and around him, taking possession of his life and becoming bigger than himself.

His astonishing memory was not anecdotal, pulling out stories like a string of sausages. But a bulb flashed on the circumference, sending a current to the centre, which lit up other bulbs. A writer sometimes finds himself in this condition, that nothing can happen without suggesting fresh material for the book in hand. It seemed to me sometimes that Mr Lyward had been writing a big book for a long time, and that he had lived for many years in the artist's exhilarating awareness of the unity of all and the separateness of individuals. Suspicious of all panaceas, he belonged to no category and put no one else in one. He would not have pigeonholed a pigeon. Once he was asked to review Anton Makarenko's famous *Road To Life* about the Gorki colony in Soviet Russia in the 'twenties, and thinking of his own doubts, his own empiricism, wrote: 'Nothing could be more convincing than the way Makarenko recalls his uncertainties about his own capacity. "Am I," he seems to say, "not an educationist after all?" Every so often he confronts us with incidents which defy simple exposition, but show that there will always be some limit past which it is impossible successfully to push any theory.'

Artists must know how to wait; many are still waiting. A boy once brought Mr Lyward two lines of a verse he had found, and remarked: 'This is what you are like:

> Learning to wait consumes my life;
> Consumes, and feeds as well.'

'Love that can wait', he wrote in one of his articles. The words might have been written above the porch.

He waited quietly while others stood around nervously, while the telephone rang, while letters arrived from parents and County Councillors. He did nothing, when action would have been a welcome but ineffectual release from tension and exasperation. He did not pump and dredge the boys; sooner or later they usually told him of their own accord what troubled them. He wrote to a boy's mother: 'Action at all times is effective and fruitful, just in so far as it follows a period of passivity, during which the true observation and acceptance of the real facts, internal as well as external, have been made.' But when a decision was taken, all the artillery moved up during the time of waiting would then be fired off, in attack rather than defence, and it was difficult to get a word in. He did not lose his temper, but sometimes exploded on purpose. 'My God!' said one boy, after one of these calculated outbursts, 'I heard the Chief's voice half a minute before he came in through the door.' If he told a boy to go to bed or to get out of the room, the boy disappeared at once.

Waiting is long-term and strategic. Its tactical expression is timing. Some actors and actresses succeed with little apart from timing. Hold back the gesture a second longer, make the pause a second shorter, and the laugh, the tear, are lost. Mr Lyward excelled in timing, which is not a matter of flair, but needs endless patience, practice, observation. Hold back the challenge to a boy for a day, or a week longer, advance it by a month, and the chance never recurs. Over and over again action came upon the chime. He wrote a letter, and it arrived the day the boy most needed it, or suddenly forbade a liberty he had hitherto allowed, and the boy complied.

He used timing in interviews and lectures. Once, expected to lecture in a room where everyone was shouting, he stood on the dais, opening and shutting his mouth but saying nothing. People near the front looked at him in amazement; soon he began. He employed his tones of voice, his silences, with a true sense of theatre—though not theatrically—and could bring down his curtain like a sunset or a guillotine. He acted deliberately at times, knowing that he was acting. As a teacher his job was to be listened to. Hence the sudden breaks in what he said and the startling images. 'I seldom lecture to people about sex without mentioning a sword.'

Whatever his gifts, whatever his experience, his work could not have thriven for a quarter of a century, if he had been off hand in his dealings with parents or official bodies, or if he had not known exactly where he stood in regard to public opinion and the law. People applaud an adventure after it has succeeded, but one slip before success may start a clamour. Mr Lyward accepted formidable risks. It was a risk to let Richard go for walks alone; a risk to let Riff stay out late at night; a risk to challenge one boy and leave another. All pioneer work with adolescents is always in peril, not from ill-will so much as from the boy who dramatizes himself or the parents who cannot understand. If the pioneer happens to be slipshod, arrogant, or only weary at a crucial moment, then God help him! Mr Lyward had no Department or Board of Governors to refer to in difficult situations. He could not share his responsibility. He was answerable in person for everything he himself did and for all that his staff did for him, and administration had to be as thorough as the original creative side of his work, if he wanted to remain creative.

His reports might fill five lines one month or five pages the next. He used the telephone lavishly, but did not care for it. He confirmed his conversations in writing, and when misunderstanding was to be expected, made sure that what he said was witnessed. Long reports about boys he could no longer help went from him to magistrates, mental homes and Borstals, although he was not obliged to write them, and he spent hours preparing lectures. I have already quoted his remark that the boys were 'seven-year-olds with an L sign'. Other phrases stay in the mind.

'Because politeness is the very signature of sanity, we must not keep on demanding "Please" and "Thank you" indiscriminately, thereby making our members draw cheques on what is not yet theirs.'

'This boy will not bring his gifts to the altar.'

Of a new President of the Ministry of Education: 'His name is Butler. May he remember that education means to nourish.'

'His parents are kind people, and will "do anything for the boy". And so they have *done* for him.'

'Adults are wise to admit their helplessness quite often. The young are more willing then to acknowledge theirs.'

'We are always in danger of becoming like the people we say we hate.'

Mr Lyward thought this last phrase a commonplace. I wonder. Anyhow, I stole it and put it into a play.

He enjoyed playing with words, which led him into some rather donnish puns, but also into some helpful rejuvenations. Analysis: 'When I was a boy, analysis meant grammar. In later years it came to mean cure', but now after years of experience he spoke of it in its original sense of 'a loosening'. 'Always, since I pondered it all, the need for looseness for children and loosening among adolescents has seemed to me very urgent and very much neglected.' And 'prep.': 'Why does it so often mean anything but preparation, and only too often an ill-timed assault upon the child, challenging him too early concerning what he has not had time to digest or enjoy or relate. If it has not prepared him rather as a sniff at the kitchen door might prepare him for a meal, has not a great opportunity been missed?'

He restored honour to the desecrated word 'revise', which has been 'scribbled on the blackboard at the end of term so often as to be almost meaningless. It brings to mind memories of fingers, often wetted, tuning pages rapidly to the accompaniment of an almost audible murmur: "Know this, know that, know that ..." But to revise is to re-see ...' A 'spoilt' child, he said, was clearly somebody needing help. 'The child has been spoilt by somebody. And why should spoiling simply imply petting?'

Words have become encrusted with associations. To restore

words to their proper use was 'One of the poet's pleasures. In doing this he may, sometimes unwittingly, perform an act of healing. If a man tells a delinquent boy of sixteen, who has been fatherless for years, that he has not the same excuse for stealing as a hungry person, a psychologist might want to blurt out: "Man does not live by bread alone". That is poetry, and there is a virtue—the word implies strength—in such a psychological approach ...'

Mr Lyward drew little on the overworked vocabulary of Oedipus complexes, mother-fixations, repressions, inhibitions, and preferred a simpler Anglo-Saxon word if he could find one. He talked of a hunch more readily than of an intuition, preferred 'crutches' to 'compensation', and wrote in a boy's report that he was 'beginning to enter a new life', not that he was 'making a successful adjustment'. Sometimes his phrases came from the boys. 'Some special skill or "subject", found to be like a stick, which is strong when used, but breaks when leaned upon ...'

The sixth sense, the faculty to receive and to transmit impressions of all kinds, belongs to artists, although it may be found in many who are not artists by profession. Some artists receive from anywhere on any occasion, and transmit in words, music, design. Mr Lyward received principally from human beings, and gave back in his response. At Glenalmond he wrote two dramas in verse, called *The Word* and *The Sword*. The third was to have been called *The World*; he never wrote it. At the time he might have been writing it, he was starting Finchden, and the trilogy was passing into life. Finchden had sprung from the creative impulse of a man who was less a maker than an awakener, offering the boys understanding and respite to discover their true life for themselves.

The reason that Mr Lyward appeared to me so 'Protean', so difficult to fix, may well have been that while I was on his staff I saw him almost entirely in relation to his work, responding on so many levels, about so many subjects, to so many sorts and conditions of people and moods. The old phrase would describe him, had it kept its first meaning instead of turning into a derogatory opposite—'all things to all men'.

He was dealing besides with boys who, by the definitions which he himself gave them, had at least two faces. 'They've been made to look small, and have been trying to look big. ... Adolescence is like January, the month of Janus. ... I knew a boy who would sell a little shilling for six big pennies. It took him a year of "being done" before he was sensitive in regard to the quantity and quality of coins. His life was a queer mixture of feeble surrender and rebellion. He would rebel vigorously enough against washing and work. Yet, physically strong though he was, he would cry out after a very brief spell of manual labour "I can't go on, I'm done!" At times Mr Lyward might address himself to such a boy's mood of rebellion, at other times to the mood of feeble surrender, or might move lightly or challengingly between one and the other, while always retaining that touch at a deeper level which kept the boy disarmed and trusting.

One of the most vivid disproportions, at Finchden as almost anywhere else, whether among adolescents or adults, was between head and heart; some people have even referred to it as the schizophrenia of Western civilisation. 'There is no difference in the emotional condition of any of them. They are all cases of arrested feeling development', Mr Lyward had written many years ago. Not all had brain enough successfully to 'plaster over the wound'. With any who had, Mr Lyward might choose to play about for a time on an intellectual level, waiting for him, running him beyond his depth, then changing the subject entirely. He had great skill in changing the subject and made a deliberate use of interruptions. 'An account of what I had been doing from minute to minute and from point to point would not exclude digressions, whether they were literary, or such as I made when I said, "Oh, look at that damage to the wall!" to a thirteen-stone seventeen-year-old who had recently knocked over his form-master. This brought us both to our knees examining the wall, "interrupting" a conversation in which I had deliberately taken him beyond his depth but which proved a considerable "loosener".'

At times obviously Mr Lyward appeared to certain boys 'like a father', one who, as he wrote to a parent before the war, was guiding their natural but arrested growth 'away from the mother and the natural dominance on certain levels of the woman, towards the father or protector or breadwinner desire within themselves'. At another time he would need gently to hold up a boy whose possessiveness for a girl had become like the possessiveness of a child for its mother, and who was crying and clutching at him. He had to give, yet not give, and often, when he did not give, a boy would take it as a deliberate but temporary attitude. Yet the story that follows shows it to be an essential part of his approach.

Throughout this book I have given accounts of my own conversations with the boys; most of the time I was listening and occasionally saying something, but never attempting or instructed to attempt any kind of 'treatment'. If it was a question of putting out lights, or giving lifts, or teaching a subject, or chasing someone I was on the staff, but if of 'treatment' I was writing a book, and that was understood. My accounts of Mr Lyward's talks are in general mine, not his. I shall therefore give his own condensed account of two conversations of his own. I suppose he had had thousands of them. The two that follow will show some of the facts about the boys that were brought out, the shifting of approach, and the way in which something said to one boy might be used to clarify things equally or more important to others Mr Lyward knew would hear it.

'Ronald Hall, Mr Lyward wrote, 'had been worrying Mr Lyward on and off throughout an evening about a fortnight's leave at Christmas.

R. H.: There are two possibilities. I could go home or stay here. I would like to go home this year.
G.L.: Right.
R. H.: Yes, but if I go home I shan't be given any money.
G. L.: Well, stay here then.
R. H.: Oh, but I want to go home. (*His mother had said how much better he was last time he went home, 'but I wish he would stay indoors more'*).

R. H. (*again*): I want to go ... (*This went on until G.L. said*):

G. L.: There seems to be a third possibility—for you to go home and for us to give you money.

R. H.: Oh no!

G. L.: You mean you won't ask? (*Gradually it became clearer that R.H. had told certain people that he intended to try to get a larger amount than most boys would have got, and Mr Lyward said*):

G.L.: Well, you can't have that. (*R.H. still could not face the facts and said tetchily*):

R.H.: What I've been trying to ask you all the evening is whether it is better for me to go home or stay here.

G. L. (*firmly*): To go home and accept the situation about money will be the best.

R. H.: Can I have three pounds?

G.L.: No.

The boy started to shout in the bitterest tones, 'That's just what I've always had to put up with.' He slammed the door. Later he ran out of the house, but was found in bed by Neville at 11 p.m., and since it was a rainy night was asked if he would like something hot to drink. He said, 'No, thanks, Nev, I'm all right.'

The dispute with Mr Lyward had taken place on the stairs. Three other boys who had been present asked Mr Lyward ten minutes later if they could be allowed to embark on an enterprise. In the middle of the talk Mr Lyward said to the most resistant of them, 'How far did I go to meet Ronald?'

'Ninety-nine per cent,' said the boy.

'Dared I go one hundred?'

'No.'

'Don't tell me why not. I can see that you know.'

Sent for next day, Ronald grinned and said, 'I lost control last night for the first time. I feel better.' He added, 'Were you baiting me on purpose last night?' Mr Lyward answered, 'No. I never bait you. But when you people persist in shutting your eyes to a third possibility and in going round in circles, I sometimes decide to call a halt. You were granted the power of reasoning, you know, and there you were, wanting something so badly you couldn't reason at all. All the others could see that. They always can—until it's their turn to go blind and discuss only two alternatives.'

This account is given in Mr Lyward's words. It does not show the length of time he spent trying to get the boy to come to the third possibility, before the boy hit his head against the facts and called it being baited. Boys at times used this phrase, because they could not feel that they had run themselves against someone who would not budge. One per cent not given was essential, but ninety-nine per cent given was not far from breast-feeding.

The account of the other incident is also given in Mr Lyward's words, as follows:

'Sam Hutton was heard grumbling. G.L. was with two or three boys in the scullery by the corridor. It emerged that Sam was hungry. It was then 10 a.m. and he had only just arrived from sleep.

G. L.: But you were late for breakfast and goodness knows that's not a quick proceeding.
 (*A group quickly gathered.*)
S. H.: I wasn't waked.
G. L.: This waking of boys is new, isn't it?
 (*Three boys all bore witness that it went back as far as 'living memory'. It is queer, by the way, how some boys remember nothing about their first year at Finchden, —as if it had been a dream.*)
GL.: Well, perhaps it's not such a good thing. I'll talk it over with the staff—oh, not with you! Perhaps you'd all start waking up of your own accord if you weren't called. Anyhow, who is it wakes you up?
Voice: The cook.
G. L.: Fetch the cook. (*Cook is fetched.*) Did you wake up everybody this morning?
Cook: No, sir. Only the ones in the guest house.

G. L.: Then who woke the house?

Cook: Harry did, sir. (*Harry is fetched. This is the kind of hustling they like.*)

G. L.: Morning, Harry. Did you wake up the house?

Harry: Yes, sir. But I forgot Sam. (*Sam was so obviously the centre of the picture. For about ten to fifteen minutes talk ranged round the importance of facts, with humorous illustrations of arguments from false premises and of false arguments. You would have thought the original matter was slipping away. Everybody was happy and even Sam involved.*)

G.L. (*suddenly*): So Sam didn't get called? Why should he be called? And missed his breakfast and hasn't said 'Please may I have some?' (*Sam grins.*)

S. H.: Can I have some breakfast, sir ... please?

G. L.: (*looking round vaguely*) : Good about the 'please', isn't it? (*Enter Maurice Newall, having just got up, to judge by the greeting on the faces of the rest.*)

G. L.: Have you not had any breakfast, Maurice?

M. N. (*laughing*) : No, sir.

G. L.: (*studiously avoiding any further talk with Maurice*): What should Sam have?

Deep Voice from the corridor (Richard, from Chapters Three and Four): Give him bacon and eggs. (*General laughter.*)

G. L.: Right. Give Sam bacon and eggs, cook. It's a comic situation, anyhow.

(*Somebody murmurs, 'May I also ...'*)

G. L.: *That* would be merely silly. (*The sudden changes of tone play no small part in the disarming, provoking play, fluidity.*)

G. L. : (*after some more chat*): Have any of you noticed that as we got nearer to the facts everybody got quieter—this often happens—facts of any kind, I mean.

Boy: And it gets funnier. (*He meant 'lighter'.*)

G. L.: I'd love to make a study of noise.

Voice: What, here!

G. L.: Not only here. (*This is discussion again, starting. Meanwhile*

>*Sam is having his bacon and eggs cooked. Presently Davidson is spoken to in a quiet friendly voice):*

G. L.: When we get down to facts, you've run away twenty-one times, haven't you, Edward? That can't be said not to have its funny side.

E.D.: It has its funny side anyway. (*This is the kind of blind reply to be expected from him, Mr Lyward becomes completely serious and says*):

G.L.: Does it, when you think of the trouble it puts the staff to, and that it's your symptom, and how sad it is for you? (*The boys enjoy the fluidity and feel released within it. Not long afterwards Stallard followed Mr Lyward to his front door to enquire about something. Mr Lyward chatted for a short while, and as he turned to go in, said to this hysterical boy, at last showing signs of steadying*):

G. L.: You often ask questions about religion when you're not playing jazz. I don't expect when we were getting more factual and quieter just now, you found yourself thinking how silent God is to most people?

'I never thought of that,' said Stallard quietly, as Mr Lyward went into the house.'

That is the end of that story. A play? Not quite, but certainly play; and perhaps, when one remembers the stories in Chapter Two, with which the boys had come, a drama.

At times Mr Lyward would turn the 'passive' attitude of one who would not budge beyond a certain point into an active shock, provocation, or challenge, suddenly—for example—sending a boy home because he knew it was time for him to go. Another boy, who has since become a good artist, arrived at Finchden with Meccano models, to which he clung.

'I love my father and mother most in all the world,' said this boy, but later, 'I love my models most in all the world.'

'I thought it was your father and mother,' said Mr Lyward. 'Anyhow, I think it's time we took your models away.'

He took them away. The boy cried himself to sleep, awoke refreshed, and scarcely troubled about his models again. More than twenty years later, he remembered their removal as something that had to be done for him.

Now and then challenges of this kind had to be made because Mr Lyward knew that he had little time. He knew a boy called Frank Cotton had to leave soon, and came across him in Mr Knox's laboratory. With deliberate intent to provoke, he assumed the same tone of voice he guessed the boy's father would use whenever the two met. He had not reckoned with someone else coming in at that moment, turned his eyes away, and Frank Cotton hit him. Mr Lyward fell back, struck his head on the concrete surround of the stove, and was concussed. Having recovered consciousness, he went off to write an editorial for *Home & School* and said later to a group of boys, 'Well, it's done something for Frank, but *please* don't all try to get clear that way.' As a matter of fact, no others did; it was the only time Mr Lyward was ever hit.

Stories of this kind, told out of their long context of the whole treatment of a boy, are intended only to illustrate the almost infinite variety of Mr Lyward's approach, which makes it difficult to find suitable adjectives for him. Sometimes he would be using two approaches at the same time, playful yet not so playful, artless yet full of art. When trying to explain himself to an adult, he would sometimes move both his hands up and down as if he were juggling. He was a master of prepared improvisation and studied offhandedness and, to use another theatrical saying, 'threw his lines away' among the boys in such a manner that they were quite certain to be picked up. He qualified almost anything that sounded like a crystallised definition, thus uncrystallising it. His determination that nobody should harden, no response or explanation become automatic, sometimes made things difficult for his staff. For these reasons it was clear to me that he could never, although I were to go on writing for years, be satisfied with my book. The result was sure to be too hard-and-fast. 'I shall ask to review it, I think,' he reflected, 'and I shall start "This account of work among adolescents, which bears one or two striking resemblances to my own..."'

The word 'Protean' is one which Mr Lyward originally used, not of himself, but of Finchden Manor, and that particular quality was one of the principal reasons for its success. Its fluidity, someone had said, was its strength. The boys' danger had been that forming of habit, that 'premature crystallization', which became impossible at Finchden. The prevention of that crystallization was continuous and the stories told throughout this book, detached on purpose to illumine certain points, were at Finchden part of a sustained experience, of which discussions, 'sessions', interviews, casual conversations, all formed a part. Something a boy had said, or understood, or failed to understand, at a 'session' or discussion, was remembered by Mr Lyward and the staff, linked with other facts in the boy's development, and left to be re-seen in other lights; and the complete story of this sustained experience can only be told, for all it is worth, either by Mr Lyward or a boy.

I have avoided making too much of the word 'intuition' in describing either Mr Lyward or his work. Yet the question must arise in many minds to what extent his success derived from some 'gift' personal to himself and impossible to pass on, and to what extent from a method which could be continued by others willing to dedicate their lives to such a work.

The immediate and continuous disarming of the boys seemed indeed to be due to a gift he possessed of bridging the gulf between himself and the boy, so that youth and maturity met, not on the level of the boy's mask and Mr Lyward's logic, but heart to heart. He himself said of this gift that 'I rule myself out as having any experience at all and became as one of them', and that, when sitting back in a chair and looking up at a boy, 'I might be the same age. I feel as if, consciously and by virtue of experience, I do know what he is like, and yet am seeking.' He spoke of a certain kind of man as unable to become 'enquiring' in that as it were innocent fashion, which had nothing to do with intellectual probing and invited the boy to respond 'as if we were both on the same side of the fence'. He approached the boys himself with so little weight of preconception. He did not await confirmation of some pattern formed about them in his mind, although his long training had made him familiar with many patterns; nor did there intervene between him and them any picture of what he wanted them to be, or thought they ought to be, or might be. He remained entirely open to receive the impressions of them as they were, entire.

He felt that many people were hindered from receiving this whole and direct communication by being too conscious of age, on finding themselves with children. They could not themselves become as children. He himself felt that this did happen to him, and yet he never completely lost awareness of his own maturity. Somehow the majority of the boys sensed both qualities. They felt him to be wise and at the same time one of them. Nigs Walker, alone among all the boys who had ever been to Finchden, insisted on referring to Mr Lyward as an 'old man'; and Nigs was one of the few who could only spasmodically behave like the child he really was himself.

Certain moments in creative work resemble the last step after arrival at the top of a mountain, and that last step is flight. One must make the climb to the taking-off point; one must also have the wings. Some people may believe that they have wings, but are without the strength to climb; others may climb, but never become air-borne. Mr Lyward could do both. Deep thought and concentrated effort over many years had enabled him to see a boy immediately, as a whole; but a special quality beyond experience enabled him to respond to what he saw in such a way that the boy, whatever his camouflage had been, became a boy, and harmless. Without this special quality, the process of weaning became impossible. The process itself was a method, and could be learnt.

These are some of my impressions of Mr Lyward. They are not intended as impressions of him 'as a man', yet it is not out of place to say that his marriage was a happy one, his relationship with his son easy and friendly. As a student, Mrs Lyward had been a gifted sculptress and would probably, but for her marriage, have been sent to continue her studies in Rome. At one time she had taught the boys. She was a good dancer and taught them dancing too. She bound up cut hands and sprained ankles, but since the boys were seldom ill with anything more serious than a cold she seldom went into their rooms and only at shows and parties into their part of the house. If Mr Lyward, humorously or seriously, sent a boy along to her, she surmised the spirit in which it was done. She had a calm character, able to take the worst, if it happened, as it came, delighting in the boys' after-successes, entertaining also 'as they came.' Several families had become her close friends. She gave sustained help and understanding to her husband's work, playing, in general, that role which appears to be in the background, but is so often part of the foundations.

These impressions are also confined to Mr Lyward's work at Finchden Manor. I never heard any of his lectures, which have included the Sir Philip Magnus lecture to the College of Preceptors, an inaugural address at Durham University, talks to graduates at London and Oxford Universities, and many talks to teachers of all kinds and to students at training colleges. He seems on such occasions to have expressed much that his hearers had often felt and thought, but he was doing, and had been doing for a long time, and he received many tributes and letters of thanks.

In regard to all these activities and to his work at Finchden, Mr Lyward seemed to me a man who had come to a simplicity beyond complexity and to a singleness which is beyond many-sidedness, while including it. Having arrived at that point where difficult things do suddenly become simple, and all the previous struggles are momentarily forgotten, he caused one almost to believe that nothing lay behind his work but common-sense. Like an artist, and some greater, he demanded everything of himself and gave everything, whether through participation or withdrawal. 'We must lie more open than we often do,' he once said, in an address to teachers and parents. 'We must risk being hurt.' He himself, open the whole time to everyone, and therefore vulnerable, shared the happy stages of re-birth, as he also shared the suffering. If he too had not felt some deep sense of security, he could no more have supported the suffering than the boys themselves.

Where did this security come from? It could only come from within himself; perhaps it is impossible to analyse, and can only be grasped intuitively. That it was there none could doubt, and without this inward strength, constantly renewed, he would have faltered, or lost hope.

CHAPTER SEVEN

A DISTINGUISHED doctor told me that work done at the depth of the work done at Finchden was badly needed. He knew of men with the vocation, but they lacked training.

To love, and yet remain disinterested: what text-book could teach that?

The staff needed to be aware of their own personal moods, determining their attitude towards each boy not by their preference, but by his need. If they felt bad-tempered, they had either to get over it or else use it, knowing they were using it; if in a good humour, they had equally to beware. Sid, to whom smaller boys often clung, coming to him in an 'aren't-I-naughty?' mood, took care never to turn into a kind of mother-figure; the whole place could do that when required. David and Neville had to avoid becoming exclusively figures of authority or else waste-paper baskets for surplus confidences.

To be prepared to urge one boy gently and obliquely for months; to cajole another, unable to join in games or a revue into cricket or a walk-on part just for one day, until he began to talk of his former inability, said 'Now I feel different', and the change began, which another could only reach through tears and violence: what training colleges could teach that kind of patience and easy alternation of approach? David and Neville had learnt much from Mr Lyward, but in them the control-tower was still perceptible; in him it had disappeared.

The staff must be prepared to find and perhaps, in a report, to explain, though the immediate trouble for which a boy had come to Finchden might disappear quite soon, and the 'offence' never be repeated, that the first signs of new growth were not necessarily amiable. A boy released from moroseness or even primness might take to obscene swearing; another stop bed-wetting and start stealing; a violent boy might become withdrawn, or the other way round. A boy who had idolised his mother decided that he hated her; one who had worried other boys chased girls; one who had resented Finchden might become smug and go about his home childishly boasting 'At Finchden we're all mad.' It was quite common for an unnaturally neat boy to become, to the same extreme, dirty and untidy.

These were some of the inevitable stages of growth: they might be either awaited or induced. 'Peter Harrington,' wrote the famous Mr Knox, 'must be a reincarnation of Little Lord Fauntleroy. He has collected a series of bottles of toilet requisites, which he has marshalled like soldiers on a shelf. His arithmetic sums show a devastating neatness of arrangement and accuracy. I deplore it, but at present dare not interfere. The picture is completed by the fact that when he meets an academic problem he cannot see through, he just goes dumb.' And of another boy, he said that he came from a nice home 'and has the untidiest room. He has now lived through this and developed a rational neatness based on his personal desires.'

When the first change was outwardly for the worse, some parents complained; when for the better, they were likely to assume that the boy was now 'cured' and could return to his ordinary surroundings. They tended to be satisfied with another false 'face', provided that it now looked virtuous and successful. Yet many masks might be formed and discarded, before true outlines were established. The process involved an awakening of the whole personality, not emphasis of any single aspect, however useful or attractive.

To expect paradox—with the boys in that unanchored state of life between childhood's haven and manhood's voyage, what was to be expected but inconstancy, what logic but contradiction?

'I hate you!' cried one boy, reluctantly returning from Finchden to his real father, although Mr Lyward knew that he was ready to go, and the next moment flung himself into his father's arms. All that was essential to Finchden involved paradox: mistrust and trust, the discipline of liberty, insecurity within security, limits without definition of limit, love and hate. Growth as always had a double face. Dying leaves clung to young branches, falling off almost unseen. Then one day most of the trees struck good roots. Thereafter all that parents or County Councils had waited for—jobs, exams, self-control, 'taking his place in the world'—began just to happen. David said: 'The boys, too, see that they and others round them are growing, and they have a welcome feeling that there isn't a moment when anyone is fully grown.'

What Professorships have been endowed for timing, what degrees are given in learning how to wait? A boy took the staff something that to him mattered greatly, and they seemed to ignore it; later, when he had forgotten, they reminded him. When, at an apparently quite simple 'level', Ivor Marples complained that his chocolate had been stolen, David appeared to pay no attention. Two days later he gave the boy a bar, saying 'I bought it for you.' Later, the secretary of the local cricket club telephoned to say that Ivor Marples had been infiltrating into the pavilion and taking his tea free with visiting teams. David asked him lightly if he could do this and at the same time grumble about someone at Finchden stealing from him. This magnification of small things, together with a lessening of big things, was part of the 'method'. Little memories reappeared round corners and became landmarks; minor events turned into chapter-headings; most of the boys' biographies, apart from the few 'dramatics', would have consisted of footnotes.

At an earlier time Mr Lyward had had several men on his staff who, like Mr D. and Mr Hannen, were not old boys. It was during the war that, partly from necessity, he began deliberately to train boys who seemed to have the vocation. I once asked David whether the work done at Finchden was of the kind that can be passed on, and in reply he gave me some rough notes, which I will summarise at this point.

'I was one of those who came to Finchden Manor for help,' he wrote. 'This means that I have been "through the mill" myself. But in any case I am sure one would have to be the *sort* of person to "receive" front the "transmitter". Personally, I made, deliberately, a division at the point when I became employed and took on a job and did not expect my "employer" to help in the ways that he had, in another role, before. This was my way.

'As well as being the kind of person able to "receive", one must also attempt, quite soon, whilst still only perhaps sensing the truth and sometimes seeing proof of Mr Lyward's statements, to develop one's own beliefs and way of life. I suppose that at some such time as this I became ready to receive a more disciplined training. I think this meant, again as far as I was concerned, an enlightenment of what I was doing intuitively at one level, and an increased awareness of the kind of "structure" I had to work in. This latter was at another level, concerned with the boys' physical and material needs etc., as regards themselves and maybe involving their parents, teachers, local education authorities, and so on.

'To restate some of the above in terms of daily contact and help for the boys, I have had to become able to *recognise* them for what they are. (One can be trained to spot camouflage, to interpret needs, actions, frustrations, help self-pity, etc.) I have had to become able to *respect* them as persons, not case histories. I have had to become able to be *responsive* to their needs as I see them, and sometimes, if I can get no nearer, responsive to their wants. All this I try to become with the object of building up a good *relationship*; and, to put this approach to practical use, I have been aware that I must remain open, at any time and any place to any thing—almost!'

David also wrote of instruction in letter-writing and the making of reports and of certain details of method, which included lightheartedness, skill in waiting, 'the employing on occasions of delaying tactics, and where necessary the taking of evasive action, while remaining true to one's convictions and belief in the best way to help the boy in question. Some of this in its turn involves leaving the door open for advance or retreat of oneself or of the boy.' He wrote of a stage arriving 'when some of the "R's" are beginning to be reciprocated', and of a third stage in his own training and development. 'Perhaps Professionalism is the word to use now. One has collected enough instruments to operate.

I suppose co-operate would sound whimsical? One uses more incisively one's instruments, and becomes glad to work for one's results. With greater maturity I still found I had much to learn about protection. Many examples can be given of the boys' need of protection; protection against parents, against themselves, against outside contacts. One can be trained to see who is suffering from pressure from outside and who from pressure of his own making. One can be told what to say to either. So often one hopes to reach some reconciliation ...'

I may add a word about one other attitude of the staff's which helped to keep the boys disarmed. Sometimes, if a child does something which irritates its parents, the parents will say, 'There, you've done it *again*!' They thereby transform criticism of the action into criticism of the child, and make the action seem habitual. At Finchden care was taken that the action should be isolated, and not regarded as 'typical' of the boy who had done it. This restraint helped greatly to free the boys from the sense of guilt and of being 'hopeless' and 'incorrigible', which had been induced in so many of them. And how many children have acquired a bad habit as a result mainly of having it attributed to them!

David's notes are not those of someone attempting to impose a discipline from without, nor even of someone attempting, in a more subtly moralising way, to implant some inner discipline which, in his view, the boys 'ought' to learn. They are the notes of someone who had once been such a boy himself, and had found his own way, which had kept him in their midst, in the same atmosphere, and still very much a member. It would not have been at all whimsical to substitute 'co-operate' for 'operate'; it would have been the truth. David, and the rest of the staff, were doing 'no more than' help the boys to find their ways; and yet how much this meant!

What it meant I hope further to show in this chapter and the next, by answering three questions I was often asked about Finchden Manor; the first about violence, the second about sex, the third about the nature of the discipline. At the end of the next chapter, which is in part built round the embarrassed though amiable figure of Mr Hannen, I shall attempt briefly to summarise the manner in which the boys' false and dangerous self fell away and the true self grew, before going on, in Chapter Nine, to tell the whole story of one boy in particular.

As regards violence: no human being would have failed to be frightened, physically, by one or two of the boys. One night Henry Carpenter lost his temper. I was thoroughly scared. On another occasion he asked for two shillings. Neville gave it him, and added: 'That's all for a while.' Carpenter threw it on the floor. When he asked for it again later, he was refused. He lost his temper and knocked things over. The next day he was given twice as much pocket money. Once he walked off the cricket-field in a fury; when he asked to come back, Neville said: '*I* never turned you off.'

'All the same, may I come back?'

He came back, scored brilliantly, and said: 'I had to blow off to have my innings.'

He had blown off, but without harm to others. Would it be far-fetched to substitute 'life' for 'innings'?

There were scraps, mostly friendly, though they might occasionally become dangerous; the staff had then to make up their minds quickly. Their decision depended upon the boys directly involved, and the onlookers. A scrap between two boys of equal size might be allowed to go on, if neither was likely to be upset and if no boy nearby might be upset. Obviously, if the boys looked like doing each other physical harm, they were stopped.

Remembering some of the boys' past stories, I reflected how little they had injured one another during the twenty-five years of Finchden's existence. Sometimes inspired casualness averted violence. When one enraged boy was chasing another with a poker, he passed Fitzy, who said: 'Oh, give me that a moment, I want to poke the fire.' The boy gave it up. At one time I made a list of 'violent incidents'. They now seem insignificant, not only because they are so few, but because the atmosphere of the whole place was one not of violence, but disarmament. Neville once had his face badly scratched, and David had a brick thrown at him. None of the boys ever suffered much worse than a black eye. During the time I was at Finchden, there was only one bad fight.

One evening Sid was in the yard and heard shouting from the kitchen. There he found Seton and Henry Carpenter pounding one another wildly. He walked between, pushing them apart, and then circled round until they stopped. Later they started again. Peter was then in the room. He managed to get the other boys out, but for once—and this, with him, was unusual—could not manage to separate the two fighters, who seemed 'possessed'. They were fairly equally matched and both strong; both, in that mood, were capable of using anything they could lay their hands on. Peter, after sending a message to Mr Lyward, followed them carefully, removing possible weapons; he trailed them into the big hall, where they went on wildly hammering one another.

Mr Lyward had just come back from speaking at a conference. He did not feel well and was sitting half-asleep in front of the fire when Peter came in. He went down into the hall, and saw in an instant that both boys were in a mood to go on fighting till they dropped, and worse. '*I knew,*' Mr Lyward wrote afterwards, with emphatic underlinings, 'that I had got something that belonged outside here. The two boys had, as it were, already removed themselves from the community, but there were their bodies still in Finchden Manor. I *knew at once* that I had got to bring them back to Finchden Manor if I could.'

Seton turned on Mr Lyward for a moment, threatening him. Mr Lyward clapped his hands, then said in effect, in a very quiet voice, to both of them, while they were momentarily separated, 'You are outsiders brawling in my house. This isn't a fight between two boys. This is something that belongs outside Finchden. You must come back here, or your bodies must be removed. If you decide that you belong outside, then I shall send for the police.' Then he walked away.

The boys stopped fighting; nor did they continue after Mr Lyward had gone. 'The word "police", he wrote afterwards, 'might easily lead a stranger to believe that I make threats. *I never do.* I state facts.

I stated it as a fact that they were outsiders brawling in my house, and did not just say that they were "behaving like" outsiders. It was the only time I have ever used the word "police" to the boys in that way, and its use then had NOTHING in common with a threat.'

Either boy could have floored Mr Lyward. He had said little, and that little quietly; but the effort he had made and the after vibrations left him exhausted for two or three days.

Sometimes I could scarcely believe that parents and doctors and school-masters had written with such grim foreboding about these boys. There was a day I especially remember towards the end of winter. I had not realised how late I had been working, and was surprised when I put away my papers and went outside to find that dawn was breaking. The trees were coal-black against the lightening sky. Nothing was stirring. When some small noise broke the silence, it sounded like the approach of many people, and I turned round expecting to see some boy who had been out poaching. The doors and windows of the house were all open. It had the stillness and beauty of a rite; I imagined that I had stumbled out of our world into some legend, in which all who came to live at Finchden lived happily and became immortal. The cock crew and the sun rose beneath gathering clouds.

I slept for a few hours, till someone woke me to say that the local hounds were meeting in the neighbourhood and that some boys wanted to go. Mr and Mrs Lyward took two in the back of their car, and I filled up mine. The day was windless and sunny, with a blue sky and frosty air. On the way the boys argued whether blood sports should be forbidden and, as usual, dashed off to all kinds of subjects, among them Plato. It turned out that Oliver Newton really had read the Republic. He admitted that he had not understood a great deal, and Mr Lyward thought it time for him to stop. Fred Stiles, a Cockney, wanted to know what was meant by Platonic love.

I told him, and he said: 'Crikey! Is that all? I thought it was something illegal.'

Soon they were discussing film stars, forgetting Plato and the language of Plato. Fred suddenly turned to me. 'Hey, Dr Singe, I'll tell you when I was embarrassed. Remember when you first came here? Remember you came into the Chief's room, and what he asked me?'

I said I did remember; it was something that concerned Fred, and does not matter.

'I could have fallen through the floor,' Fred added. 'Shall I tell you what I said to myself? I said, "This geyser's going to be here some time, so he'll get to know sooner or later about me. So he might as well know now".'

'I was embarrassed, too,' I said. 'I wondered if I ought to leave.'

'That would have made *me* more embarrassed,' said another boy.

'I'd have said "O.K. I don't mind",' Fred went on. 'Matter of fact, it was all the hell of a joke to me.' And then, without stopping: 'Do you know what I said when we heard you were coming? I said: "Another one on the —— staff. Haven't we got enough?" Still, you're better now. You were pretty shocked by all the language at first, weren't you?' (I wasn't).

We arrived at the meet. I was always interested to see the boys in another setting. They contrived to remind me that it was only a setting, and that all these so assured and busy people, whether at a hunt or in a factory or at a theatre or in a private room, were all individuals, and away from the setting likely to be quite different. The setting protected and might even disguise; the boys suggested insecurity in everyone, and made me curious how other people managed theirs.

Mr and Mrs Lyward stood patting the horses. Mr Lyward wore his brown Trilby and a thick coat and muffler, and was looking in an abstracted way at the faces of the hunt-followers. He seemed to have taken to a Jorrocks-like character, with leggings, stock, and a wind-bitten face.

'I like people who are real,' he said as they moved off. 'I can get on with that kind of parent, even though they disagree with everything I do.'

Two boys wanted to walk. We left them on the road, and after we had followed the glimpses of scarlet for a while, drove back to Finchden. I found Sid in the Guildables room playing with the monkey. The boys had alarmed it, and Sid was coaxing it along. It was trying to crack a nut. Sid showed, and the monkey copied. Sid sneezed and the monkey sneezed. Sid shook out his handkerchief, then gave it to the monkey, who shook it out in just the same way. Sid put some sticks together, and said to the monkey 'This is the jungle', then scattered some grains of earth above and said: 'This is rain.' The monkey neatly collected all the sticks and scattered some earth. By evening Sid would probably have taught it to play the piano.

The day continued merry. Nigs Walker was in one of his boyish moods, more like the others, less of the infant camouflaged. I took him up Tenterden Church tower and we waited for the bells to ring. Back at Finchden, someone was searching for Mr Hannen to make him pose in the position of the Rokeby Venus, which the boy said was physically impossible. A conversation began in the dining room, among the debris, in the middle of which Flynn asked artfully: 'Are you writing a book about Finchden?'

I said that it deserved a book, and they began to remember.

'Remember the day the psychos came? Remember the bloke who sang all night? Eight solid hours, at the top of his voice. Wasn't there a guy who used to ride a bike into Tenterden dressed as a woman? Who was the one who set fire to churches before he came here?'

A boy turned to me: 'If you go off and write a book about this place without asking the Chief's permission, I'll knock your block off! Some journalist bloke did that.'

'Why shouldn't Dr Singe?' said Flynn. 'He used to be a journalist.'

'Because it'd be too easy. Crikey, though, I'd like to put the Chief into a book. What'd you call him, Dr Singe? A trick cyclist?'

Chorus of 'no'.

'Why not?'

'They just dope you and try to make you talk.'

'What would you call him then?'

'God knows. He's certainly not a ruddy school-master, or none

I've ever come across.' And they began to tell stories about the places they had been to before, with singularly little malice—the past was the past—and a lot of comedy.

In the evening came one of those informal concerts which Mr Lyward would demand at a few days' notice. It was an intimate occasion, without guests. The boys put on some cross-talk and slapstick; a trumpet solo; an aria of Handel; and a take-off of an Oedipus complex, which began with a mother carrying a difficult child and ended with the child carrying a difficult mother—a story that had occurred more than once in Finchden's life. The unrehearsed standard was not high, but the concert gave pleasure because of its lack of self-consciousness, and because some of the boys were taking part for the first time and it had meant a struggle for them. After community singing, they danced with one another, or stood discussing by the smouldering log-fire. Nigs Walker gave Mr Lyward another lesson in the St Bernard Waltz, and a boy accustomed to hunt balls taught an eightsome reel. Mr Lyward accompanied old songs on the tired piano, the boys gathering round him to turn the pages and join in the choruses. He remained until past eleven, playing Bach and Brahms and Beethoven, stopping to discuss a composer for a few moments and continuing to answer the boys' questions as he played.

They stayed up for a time, and I wondered, as I had the first day Mr Lyward had pointed them out from his window, if anything was really 'wrong' with them. If they were all so 'normal' and contented, as they had seemed during the whole of this day, was this prolonged respite necessary? Why should they not be studying all day and made to do the same as everybody else? Especially a boy like Drake. Look at him, talking to Neville in the corridor. He was nearly twenty. He had been at Finchden four years. He had an extremely good brain. He ought to be in a University. Suddenly Drake's intelligent face became red, then white. His voice blazed up like a paraffin thrown on a fire, and he hit Neville ferociously on the side of the head. 'Come on!' he screamed, 'what about that fight!' Neville did nothing. Drake hit him again. Neville went to bathe his face, and Drake rushed into the staff room. Old early resentments poured out. 'I felt it boiling up for days,' he said. 'I'm confused if I do lose my temper, and I'm confused if I don't. I feel utterly unwanted.' I saw him later when he went to bed, again looking calm and intelligent, the one who ought to go to a University. Neville had a black eye and was lucky not to have worse.

So ended the perfect day, far from perfectly; yet for Drake perhaps something necessary had now happened. Occasionally a day might be all disturbance, and no scherzo, and yet have some healing close.

That evening was the only time I ever saw one of the staff hit. Why? Why did those few boys still given to making passionate threats carry them out so seldom? Ned Barclay, for example, was officially hating Finchden. He once warned Neville that if he didn't stay to hear the reasons, he would chuck Neville's belongings out of the window. Neville went to Tenterden, leaving the door of his room open; his belongings were there intact when he returned.

Two reasons that there was so little violence have already been given; one, that the boys needed Finchden, and knew they needed it; the other, that the staff, by virtue of their training, did not provoke the boys.

The boys also knew they would get little satisfaction out of attacking the staff, who were not going to hit back. In some indistinct way they themselves felt diminished by certain kinds of violence. If a gang of (physically) grown thugs had come to Finchden all together, they would probably have laid about everybody; if one or other had come alone, or if they had all come at a sufficiently early age, they might have quite naturally grown out of this kind of showy violence. Certain boys who might have become thugs did in fact manage sooner or later to recognise themselves as members of a community; just as their specific violence diminished, once it was seen steadily as part of a more general disturbance.

The story which best illustrates what became of violence was a stock story, told best by the boys, and of the kind that loses most of its point without elaborate preparation. One has to know the boy concerned— 'dear old Ed'. He was a square stolid gruff 'tough' with a ponderous voice. 'Before I came to Finchden,' he used to lecture new arrivals, 'I was no good. No good at all. After three months, I stopped being no good. I was *born*.' Towards the end of his time there he became restive again and now and then threw things at the staff. David said something that enraged him. He rushed into the garden, picked up a brick and stood fingering it under Mr Lyward's window. David went after him and was in time to hear him growl, 'No ... no ... perhaps not. After all, the old ——'s only doing his best.'

Adolescence is impressionable and unsure enough, whether or not childhood has been disturbed, to make crucial anything said about sex by a person the adolescent respects. Many young lives have been made miserable or left unfulfilled, because the parents' attitude towards sex was too embarrassed, too trivial, or too matter-of-fact. Mr Lyward thought of the boys in his care not only as adolescents, but also as parents of the future. He had an exceptional influence in his own right and by virtue of his position; they respected and remembered for a long time everything he said, even on unimportant topics. He knew that much of their future happiness might depend on his response to their direct or indirect questionings about sex.

It is therefore not strange that there was no great expression of human personality about which he talked less, unless religion; and no theme concerning which deep thought had to be combined more carefully with lightness of approach. The result of it all might be no more than a few words amongst a group, or five minutes of a private interview apparently about something else.

He neither kept sex dark, as under the older education, nor chalked it on a blackboard, as under some of the new (now, perhaps, outmoded). Consequently, however reserved some of the boys, or crude others, sex gradually ceased to appear as either sinister or commonplace. Nobody announced: 'Thursday, 10-11. Chemistry', or 'Friday, 11-12. Sex.' There was no programme Confirmation at sixteen for boys who might be in no mood for it; and there were no organised fireside chats on venereal disease for boys who either knew all about it already or did not yet want or need to know.

A man who never used the word love in a trivial way was unlikely to think or speak of sex as just a biological function, unrelated to feeling. A man with his feet firmly planted on the ground was unlikely to disregard the importance of information. Mr Lyward had wide and long acquaintance with unfulfilled marriages, and was unprepared blithely to explain them away merely by some physical ignorance or inadequacy on the part of husband or wife. Such inadequacy there might be, as there had been physical defects in some of the boys. But he traced failure—and happiness—to a deeper level, and applied words which many habitually apply to sex alone, to the whole personality. And so a boy who in some conventional schoolmaster's words was 'beginning to show unnatural tendencies' became one who was really beginning, in all ways, to lead an unnatural life, in defence perhaps, or revenge, against the life which others had imposed on him. Prostitution did not only take place on the streets; it happened in heart and mind. Masturbation was 'perhaps the most honest form of self-abuse'.

He lifted these words out of their context and gave them a larger meaning, just as he spoke of divorce as a condition which often exists at the heart of a marriage. Many of his boys later made happy marriages. This would have proved far more difficult had Finchden not repaired the damage wrought to their feelings, in years when they were scarcely conscious of the sexual impulse.

The boys inevitably corrected much of their sexual knowledge (as they did other knowledge) by listening and taking part in the conversations all round them. If one boasted, there would be many ready to deflate him. A boy who went about exposing himself on arrival was obviously trying to prove that he was grown up, and unwittingly disproving it, in the simplest way. At certain stages the boys all bluffed, as most of them soon realised.

Talk about sex played a large but not abnormal part at Finchden. Some boys could listen unharmed to its crudeness, as they could watch a scrap; but there were others who at some stages might be harmed. A scrap could be stopped. It was much harder to stop talk about sex, which might prove harmful to some boy, without over-emphasising its importance. Such talk would certainly not be stopped in the more usual ways. The boys at Finchden were fairly shrewd, and sometimes discerning. A group might hang lewdly or furtively round an old boy who had left before his time and who had nothing better to do, while waiting for Mr Lyward, than to tell crude jokes. Some boys were certain afterwards to repeat this stuff, while at the same time they inwardly had a feeling that this old boy should have stayed and 'got beyond it', and wondered, anyhow, why had he come back for an interview.

If one of the staff were about, and felt that any conversation about sex, whether serious or salacious, should be brought to an end, then he had the skill to turn the subject lightly. Most of the boys would realise what he was doing, and might even understand that he did it on account of one of them. The more they absorbed of Finchden, the more sensitive they became to those who were still vulnerable, and the better able were they to help the staff in their protecting or releasing of frailer boys. There were some, usually at a kind of half-way stage, who, having 'a lot of muck to get rid of', were busy excreting it in words. Such boys usually wanted a companion. With them, there was seldom anything to be done but to leave them work out their need; but ways could always be found of protecting the companion.

Living so close, the staff could not fail to notice if one boy listened to conversation about sex with that half-moral, half-fascinated embarrassment of the curious who are afraid to appear curious. They would notice if one appeared obsessed with one particular sexual aspect, or if another was not interested. A boy might talk about a revealing dream. All these indications were stored into the memory; to be used, probably without specific reference, at such time as Mr Lyward might decide. At certain moments, after rage or tears, or when alone with one of the staff, the boy would mention a troubling sexual uncertainty, or he might bluntly ask to see Mr

Lyward. Then he would be answered according to his mood, and always within the wider context of person and life, of which the sexual questioning was a part.

Mr Lyward's answers might include fact, but his approach was never matter-of-fact. Some dreams he cherished. He saw into the touching reticence and chivalry of the adolescent which, worlds away from squeamishness, did them no harm. Direct when it was necessary to be direct, he none the less moved gently, so that the sensitive, the young, the lyrical, should not be rebuffed; so that one of the greatest of human adventures might not be closed for ever with some textbook answer. 'The adolescent,' he wrote, 'has his eternal child within, sometimes more happily related to his surface self than all the adults round him. This is especially noticeable in relation to sex and religion, themselves so subtly connected. Reserve about sex may be the distinguishing mark of these particular adolescents, and is not to be confused with inhibition; and they are also likely to be aware of the unseen to an extent which may bring them into conflict with those matter-of-fact adults, who would not be so proud of their matter-of-fact attitude, if they could remember how it started.'

'For too many readers,' he wrote, while still a house-master, in an article intended to form part of a symposium for parents, 'guilt may mean sex. Fathers are more prudish than mothers. Those who can talk easily with their sons about 'the facts of life' (may Heaven forgive us for that phrase!) are still in the minority. This must be due to the fact that mothers do not always play their part and answer adequately the questions asked by children from about four years of age onwards. ... After puberty, any information given by the father on a subject touching the emotional life will be collected intellectually, that is to say, hoarded in the attic. But I can imagine something worse, and that is delayed instruction given by a mother who has scientific leanings. Not long ago I was actually asked: "Shall I do it? Or his prep. school master? I should love to, and I am qualified. I am a Doctor of Science. His father won't. Shall I?" My reply was: "Not you, Madam".'

Mr Lyward wrote elsewhere of 'an undue emphasis on the biological aspect' as, at its worst, 'the attitude of those who are dangerously unaware of their own repressions'.

And Sid told me a story. 'One of the younger boys asked me to teach him biology. The boy was intelligent and keen, and we got along splendidly. Then one day he came up as usual and I had some extra work to get through for Mr Lyward, so I told the boy to do some reading instead, which we could discuss next day at lesson time. I picked up one of the three books from which I was teaching him, and handed it to him.

Next morning he came up at the usual time and I saw at once that there was something wrong. His face had gone quite dead.

So I said, "Something's gone wrong, hasn't it?"

"Yes," he said.

I didn't enquire further and started on our lesson. After a time my eye was caught by a diagram illustrating the workings of a wireless. "It's something of that sort that's worrying you, isn't it?" I asked.

"Yes," he said.

I left it at that and carried on with our work. He seemed to have lost all the lively intelligence which had made our lessons such a pleasure, and it wasn't until the end, just as he got up to go, that it all came out.

The book I had picked up at random had a chapter explaining mechanically what is known as the "facts of life".

"They say it's just a reflex action," the boy blurted out, and then, like a cry from the heart, "It takes away the magic".'

The letters quoted earlier, by which the boys were heralded, have shown that some aspects of adolescent sexual behaviour are still treated in some homes and schools as an 'offence'; and how willingly some boys came, outwardly, to believe that they had been wicked and were 'never going to do it again'. They arrived at Finchden feeling guilty, 'though they were not quite sure about what'. The first step was to oust this guilt from its obsessive place in their consciousness, and afterwards to arrive at the boy's true feelings, which would lead far from the actual 'offence' to deeper wants and deprivations. At his interview with Charlie Ashmore, Mr Lyward did not mention the 'offence' at all.

Nor did he offer parents the swift and easy 'cure' for which they hoped. Games were one 'cure'. One father explained that as his boy had broken his ankle, he could not play football—'hence the trouble about sex'. Another offered Mr Lyward some rough shooting, because 'I have always thought that, if the bodies of healthy boys are not kept fully exercised, their minds are apt to turn to sex and the practice of self-abuse.' Other parents said: 'If only he would settle down to some serious study.'

Many parents held these views. Sport, books, physical and intellectual enjoyment are each or in combination often substituted for the adventure of the whole personality. How many of those who boldly confront physical obstacles are afraid to confront psychological obstacles, and may mistake an external conquest for an internal victory. During the 'thirties, Mr W. H. Auden composed a beautifully over-simplified and funny play called *The Ascent of F.6*. The hero was shown as socially the pawn of a newspaper Imperialist and personally the victim of a mother-fixation, and got to the top to find Mum waiting for him. Something of that kind had to be written at that time; now it seems a bit dated. There are mountaineers, sailors and poets, who are what they are regardless of those who financed them and in spite of whatever their mothers may have done. Motives can be complicated to a point of silliness; all the same, I certainly remember meeting men during the war, who though sane and clear-headed at sea or on precipices, were curiously muddled ashore and on the flat. I would have trusted a son to them on a rope or in a typhoon; but if they had become school-masters, I would have kept him miles away from their schools.

Mr Lyward did not believe in either games or hard work as a 'cure', and therefore refused the offer of rough shooting. Flynn later went on a course which offered the 'solution' of inner difficulties through sailing and mountaineering. He enjoyed it as a vigorous holiday, but said that, after Finchden, its organisers 'laid too much on', and should not make claims to 'build character'. Often, in Mr Lyward's opinion, these physical outlets were substitutions, not solutions. They failed to disclose the real unrest. Its disclosure might probe the parents' relationship with the child extremely deep. One often felt, at first interviews, that this was about to happen; and so, while parents continued to think in their own terms, they stayed understandably reticent, as the boy, alone with Mr Lyward, was forthcoming.

Mr Lyward's approach to two particular boys with some kind of sexual difficulty may be seen from two particular interviews. Neither is 'typical'. I wonder if anything at Finchden can be called typical. He would have behaved quite differently with different boys. I only quote these two interviews with the proviso that they do not represent any 'general approach'. The first is his own verbatim account; and because it is only meant as that, and lacks the tone, colour and shifts from lightness to seriousness that carried the words to the boy's understanding, I have supplemented it with another interview I myself witnessed.

In the first instance, a public school head-master had sought Mr Lyward's advice about a boy of sixteen at his school. Mr Lyward wrote as follows:

'I saw this boy on November 30. Any summary of a long interview is likely to be inadequate. But I feel that an attempt may be worth making. Although the immediate need was to arrest whatever tendency there is towards repetition of the "offence", which was the occasion of his getting into trouble at school, the boy's own need is something bigger, with that as merely one aspect. It is good to know that the school have recognised this and have shown understanding.

Clearly, it would have been wrong to plunge straight into any discussion of the actual offence. Such an approach would be most unlikely to do anything but increase inner confusion, and might well pervade the whole mystery of sex with a deep sense of guilt.

In that way it might actually increase the risk of further irresistible attraction towards such shared uncreative "enjoyment" as he has already sought.

Furthermore, it is not easy to be sure how intelligent he is and how far capable of dealing with any sort of abstraction.

I therefore set out to play at length around the word satisfaction. It was not long before I realised that his troubles are largely intellectual, in so far as words, such as satisfaction, are only the vaguest of symbols with no sort of intellectual content.

On the other hand, he is well able to put his personal experiences together. He is keen on swimming and could easily be helped to distinguish in detail the difference between a good morning by the sea and a bad morning, which (shall we say) started by his stubbing his toe. One gave satisfaction; the other did not.

This distinction established, I passed on to the word "achievement". He knew the word, but (again) it conjured up only the vaguest feeling. It was, however, he who suggested looking it up in the dictionary ("I like using the dictionary") and he was not slow to appreciate the significance of the statements: "To carry on to a final close", and "To get by effort".

From that I made (from his point of view) a diversion and contrasted "satisfaction through achievement" with "satisfaction through sensation". I took pains to make it clear that the latter was quite legitimate and indeed vital to the baby and the small child.

He took about an hour to reach the point where we were able to illuminate, with examples, the difference between the two "kinds" of satisfaction, and it was he who volunteered that "one would be deeper than the other". This is worth noting.

Not until then did I refer to the episode which had recently got him into trouble. He showed very little sign of being ashamed—and in view of what had gone before I did not expect him to do so. Nevertheless he did say that he "knew he was letting down the moral of the school"—(his words).

MYSELF: That is what your masters feel?

Boy: Yes.
MYSELF: Do you feel it?
Boy: Oh yes! (Warmly)
MYSELF: But why? Why should you feel that by getting a particular kind of satisfaction you are letting your school down?

Of course, he had no answer. But he was now beginning to be moved, not so much by guilt as by healthy curiosity.

Presently I substituted for "the moral of the school" the expression "tone of the school". He knew the word "tone" used in this connection, but it meant nothing to him—there was no significance.

I talked to him about muscles and, of course, he was quick to decide in favour of good muscles rather than flabby ones—"good tone". He could be seen arriving gradually at a personal (and not echoed) realisation that a number of boys *seeking* "sensation satisfaction" would tend to give the school an infantile flabbiness. They would only be performing repetitive rather than constructive actions, going round in circles instead of building; and so on.

It did not need anybody else to tell him that he *ought* to prefer good muscles to flabby (that is, to "sensation"). He just did prefer them. The words which were previously part of his general wooliness were already becoming "words with power".

From such a position it was possible for him to "confess" that he was slow, and so got behind and disheartened, then gave things up; in other words, that he was not getting enough "satisfaction through achievement". That, he could agree, was perhaps why he had been drawn (backwards) to seeking alternative satisfaction through sensation—at a shallower level.

He talked about French, History and English (in that order) as giving satisfaction; and about this term at school as his "best so far", because of his new satisfaction in rugger. He says that he "loves dancing" and this, with his delight in swimming and rugger, points to a possible need for further integration through "body achievements".

He also talked about the pleasure he derived from some of his scout activities; but added: "there are things I don't like, such as having to change in the evenings". This latter qualification led to a talk about achievement as dependent upon acceptance of challenges, situations etc. "as a whole". He appreciated the pictures presented to him by this "as a whole" notion and thought that sufficient satisfaction might come "to make you quite keen next time to do the less pleasant parts as part of the whole", i.e. to will the means with the end.

Finally, it emerged that if he could aim at more exact and thorough work, *regardless of the amount* and with less thoughts about marks or "position" in relation to other boys, he might often go to bed with a sense of "achievement satisfaction". "You mean quality not quantity" was his unprompted remark in this connection.

I made no attempt to deal with his recent shortcoming in terms of right and wrong. He is not equipped for that approach—how many boys of his age are?

What he needs is enlightenment—not so much (say) biological information about sex as that more exact and detailed hold upon certain commonly used abstract words.

His chief problem, as I see it all, is his failure to discern adequate significances. He is certainly not incapable of being helped to discover significance. I cannot yet say whether or not I consider him intelligent enough to go forward in his present environment. But I know that in his own way he is happy at school and that he still has a strong (vague) regard for his house-master.

He is keen to have a "test" during the coming holiday. (I didn't call it an intelligence test.)

I should be happy to learn that his school had been able to meet him in the matter of "quality" and "quantity", so that he passes well and truly into the world of adequate "achievement satisfaction". I should then be pretty certain that he was unlikely to be one of those whose regressive behaviour lowers "the tone" of a school.'

The other interview took place after I had left the staff. I happened to be on a visit. Mr Lyward was just going to see a boy called William Hallett, motherless, brainy, over-studious, who had lived at home with a brilliant, successful and extremely busy father. The father had overawed the boy, who tended to remain solitary at Finchden as at home, and lately had been upset by some remark suggesting that he had 'made advances' to another boy. He had come to David, asking if he should take it seriously, and then said that he wanted to see Mr Lyward 'about homosexuality.' There had been a good deal at that time in the papers about homosexuality. William had also been worried through reading of a woman who had changed into a man, because he imagined that he himself had strongly developed feminine characteristics.

Mr Lyward reminded me of what I already knew, that interviews of this kind were rare, and that he deliberately avoided making too much of sex. He said that the 'isolation' of William Hallett should not be related to the isolation of a homosexual 'which he is not', but rather to certain boys who had strong sexual pressures, and were ashamed of them; they strove to hide their inward conflict behind a facade of cleverness, which their brains or practical sense helped them fairly successfully to construct. He made a gesture with his right hand of brain sailing into the air, and with his left of the emotions connected with sex remaining behind, with a huge gulf between. There were several such boys at Finchden.

William came in and sat down. Mr Lyward greeted him like a guest, and said: 'David's been telling me about you.' He sat at his table by the alcove window. 'You should know some quotations,' he went on. 'What's the one about "We something for what we have not"?' He turned to me. 'Come on. If William doesn't know, surely you do?' I had forgotten, and Mr Lyward told David to get the Dictionary of Quotations and look it up.

'Do you know London?' he asked William.

'Yes, sir.'

'You know you sometimes see a big house with a front and back entrance, and the back entrance is called the mews? They were once stables, though they aren't used much as stables now.' He made a bad pun on 'mews' and 'used', and David produced the quotation. 'Shelley. I thought it was Shelley,' said Mr Lyward, innocently.

> 'We look before and after,
> And pine for what is not:
> Our sincerest laughter
> With some pain is fraught.

Do you remember it?'

'Yes sir. I think I do.' The boy was listening quietly, neither stiff nor hostile.

'Who goes in at the back entrance?' Mr Lyward asked.

'The servants, sir.'

'Yes. And who go in at the front?' William did not answer. 'The sons,' said Mr Lyward. 'If someone has usurped your life, if your rightful self has been taken from you, you go in at the back, don't you? You're afraid somehow to go boldly up to the front. I'm not saying you wouldn't go in at the front door of some dilapidated old house.' At this point I registered a mental exclamation mark, since Mr Lyward had told me of a sentimental association William had formed with an elderly spinster, to whom he was clinging. 'Aren't you always getting round things, going to the back door?' Mr Lyward continued.

'Yes.'

'Or were?'

'And now I'm in front of the front door?' said the boy, almost eagerly.

'Yes. And it will open and you'll go in. I'm not saying anything about what is good or bad, but merely that the front door is better. Now, when you see a woman, for example, she may be rather frightening, but you want to get over the trembling. To go in by the front door is' (and he emphasised the word) 'happiness'.

A small girl happened to be staying with the Lywards, and some tiddley-winks were on Mr Lyward's desk. He noticed them and suggested we should play. William took it without surprise—but sat stock-still.

Mr Lyward said: 'What I wanted you to do was fetch the table, get us three into the game, decide what colour you wanted—*you*, not *we*—and tell us to begin.'

So the boy fetched the table and counters and we began to play. To begin with, his attitude towards the game—as to life—was apologetic and awkward. After a few minutes, and with a little provocation, he became aggressive. At one moment David's counter was under mine, and I looked like winning. William devised a quick strategy to release David's counter, so that I should not win. Mr Lyward, who had been gay and ordinary, became serious for a moment, and said: 'Now that's where thinking is useful. That's what thought is for. Go on, William. Win.'

Suddenly William said something relating the symbol of the front door to the positive attitude, and Mr Lyward—as if it was William who had thought about it—equally suddenly added: 'Yes, and don't you get the idea into that clever head of yours that you're what they call homosexual. You aren't. Something has been done to you which has deprived you of your guts. It's the wrong sort of word, but I can't think of another, and sometimes we have to use the wrong sort of word. You haven't been able to live your own life, have you? Well, soon you will. Gradually the door will open. You may open it yourself. Who knows—the good God may open it for you. But I want you to start things. "Let me be in a play. Let's have a ping-pong tournament. I'll be this! I'll be that!" But it's *you*, not someone else.'

That was all, except that later, and with the same kind of casualness, the boy thanked Mr Lyward; and months afterwards— when, on being asked about Mr Lyward by some friends, I used this interview as one illustration, a man came to me and said: 'I wish someone had talked to me like that when I was young. Instead I took fifteen years to find out.'

Both interviews have one or two characteristics that may serve to illustrate Mr Lyward's approach to boys, and their eager responsiveness to his sympathy and insight. It was left to William Hallett, not Mr Lyward, to point the symbolism between the front door and the positive attitude to life. It was the boy, not Mr Lyward, who made the distinction between quality and quantity. Over and over again boys understood, where adults with their fixed ideas failed. One boy wrote to his father: 'You didn't show much understanding of the place, as the thing that should be looked for is that it's a school which one person runs for the good of everyone, not academically but (*sic*) psychologically. There are thousands more people in the world who should be in a place like this, so the sooner I am ready to leave then so much the better for some other who needs help as much as I did.'

In the second interview, fear about sex was 'put in its place' as part of a general timidity. A general reference was made to past events and attitudes which were really responsible, without pinning them to the boys' parents or attaching blame. Release was suggested through a more positive approach in much smaller things, by which a general increase in natural assertiveness might be built up.

As a last illustration, here is an extract from a longish letter Mr Lyward once wrote to a father who had withdrawn another boy too soon. The boy had been in the same kind of trouble that William Hallett feared.

'Fear of life includes fear of the opposite sex, and that prevents their having any attraction, and so throws the boy back, as your son has been, upon perversion. General inversion is a better way of putting it. He has never realized that contact is the true way of safety, but has tried to remain intact against being found out. I hope that he now knows a better way of responding to the general challenge of life. He would have been sure of getting through if you had let him stay here. I have done what I can in a short while, and this letter is to give you some indication of the root trouble (as distinguished from the symptom).'

Some may find the imagery used in the interview with William Hallett irrelevant and think the abrupt transition to a child's game flippant. Such critics may ask themselves whether they are not thinking in their own terms, and not those related to the boy's needs and stage of growth. They may even find it painful to inquire deeply into themselves, and to ask why they might have preferred something more 'intellectual'. Whatever their reaction, the boy alone mattered. One such vivid quarter-of-an-hour might turn out to be worth more than long sessions of benign or clever exposition. Dreams are often irrelevant and flippant, and yet they may throw light on a 'total situation' which they symbolize or caricature, as nothing else may, and perhaps in consequence haunt the memory, and illumine a whole life.

'I suppose,' said a well-known man, who had asked questions about Finchden and been told that girls came to the boys' dances, 'that you have the usual trouble afterwards.'

Why? The girls were simple and unaffected girls, and the boys adolescents who had been pretending to be grown up and had returned, although belatedly, to being boys. Most of them were uncertain of themselves. Most of them, with girls, kept naturally at a gay and unemotional level. Some, not necessarily the older ones, may consciously have avoided anything else. Some, afraid of life, were afraid of girls and took a long time to get over their fear. In the whole history of Finchden a few, extremely few, became involved in prolonged and complicated relationships with a girl in the neighbourhood. In the past all these relationships had subsided without harm and without scandal. There was a great deal of talk about girls and women, which remained talk. On the whole the boys' behaviour seemed to be composed of chaff, usually light, from one or two slightly portentous; primness; and adolescent chivalry; a natural relationship between boy and girl.

CHAPTER EIGHT

Mr Lyward had taken Mr Hannen on to the staff for a probationary period at the urgent request of a friend. He had arrived just before me. Now in early middle age, he had done well at the University and had taught at a number of schools. He had lately suffered a breakdown, and Mr Lyward had written to him before his arrival 'when I saw you I felt that you might find Finchden Manor almost ideal for your rehabilitation, if you didn't (consciously or unconsciously or both) avoid its rather unusual challenges ... There was never any idea in my mind of taking you unless it were for a real job, however much time you were likely to need to get into your stride.'

He had added in the same letter: 'The difference between Finchden Manor and a school is so vital that by its very nature it is liable to tempt an erstwhile school-master into adopting "school mastery" attitudes, which are more akin to those he may at one time have deplored than he would believe possible. Therefore it is essential that I should say now that there are certain pullings away or fallings away from the centre about which we have to be even more strict than a school. ... One example will, I hope, suffice. Finchden Manor offers boys certain things which are vital and valued, but it is not difficult for any individual adult to outbid it by offering something more immediate, i.e. cosiness. In an ordinary school a master might, rightly or wrongly, be commended for showing individual interest in a lonely or unhappy or troubled boy. He might be thanked for inviting the boy to his room, where "we can make toast together and it can feel like home".

'Members of the staff here would know when they could safely do that, or do it with advantage to a particular boy. Nobody, who has not been told that he is a member in the sense of having begun to "find himself", would be wise or kind to take such a risk of ruining or disturbing a boy's relation to a community, which is always (as a school is not always) mindful of every individual boy and his needs.

'The granting of permissions is likewise not something which can lie freely in the hands of each member of the staff indiscriminately; and so on.

'If you quickly sense all that I am trying to convey you will as quickly begin to draw strength from life here ...'

I enjoyed Mr Hannen's civilized talk, his erudition, and his rather forlorn and rueful humour; it was a change from the boys and the bleakness of my own room, to enter his, to find a comfortable chair, books, and Mr Hannen to discuss them. He brewed coffee, buttered toast, and scrambled eggs; I used his cooking things and forgot to wash them up.

He had an anxious benevolence of expression, seldom gave a firm opinion, and if he did, looked at you sideways as if he had said something *risqué*. He painted neat paintings, and was an intelligent if pedantic critic.

He was generous with his coffee and cigarettes, and the boys called his room the soup-kitchen. But that was not the only reason why they liked him. He was a trained teacher of arts and letters, who knew the literature of several centuries. He could 'place' T. S. Eliot and tell a Picasso when he saw one. He taught boys to draw and recite Shakespeare. He took a part in *Hamlet*, spoke beautifully, and as the player King died realistically. If anyone asked, he was ready to spend hours explaining Dr Leavis and the higher literary criticism.

Having spent a few days at Finchden before finally asking to come on the staff, he knew what it was like. I cannot say if he expected it to be a refuge. Once in residence, he remained in his room almost the whole time. As the noise at the boys' meals was too much for him, he ate upstairs. He seldom put out the lights, never stayed long in the staff room, and since he went downstairs so rarely got to know only a small number of the boys.

He was frightened by Mr Lyward, who was kind, but saw into

him. Mr Hannen did not want to be seen into or to see too far into himself, or to pass through the eye of any needle; in any event, not at Finchden. When he realized what sort of a place it was, he began to talk of leaving for a monastery.

Perhaps he should have come later. Perhaps he was too unwell or merely had not the temperament to live there as a teacher, though elsewhere he might have been at home. While he remained, the place inevitably presented him, as everyone else, with those 'rather unusual' challenges, which he found uncomfortable. So did the boys; so did a number of parents; and so at first, did I.

I found myself wondering how much my own development had been, at one time, arrested, and how much I had once resembled the boys in developing a false defensive self and in needing to depend upon attitudes and external things. I felt at first as if I were passing along an identification parade, all the people being myself. Which was I, really? I was not sure even now that I wanted to admit which I was, or had been, or what I could not do without.

I had a nice car, could make trips to London when I chose, had been in the Commandos and a prisoner-of-war in the Castle of Colditz, about which the boys had read exciting books. All this had a sort of glamour. Could I do without it?

The same with my experiences as a foreign correspondent and those quotations Peter Storey had said 'It must be lovely to bring in.' All useful, but ...?

Could I become interested, like Sid, like Mr Lyward, in all the boys; and not only, like Mr Hannen, in the ones who interested *me*? How well at times, with some of them, I understood the child, who prayed: 'God bless everyone-except the Japanese.'

After reading the boys' stories, how much I longed for a scapegoat! 'Someone is to blame for all this,' I said to myself. 'It must be the parents.' That need for certainty, that yearning for an all-explaining theory! 'Here is the cause,' I wanted to proclaim, 'and this is the cure'.

I had once thought I was not sentimental; I found that I was. How unpleasant to be unpopular; how difficult—particularly to these boys—to say 'no'. I began to have a dreadful feeling that I could not do without (1) flattery, and (2) cut-and-dried explanations of 'human problems', that I might be a mixture of Nigs Walker and Arthur Ney, or of the vainest mother and the most rigid father. These challenges, which of course had been presented by life on many occasions, seemed to become clearer in a small community. They interested me and later I found that I had certain challenges to present to Mr Lyward and his staff. They do not belong to this book, though possibly to a novel.

The challenges Finchden presented to the boys reminded me of the Hound of Heaven, in very slow motion. They were felt in the midst of laughter and enjoyment. To Mr Hannen they seemed menacing and urgent, more like the Hound of the Baskervilles. He did not care to forego regular hours. He preferred to confine himself to the more obviously intelligent élite. He sometimes gave me the impression of believing that his recent troubles had made him special and apart, and that, if anyone took his apartheid away, by probing the real fears and deprivations which had produced it, he would have nothing left.

And so he stayed in his room, like Jonah in the belly of the whale, but with no indication of emerging.

Instead of passively allowing Finchden to put him on trial, Mr Hannen could have given it a trial himself by making at least an occasional sortie among the boys, for he soon lost his fear of them as 'toughs'. He appeared to remain as an urbane critic of the place, into which he did not too laboriously enquire. Most of his criticism had already occurred to me, but while I was on the staff I did not think about it too much—except at night. Mr Lyward and the rest were doing devoted and successful work, bringing to creative life boys whom no other place had been able to help. Mr Lyward had been at it twenty-five years. I preferred to take what part I could, absorb as much as I could, and ask questions afterwards.

Mr Hannen often used to ask what would have become of a genius at Finchden.

'Suppose Rimbaud had come here?' he murmured. 'Or Baudelaire?

Or Verlaine? Or Byron? Nowadays they would all have been deemed maladjusted.'

'I suppose they would,' I said. 'I think they'd have enjoyed themselves.'

'But what about their genius?'

'What about it?'

'If they'd stayed, might it not have been adjusted out of them?'

This was his theme, if I understood him aright; if I did not, I apologize. He seemed to be saying not that many men of genius have been unhappy, which may be true, but that a genius depends on maladjustment, which is a matter of opinion. Sometimes he said 'artist' instead of genius. I could not help feeling that he was thinking of himself and used this argument as an excuse for taking no part in Finchden's ordinary life. He would remind me how much creative achievement had sprung from unhappiness and loneliness. His doubts concerning Finchden did not seem to be exhausting angry disputes within himself, but part of a vague antagonism, which passed the time of day. At night my own thoughts used to meander round the same argument.

Riff, for example, had extraordinary vitality. He played the piano well, and his paintings and writings showed originality and force. His life had been stormy for a boy of twenty. Mr Lyward was one of the few people he had been able to respect, and Finchden Manor the only place at which he had agreed to stay. Apart from one specific limitation which still kept him outside the community, he had certainly become disarmed to a surprising degree. He was making contact with the community in a relaxed and easy way which had once been impossible for him. He also felt the selfish impulse of a creative artist, but it was not yet particularly vigorous; the energy it needed was not yet free. He sometimes talked of a tussle with what he called his feeling of responsibility towards other people. How could he reconcile the two? Ought they to be reconciled? Had not a great number of creative people just gone straight ahead without caring a damn for others, and created, leaving people to gobble up their pictures, hang on their music and their poetry, and agree they were exceptional? 'I am myself,' Arthur Ney had said, 'I've got something that is *myself*. Why should I give it up? What proof do I have that I'll gain more than I lose?'

Flynn saw himself as an adventurer and explorer. Perhaps he really was a born explorer. To what extent had the great explorer he so much admired and had gone to visit 'accepted the community'? —and to what extent had his explorations, and so many other big achievements, sprung from something in the achiever which could not and would not make this impalpable surrender—from some maladjustment?

One answer is, I suppose, that had all these boys, and Mr Hannen, and adults like him, commanded the energy to do what they saw themselves as doing, they would have done it. Later some of these boys might do it, after the energies expended in their struggle with the community had been released. So it might be for them. Nonetheless, I wondered if, out of such a struggle itself, creative achievement might not come and had not often come in the past. This argument went on within myself, until one night I found myself imagining two boys of potential genius, both seventeen, both with a disturbed childhood, and the same kind of upbringing and constitution. Both, I thought, are impossible at their schools, or their schools impossible for them. One goes to Finchden, the other does not. What happens?

Call the one who does not go to Finchden Z. He bashes himself against himself and everybody and everything all round him. He may go to a remand home. He falls wildly in love and is wildly happy, then is disappointed and wildly wretched. Jobs come, jobs go. All the time he writes, and sooner or later his first work is ready—say a novel. It is a magnificent explosion of rage and bitterness and struggle. Parents, school-masters, clergymen, appear as monsters, unrelieved. The world is dark and cruel, society corrupt, happiness a delusion, God a fabrication. The hero is himself, and all is coloured by his own distress.

Call the other boy Q. He goes to Finchden. He feels like a refugee from a tyrant state reaching a free country. (Shelley would have been in his element there.) Gradually he is asked to surrender all or part of the picture he has formed of himself. He passes through pangs of rebirth, but feels them more acutely and suffers more intensely than the other boys. Z's volcanic book comes into his hands, exciting him, making him exclaim: 'This is what I am, this is what I should have written.' At a certain moment he furiously resents Mr Lyward, all the more because Mr Lyward understands him. But as the character which had been foisted on to him, or with which he had protected himself, falls away, perhaps a new kind of growth begins, rooted not merely in his own dilemma but in humanity. Other deeper rhythms begin to be heard, and with this new growth comes a widening awareness which Z so far is without.

Q leaves Finchden and takes the road to London. Like Balzac's de Rubempré, he sees the metropolis glittering at his feet and dreams how he shall conquer it.

Some people, I thought, would say that nothing happens; or not a work of art. Instead of writing, Q would live. This is the familiar argument of all who believe art to be nothing more than the sweat of a sick world. If it were true, in a happy world we should have no art. I thought this rubbish, and therefore assumed, as the duck which woke me early every morning quacked under the window, and Mr Hannen's snores came softly through the wall, that Q does not forsake 'art' for 'life', but writes—also a novel. His early troubles will still be close enough to colour the story and contribute to the plot. The book will therefore include many experiences like those of Z.

But how different it will be!

Q will have ceased to see himself only in his role of sufferer, and other people only as they have affected him. All will be more rounded, nearer the whole. Beyond the drunken mother, who neglected him, are circumstances which helped to make her drunken and neglectful. And his 'cold' father with whom he was not on terms—what made that father cold? What other facets did he have, and may his life not have been tragic in a way? The book will have humour; humour will play about the figure of the author, Q, himself. Q's book will be more objective than the one Z has written, whose characteristics will have included subjectivity and force. What Q writes will be coloured by himself, but less violently, and the force be distributed over a wider field. The new sense of values which will have come to him as a result of his greater awareness will also, probably, be expressed in a stricter style.

And what will become of these two afterwards?

Unless Z meets a wife or mistress, friends or surroundings, which may prove to be for him just what Finchden was for Q, he may continue to strike the same note. It may continue magnificent, if he has a keyboard with innumerable octaves. It may, if disease, poverty or disappointment pursue him through life, grow steadily more profound and more terrible. Then, especially if he die young, sublime he will remain within his limits, the genius of one emotion, like Leopardi's 'firm foundation of unyielding despair'. But if he never meets anyone to awaken other chords, and fails to experience enough misery to deepen his own, the first-fruit may remain an only child and all the books that follow phantoms.

I saw the genius who had passed through Finchden as likely to develop in range and depth for many years. Inner turmoils are exhausting. They consume energy which creative people need for their creations. I set against the works of art that may have been composed in release from personal turmoil, the great number that might have been composed, had the potential creator known better how to direct and use for others his inner disturbance.

Great artists have loved life and seen it whole; how can a man depict life whole if he remain preoccupied with himself? Maxim Gorki, whose autobiography is for many the greatest ever written, witnessed and suffered ignorance and cruelty enough to keep twenty writers busy for a lifetime. He called himself Gorki, because the word means bitter. Yet his story is not one of personal embitterment; nor is it shot with bitterness only against or on behalf of others, but with love, poetry, humour, quiet observation and compassion. As a result, the self-portrait becomes a portrait of mankind, and in his case a panorama of all contemporary Russia.

There are men of genius who have made their greater troubles serve creative ends. That possibility at least Mr Lyward taught the boys at Finchden, within their lesser range. He had had his own troubles in youth, had overcome and harnessed them. He may often have wished to shake off his responsibilities and go away, perhaps, to write his own story. The lack of clarity in some of his writings may have been partly due to lack of time; it was surprising that he had found time to write anything at all. But he had chosen his own course, his creative impulse had expressed itself in life. Had a genius come to Finchden, I reckon the boy would have been enriched. Is not the creative impulse often enriched, when men of a particular type turn outwards from themselves?

'I hope old Hannen stays,' said Riff. 'He's so nice. And he could get so much out of the place.'

It was curious that this remark should have come from Riff, the one boy with the originality which, Mr Hannen was suggesting, Finchden might destroy.

But Mr Hannen remained in his room. He talked wistfully about his troubles, and the staff, busy with the boys' troubles, had little time to listen. 'What good can he do?' my wife wrote to me, 'by his own confused fears? He seems to be growing old under a shrinking horizon, and there is nothing magnificent in his "revolt" against the community.'

One night Nigs Walker ran away. David, Neville and I foresaw that we should be up till all hours looking for him. I told Hannen that I should be unable to take coffee.

'I don't know why everyone makes such a fuss,' he murmured,

deep in his armchair. 'Why don't you leave the boy? By the way, did I ever tell you how I ran away?'

But I could not wait. He was constantly beginning something, the end of which I never heard. He once started an interesting and important discussion about discipline. This I had to continue by myself, for one morning he and his troubled spirit mounted a bicycle and pedalled away in the direction of a monastery; where (if they have arrived) others will ask for some surrender of himself. Perhaps it will be easier, because surrender in such a place is made to something which in its visible form includes rule, ritual and centuries of tradition, all of which were lacking at Finchden.

The boys regretted his coffee and missed his culture. Now and again they spoke of him in a friendly way, or argued from their own experience that he 'should have stayed'.

Mr Hannen's departure prevented me from discovering his views about the discipline at Finchden. But other people outside Finchden, who had never been there, often asked me the same questions. Doubts were expressed in three ways.

There were those who take discipline to mean only the outward discipline of rules and punishment, and attribute 'softness' to anyone who deems it of secondary importance.

Others considered that what they vaguely termed 'psychological treatment' was merely a high-falutin' phrase to exculpate those who failed to make sufficient exertions on their own behalf. In the opinion of such people, Mr Lyward was 'pandering' to the weak.

A third group had no prejudice in favour of rules and punishments, and no prejudice against psychologists. They merely asked: 'Mr Lyward does not depend on outward discipline, but there must be discipline of some kind. What is his substitute?' Put in this way, the question had some force.

The boys at Finchden were all the while being helped, most of them *unconsciously*, to make a harder choice than others brought up under regulations which they had either to obey and be rewarded, or disobey and be punished. The reason, of course, was that at Finchden both prizes and punishments were absent, and the boys in consequence were compelled to choose for themselves, without fear or inducement. As one old boy, now a probation officer, wrote: 'The probation service has the sanction of the law behind it. Finchden has an inner discipline.'

One may imagine oneself, as I often did, sent to Finchden, and it is not extravagant to assume that a large number of us, in adolescence, might easily have been candidates.

The boys found themselves with a freedom that at first appeared to be 'complete'. That only meant that they noticed the externals (no locked doors, no penalties and so on) in contrast to those other externals they had left behind. With nothing either proscribed or prescribed, they were thrust back upon themselves.

It became difficult for long to make anyone else responsible, either for the action or its result. A gifted boy wrote home a stilted but revealing essay on Finchden. 'The essayist was suddenly upset by some trifle,' he remarked. 'He immediately started to find fault with all kinds of things. He failed in his purpose, for he only found fault with himself.' It dawned on some slowly, on others quite fast, that 'to be a person, not a pawn' was not easy; and several (for example, those who talked of changing into the Army, or living according to 'scientific rules') soon seemed to want to be 'pawns' again. They felt confused and insecure. One evening Henry Carpenter lost his temper. I managed to clear the other boys out of the room, and he and I were left alone, like boxers, in opposite corners. He was speechless, and I did not know what to say. For quarter-of-an-hour we said nothing. Then he burst out: 'We're sometimes so —— wide open here.'

The more sensitive the boy, the more deeply this openness was felt, and the greater perhaps were his later possibilities. The vulnerable feeling could not at times be avoided. On this account Mr Lyward was particularly concerned to maintain the security within which the boys could feel insecurities in their own way, without further pressure from outside, and to ensure that insecurity, or doubt, was not falsely eased by automatic responses, or explanations, which they would come to expect on all occasions and start clinging to as rules.

If they had had nothing at all by which to measure their actions, nothing either to surrender to or rebel against, they would simply have been adrift, and the whole place, not to say all the love and energy of the staff, worse than useless. In 'old days' their 'standard' might have been a tradition or an ideal or a person. Now it was a way of life, to which they were either to belong or not. The choice was theirs. Mr Lyward did not lecture them on this or any other point. The community at Finchden did without lectures as it did without rules. In comparison, the freedom of all other adolescent communities which relied on rules was limited by those rules, those lectures, those sermons, and the boys' horizons were possibly enlarged, possibly limited, but certainly less fluid and seen to a great extent through other people's eyes. Sid once had a dream. He dreamt that I was writing this book and that he was reading it. What I had written worried him, and he was frowning and exclaiming: 'For God's sake, don't say that! Only say that it's unlimited. That's how our boys arrive at limits.' His dream might have added to 'unlimited' the words 'not crystallized'.

If the boys decided to 'contract out' of the community by running away, nobody could stop them; the resultant damage to themselves is shown by most of their later records and by subsequent appeals to Mr Lyward. The story of all who remained is a story of a largely unfelt struggle between their false self on arrival and the community. The surrender was asked, but not demanded; there were no threats if it was not made.

This inward perplexity might burst into the open in some highly dramatic form, as was to happen to Flynn. It might show itself in tears, or blows, or hysterics, or passionate letters to a parent or to Mr Lyward. The following is an instance:—

Dear Sir,
    I am writing this in the hopes that I may see you when you

have time. I know you are a busy man whose interests are entirely (*sic*) for the community. But I must be released from this tomb which I have built during the past and which is suffocating me as the days go by. *Please* help me, *please*.

This letter, written by a boy of seventeen, was accompanied by a drawing of a bottle marked 'Repression', with a matchstick figure inside holding out its arms, marked 'Me'.

Naturally, a struggle expressed itself in dreams. A wish to 'postpone' decision might be detected, for instance, in a much older patient of Mr Lyward's, who dreamt of sharing a railway carriage with someone he vaguely recognized.

'Haven't I seen you somewhere before?' he asked.

'I expect so,' answered the stranger. 'I am Jesus Christ.' Later the stranger got out.

'Where are you going?' asked the dreamer, and received the reply: 'I have to send a telegram putting off my crucifixion.'

Occasionally a boy's doubts might patently reach a crisis. But since, so often, Finchden's respite and relaxation forestalled crisis, and since the boys' rebirth was so gradual, which allayed the pain, crisis was rare. One saw instead a succession of small changes or failures to change. These, though not superficially dramatic, could be deeply moving, or sad, to people who saw and understood. A visitor could not be expected to know how much it meant that So-and-So, silent for months, had suddenly begun to ask questions about himself; or that someone like Arthur Ney had stopped worrying; or that So-and-So, having refused to clear up the dinner plates, came back and finished the job; or that Henry Carpenter, too vulnerable to be given a 'no' for months after his arrival, had at last been able to take a 'no' in his stride; or that one boy, who had detested his mother, went home on a visit and then rang to ask if he might stay a few days longer, returning happier; or that another, who was always begging to go home, suddenly wanted to remain at Finchden; or that Riff, who had stayed out late for weeks, began to come in at or near bed-time.

These small signs were indications of a change; and the change was evidence of re-birth. 'Whenever a man catches himself acting through impersonal interest or real concern, he knows that something big has happened. ... Always something has to go, a hold has to be released, values revised. ... There must be alarms, fumbling, indecision, ineffectualness, pain, a temporary feeling of helplessness ... and individuals vary in the degree to which they "go through it"...'

Sooner or later the boys were involved in a surrender. Something to which a boy—or adult—had clung, in order to keep at least one foot outside the community, was challenged. It might be the picture he had cherished of himself. It might be one of those almost fanatic attachments to which reference has been made. It might be a connexion in the town; very likely a girl. No moral judgment was delivered; the boy would not be told that one thing was 'wrong' the other 'right'. It was sometimes, however, suggested to him that he might just live, for a while, among his neighbours, without seeking any artificial aid to prove himself separate or different; until, merely by contact, the natural separateness or difference, which exists in everyone, might grow up in him, and a strength be gained that would stand him in good stead in the world.

Later he might possibly return to the same person, or thing, but having passed through 'the eye of the needle', as a new man. A boy too closely tied to one of his parents might return to them far more truly their son; a boy who had merely taken refuge in art or science or the woods, return as a true artist or scientist, as an explorer or a naturalist. An infatuation might later become a love. There were instances of all these 'changes' and 'returns'. Sid, the East End intellectual whose science (a real love) had at first been confused with a personal need to prove his difference and superiority, discarded science for two years and came back to it, with a far more mature attitude, for life. There were many instances, where a boy's discovery of himself led to a happier relationship not only with his parents, but also between the parents themselves. I vividly remember one boy saying of his mother, with whom he had been on difficult terms: 'Perhaps now *I* shall be able to help *her*'; and another: 'I now see how well my mother walks'.

Clearly human development of this order is not assisted by being 'soft'. Clearly too no 'soft' person could possibly have faced, relentlessly and without illusions, the unavoidable conflict with so many parents. No 'soft' person could possibly have lightened the burden of so many boys. Perhaps if one takes certain words, which express the relationship between an adolescent and an externally imposed discipline, and transfers them to Finchden, they help to explain what happened there. A struggle, which might elsewhere be made against visible authority, at Finchden might seem at times, and rarely for long, to be against Mr Lyward, but be really to keep an inward picture of oneself. An anger, felt elsewhere against rules and penalties, at Finchden might be against oneself; and the prizes, which elsewhere are medals and success, and for the Finchden boys too might afterwards be expressed as 'cure' and 'success', were really inward and lasting.

This chapter and the last were in part written to answer questions I was asked about violence, sex, and discipline. It may have been noticed that I have seldom used the word discipline, or self-discipline, but instead such expressions, in regard to the boys' 'cure', as 'falling away' or 'loosening' and, in regard to their growth, as 'widening awareness' and 'change of values'. Mr Lyward two or three times altered 'self discipline' to 'widening awareness' in my original text, and the alteration is illumining.

The boys did gradually acquire a self-discipline. It was not narrow or moralizing. It grew naturally as part of that widening awareness of themselves and others, which accompanied the happy and relaxed enjoyment of their boyhood. Their landscape became bigger, their movement spontaneous and free, and the growth of many of them almost unconscious, like physical growth; so that the troubles which had once beset them did 'fall away' and were indeed 'lost' rather than 'conquered' or 'discarded'. Self-discipline was not inculcated as an ideal; but self-limitation developed out of their easier and expanding relationship with others. In this recognition of limits they found a new kind of freedom. The process, like most natural processes, was slow. (Even after losing his burden, Christian still had more than half of the Pilgrims' Progress to travel.) The change in the boys was often only perceptible to the trained eye or to someone, like myself, returning after some weeks or months of absence.

'How does a child learn to walk unless by walking?' Mr Lyward once asked. He might have added, 'How do these adolescents, who have become children again, learn to live except by living?' One day I asked Henry Carpenter what he had meant by the answer he gave General Percival, 'We learn to live'.

'Just what I said,' he answered curtly, and added, 'I meant learning to fit in and at the same time to cope. I accept now. I don't worry about defending myself. My energies can branch out'—he splayed the fingers of both hands—'instead of all going into one clot', and he indicated a point at the end of one finger.

I asked if he felt that this was rendering him passive.

'Yes,' he said. 'Passive about offences to me. In regard to other things, exploratory.'

'Attacking?'

'No. Exploring. And all this happens automatically. Casually. It can't be forced. I don't want to be given too many ideas. That's why I don't want to see Mr Lyward at the moment. I've got enough.'

These two gestures of Henry Carpenter's have remained a most vivid clue. Beyond them I saw countless people, never recorded as delinquent or deemed maladjusted, with all their energies driven down one single lane, piling up, entangled in too cramped a space; and in my imagination those two splayed hands became the paths along which others advance to many-sidedness. Henry Carpenter, with no home, and no schooling to speak of, had had his vision of the fullness of life; three years earlier he had almost been given up as hopeless.

The boys did not only feel outwards. They felt more deeply. Indeed their movement outwards was a result of the releasing of those abundant impulses which the absence at home or school of a diviner had caused so unhappily to remain sealed. 'Joy ... comes to those who are finding an increasing self-awareness in co-operative effort, carried on not so much as an intellectual ideal as the overflowing of a self fulfilled.' Sometimes there came to Finchden boys who had been at institutions, where for a time they had seemed to be normally happy and normally law-abiding. 'In every instance these people seemed to have an institution-produced layer wrapped around their original life of loving and hating and being hurt. One such had spent his earliest years in degradation, but from then onwards, for eight or nine years, the staff of a Home had done everything they could to make amends to him for those earlier years. He knew all the language of gratitude, but any keen observer could see that he never overflowed, ... nothing welled up ...' Many a boy who came from an institution felt that 'what he receives is only his due and what is withheld sure evidence of "their meanness".'

The appeal to this impersonal and mercenary approach is, as many but not yet enough people understand, one of the dangerous ambushes which, together with good foundations, have been laid by the Welfare State. 'The Queen will give me a suit', a boy once said, and another like him, while still new to Finchden or unable to form a living relationship with it, would speak of Mr D. and the Office on the top floor as all at Finchden that mattered, an impersonal 'They', denying money or disgorging.

In my original text I had written of the boys' 'struggle between their false self on arrival and the community'. In front of 'struggle' Mr Lyward inserted the words 'largely unfelt'. I had also written that they 'had sooner or later to make a harder choice than others brought up under regulations'; this he altered to 'were all the while unconsciously being helped to make a harder choice'. It was this unconsciousness which makes words like 'conflict' and 'self-control' —the kind of self-control that implies tenseness and clenched fists —inapplicable to nearly all the boys. One might suppose that the older a boy was when he came to Finchden, the more conscious he would have become of anything that happened inside him, and the more likely therefore to suffer from wearying conflicts rather than tangles gradually loosened. Yet it was not always so. I remember in particular a boy of over twenty, outwardly most sophisticated, who became a child not only in his relationship to the others but in facial expression too, almost at once. Those who were likely to feel 'conflict' were those who, having built up the most stubborn resistances, were therefore the most difficult to disarm; these were the exceptions and might be of any age.

'Pain' many of the boys did feel, not 'conflict'. 'Finchden Manor afforded to some the sternest experience they have ever had. The pains they endure during some period of their stay represent something that no ordinary schoolboy has ever had to experience. Although a happy place, it is no easy place. Unhampered by fear of criticism, they are forced back upon their real selves. The bubbles of fear rise to the surface, explode and are gone.' While those bubbles were rising and exploded, a boy might suffer. 'You've grown,' I once told a boy. 'Oh—physically,' he answered ruefully. The pull forward to adult life and backward to childhood might well have made that particular boy more than rueful. Another reached a stage when he realized what it meant never to have known his mother, and suffered. Another, whom his mother had dominated, began to break free of her, and in that phase suffered.

In offering this relaxed and happy atmosphere, in which—late but not too late—each boy's deepest and often tenderest feelings could at last well up, and his whole cramped arrested personality branch out in his own way, Mr Lyward gave to those 'deemed maladjusted' an extraordinary chance, not given to many adolescents in many schools. My thoughts went often to boys who were not emotionally disturbed, or who were believed not to be disturbed. Some might be in crowded classrooms; they must learn, learn, and when the clock's hands stopped at the statutory hour, they must hurry forth and find a job. In the great public schools, routine and rule might produce self-discipline, but make it in part formal, artificial, not spontaneous. Tradition could still stifle, while the pressure to get on grew ever more urgent. At Finchden the tyrannies of both past and future seemed held at a distance. There youth discovered its own way, not along any beaten track, and for a while not hectored by the clock. There youth seemed long, and the future everlasting, and all that one could wish to grow had time to grow spontaneously. Coming back to London, I wondered how sometimes men could seem so uniform, when adolescents were so diverse.

Perhaps, after all, those responsible for the disturbances of the Finchden boys had done them a good turn? Small wonder then, at the many grateful letters. No wonder a boy, diagnosed on arrival as a 'possible schizophrenic', hid tears on departure.

The reports which Mr Lyward wrote about all the boys went deeper than I remembered elsewhere; as if he were trying to present an inner essence, from which all other secondary accomplishments flowed. I thought often of that wonderful passage about childhood from Thomas Traherne's *Centuries of Meditation*: 'The corn was orient and immortal wheat which never should be reaped nor was ever sown ...' I should like to quote it all. ... 'The skies were mine, and so were the sun and moon and stars, and all the world was mine; and I the only spectator and enjoyer of it. I knew no churlish proprieties, nor bounds nor divisions; but all proprieties and divisions were mine, all treasures and the possessors of them. So that with much ado I was corrupted, and made to learn the dirty devices of the world, which now I unlearn, and become, as it were, a little child again that I may enter again into the Kingdom of God.' And from this I was led to other words: 'Seek ye first the Kingdom of God, and all these things shall be added unto you.' Was it this, perhaps, by which at Finchden so many 'cures' had been achieved? Was it this that had been meant, when I was told that only a poet could write about such work?

CHAPTER NINE

I HAVE chosen to tell the story of Alastair Wilton in full for two reasons: first, because it illumines a relationship between boy, Mr Lyward and parent—in this instance the mother; secondly, because Mrs Wilton had many feelings which a majority of parents—and possibly educational authorities—naturally shared about Finchden. She stated them vigorously and at length, before her son went, while he was there, and later, when she decided he ought to leave. The doubts and recurring anxieties, which might be felt by any mother or father faced with the same problem, were put with particular force by Mrs Wilton.

Alastair Wilton went to Finchden three years before the war. He came of well-to-do parents. His father, who had been a naval officer, was dead. His mother loved the boy, her only son, deeply, but had spoilt him. She was a Scotswoman and lived near the Border with Alastair and his sister. This sister was several years older than the boy, and of a vigorous and dominating character.

Alastair often dreamed of Victorian surroundings. Mrs Wilton had many of the solid characteristics of that period, and when people spoke of her I thought at first of Queen Victoria. She was small and sturdy. Her letters were seldom fewer the four pages long, with strong underlinings; 'must' was a favourite word. But she was not stuffy. She had vivacity and vitality, loved to fill her house with young people, and gave hilarious parties at Christmas, at one of which she dressed up as the old Queen.

She had firm religious faith and went regularly to church, but did not insist that her son should go. She had high ideals and definite standards of right and wrong and did many kindnesses to many people. Much that she said or wrote sounded excellent; in relation to her son some had proved mistaken. The inflexible side of her character was softened by an endearing honesty; at a fairly advanced age, she could admit and adapt herself to unfamiliar ideas and even reveal her vulnerable real self. Consequently one ends her story with admiration and sympathy.

Her spoiling of her son had been in part brought about by a serious illness of his. One boy at his school had died. He had nearly died and this crisis had affected both mother and son deeply. Alastair had already begun to play upon her at his preparatory school, begging her to take him home. During his first term at a public school he caused such commotion that he had to be taken away and handed over to a tutor, Mr Greenacre. At the end of the holiday Mr Greenacre took him back, but the boy 'worked himself into so hysterical a condition that neither house-master nor school doctor (wrote Mrs Wilton) would consent to his remaining at College. His present firm intention is never to return to any school, large or small.' Whenever return was suggested, he threatened suicide or chewed playing-cards. 'He is dominating the situation at home,' wrote a psychiatrist to the family doctor, 'and being extremely difficult and unpleasant. He clearly needs to be away from home with someone much stronger than Mr Greenacre, and there are many other problems. He is primarily hysteric. ... I am not sure whether you know Mr Lyward of Finchden Manor, Tenterden. I have great confidence in his capacity to handle difficult situations ...'

A few days later, Mrs Wilton paid her first visit to Finchden. She took to Mr Lyward, *but* (and there were to be many 'buts'), 'We are a rather critical and observant family. What perplexes me most is the effect his surroundings and above all the other boys will have on Alastair. They struck me as having been, or being, far more nervously ill and less normal to all superficial appearances than he is. I recognize that there are serious things wrong with Alastair's outlook on life. Probably that is the case with *all* of us (I mean most of us); but whether he would not feel—"Good heavens, they must think things pretty wrong with me if I'm sent among boys like that!"—and what effect this might have on him, I don't know.'

Mr Lyward answered: 'I sympathize with you because it must be a difficult decision to make. The simplest answer I can give is that I have seen many parents grappling with the same problem and making the same criticisms, and finally months later expressing their gratitude and satisfaction that they had accepted this place as a whole and not in part. It would be comparatively easy to run a place which would appeal to visiting parents, but would not inevitably help the boys. ... I could put you on to many parents who would reassure you, but I would rather you made a venture of faith.'

This skirmish recurs at the beginning of many of the boys' stories. Other parents were doubtful about untidiness or bad language or absence of curriculum. Mr Lyward wished them to accept Finchden as an 'act of faith'. But once or twice, if he felt that the parent was likely to be more than usually upset by appearances, in the boy's interest he made an exception and deliberately set the stage. In preparation for Mrs Wilton's second visit, he sent for a dozen boys of Alastair's age, all from public schools, and asked them to arrange a formal tea. He explained that he had never done such a thing before; there was now a reason. ... 'The mother is genuinely puzzled, and you can't blame her.'

So the furniture was polished, and the tea laid on a table with a white cloth. Mrs Wilton arrived, with Alastair and his sister, to be met by a gathering of tidy boys in their good suits, with clean nails and smarmed-down hair.

'This is a plot,' said she, in an aside to Mr Lyward.

'Of course it is,' he answered.

She was displeased and remained stiff. She refused a cigarette offered by one of the boys, suspecting poison or a practical joke. 'Thank you for our pleasant visit,' she wrote, 'although I did not very greatly appreciate my reception! Alastair was quite favourably impressed. I think his chief misgiving is that his many gifts will not be sufficiently developed. My principal misgiving is that I don't feel now that there could be any real reason why he should stay at a Clinic like Finchden Manor for more than six months at the outside. The aim we should all have in mind is to restore him to the normal as rapidly as possible—he is putting himself on the right road fairly rapidly by his own efforts ...'

Mr Lyward answered; and thus a correspondence was fully launched which was to continue almost weekly for five years. (With Alastair himself it continues to this day.) 'I am not at all sure,' Mr Lyward wrote, 'that you would ever be able to trust anyone or any place which had challenged your views even as kindly as we have done; and in that case we should be in the impossible position of being only nominally free to help Alastair. I must know how far you are likely to go on for ever spoiling Alastair's chances, even should he come here. I am therefore going to suggest that you try to recognize that you have now reached a limit, past which it would be unwise to go. In other words, I must reject your suggestion of visiting here again to-morrow. It cannot do the boys here any good if you should come again so soon, or that you should so obviously question our suitability for a boy whom they recognized as like themselves. Nor would it help them if my patience was strained by parents too often past a certain point.'

I can now leave the letters to speak for themselves, commenting only where necessary. On the one hand there is Mr Lyward. At that time he had already taught for nearly thirty years. His independent experience with maladjusted boys so far extended only over six years, but he had spent many more in charge of his junior house at Glenalmond. On the other hand there is the boy's mother, (or in other instances his father, or both mother and father),—unwilling, naturally suspecting the unorthodox, to trust their son by 'act of faith' to a total stranger. Yet all parents—in this, as in scores of other cases—felt with varying degrees of awareness and honesty of mind, that they themselves had failed somewhere and that, if they did not agree to some kind of special treatment, they might ruin their son's life. Many, like Mrs Wilton, thought in terms of a few months' stay. Many again thought of some slight adjustment back to 'normal', of some quick 'cure' for the original 'offence'. Many found that the boy's real disturbance lay far deeper than they had dreamed.

'I am sure you must realize,' wrote Mrs Wilton, 'how unhappy and worrying is the slow realization that one's child has passed more or less (no doubt largely through one's own fault) out of one's control and power to help. I am afraid I don't take things on trust at all easily; partly owing to special circumstances of my own up-bringing. ... A very large number of people, including my doctor, urged me to leave Alastair at his first preparatory school. I did so against all his own entreaties for three years, a course which I am sure has contributed very largely to his present unsatisfactory condition. ... If Alastair comes to you, I will certainly endeavour not to "spoil his chances", but I don't quite know what you mean by this accusation.'

July 6, 1936.
'Dear Mrs Wilton,
One of the things I am most grateful about is that I still feel for each parent as he or she comes here, as I did when I started this work. If anyone has been brought up so that she feels insecure, then how can she be other than possessive? It is not a question of blame, and you would be well advised not to blame yourself at this juncture. It is much harder for me to take the line I took in my last letter; and yet I had no alternative, if I was to introduce limits and thereby give you some temporary rest from the wearisome inner urge to press on and on in the forlorn hope of finding a hundred per cent certain solution. Alastair's trouble is just that he must be completely certain before he moves. Do you remember the line in the Psalm—"Thy word is a lantern unto my feet"—not any more light than is necessary to make the next step.'

July 7.
'Dear Mr Lyward, (Mrs Wilton wrote)
Thank you for your kind letter. I admit a good deal of weariness, thinking by day and dreaming by night of what is really best for

Alastair. As you say, it is the vain search for the hundred per cent certainty. What I do not quite see is how your methods will give him grit and pluck and energy to fight all his tendencies to laziness and unreliability. However, we can "wait and see", and I will do my best to trust.'

Alastair and Mr Greenacre paid a visit to Finchden, but nothing was decided. Mrs Wilton and Alastair spent their holidays with cousins in Ireland, where Alastair was 'very sensibly sociable with other young people, both boys and girls, and was quite willing to make his own plans with them if ours were too energetic for him.'

He had also begun to paint 'and hopes for opportunity and encouragement in this creative effort when he comes to Tenterden.'

A change now appeared on the Wilton side of the correspondence. Mrs Wilton, tired of Alastair at home and anxious to *do* something, began to press Mr Lyward. The boy 'will come to Finchden Manor as soon as you return from your holidays, which I hope may prove restful and enjoyable. Will you be so kind as to let us know later when you are ready to receive him?' Alastair meanwhile began to stall; it would soon be his birthday, and Mr Greenacre had promised to help him with his paintings and to give him drawing lessons. Mrs Wilton wrote to Mr Lyward again: 'I sometimes feel that some step or sign from you at this juncture would be of great help. I and my daughter are the only source of pressure on Alastair to come to you.' A week later Mr Greenacre had found another pupil, and had less time for Alastair's art. The underlinings to Mr Lyward became more frequent. 'The time is very ripe for you to *move*. I think Alastair should come to you after a *quiet week-end* on *Monday next*.'

Mr Lyward was not to be hurried. He would never permit any parent to think that he had 'forced' a boy to come. Alastair dashed off several more canvases. The last letter before his enrolment at Finchden came from the boy himself, typewritten but mis-spelt, and showing more than a trace of hauteur:

'Dear Mr Lyward,

I hope that when I arrive, I shall find you all arguing, then I shall not feel so homesick. I am very anti-psychology, but of course I have very little knowledge of it. It seems that psychology is a great help for some people, but me—NO. Whether or not I wish to swallow a pack of cards is a matter not yet decided.'

At the end of October, aged fifteen, chauffeured and with several canvases and a large sketch-book, the difficult one arrived.

Alastair took against Finchden at once. Of course he wrote to his mother, and, as at his preparatory school, demanded to be removed. He gave her a feverishly exaggerated account of the place, which, as it was meant to do, thoroughly upset her. She telephoned Mr Lyward in distress, and wrote Alastair a letter of wounded but sensible reproof. 'I think you are making a desperate attempt to get me under your thumb. ... I refuse to be a source of endless sympathy to your dramatized version of yourself. You don't give me facts in your letter. Why not? If you are convinced of them, tell me what they are.'

Mr Lyward's answer filled three typewritten pages. Many of his letters to troubled parents were at least as long. The documents in Alastair's story, covering five years, run to at least two thousand pages.

'Dear Mrs Wilton,

First, I want to reassure you, if I can, that you have my sympathy. If you imagine that I am not taking into account how perplexed and pained you must be about all this, then you will be wrong. ... Alastair cannot be expected to be completely happy anywhere at the moment, or completely satisfied that any place whatever conforms to his conception of what is desirable for him. ... Long after he is quite happy, he will find it impossible to say so, because that would constitute a climb-down. Meanwhile the only line he can take is to ferret out whatever would make a good story and exaggerate it, keeping in mind the things which might worry you. ... In this way he keeps you on tenterhooks, and hopes to keep me on tenterhooks too. It is vital to his well-being that we should not be caught so easily. Remember that fear lies behind all this, and therefore every time the trick succeeds, the fear is kept working below the surface, whereas each time we can defeat the trick, we reduce the fear. The world will not stand for this sort of trickery, nor can his real self ever be satisfied that way. What we do here is to defeat the trick so gently that sometimes he never knows. We do not leave him, as the world would, but help him through these moments towards more wholeness of life.'

This letter gave Mrs Wilton 'great hope and comfort', which was undermined almost at once by another 'terrible' letter from her son. 'He does not threaten suicide or even running away. He only begs me to see him and learn what he calls the "truth" from his own lips. If I don't, he says he will turn away from me and withdraw all confidence.' She begged to see Alastair *alone*.

'Dear Mrs Wilton, (wrote Mr Lyward)

So soon as Alastair is with you or writes to you he takes on a new personality, one which needs to do two completely opposite things: (1) to win his way back to an exclusive position and capture a monopoly of your interest, affection, time; in fact, your soul; (2) to hurt you as much as possible. This he needs to do because he himself has been robbed of his manhood by the over-dominance of the feminine element at home, and by such lesser but important things as being kept ignorant of sex and therefore compelled to bluff and feign knowledge which he hadn't got. It sounds simple, stated like that, but it all goes in a vicious circle and the two opposite needs stated above keep the circular movement going ...

Can you see at all from the above that the one fatal thing at the moment would be for me to respond thoughtlessly to either your plea, or his, that you should come together at this moment? If I did consent to your meeting, the maximum need for mothering and the maximum need for hurting and dominating mother would be joined. It is our job here to stand between the two forces in conflict and bear the brunt, but I would not have *you* in your old position ever again, and you cannot call that being unkind to you...

I believe, if I wished, I could fix upon the actual time when Alastair wrote his letter to you. I was informed that when he enquired for ink he was quite cheerful.'

Alastair was quite cheerful. He had been given a private room and was allowed to furnish it himself; he asked for a fire, but this was refused. A visit to London followed, with Mr D., to buy a wireless set. 'He assumed the part of guide,' Mr D. reported, 'anxious to impress me with his knowledge of London. ... He told me he knew where Selfridge's was, namely in Regent Street, and was surprised when he failed to find it. Was assured by myself and several dealers that a wireless set which would do what he wanted had not yet been designed, and probably never would be. Showed a preference for sets of flashy appearance, with an obvious lack of internal finish. Wanted to go to an expensive place for lunch. I took him to Lyons Corner House. He was rather disdainful and said that he didn't like crowds. Suddenly said: "I suppose really it is awfully good for me to come to a place like this". We went to a film and he proposed another visit next week. I said I might not want to come to London next week, to which he replied that he thought the present visit had been most enjoyable and successful, and that he would ask Mr Lyward to let me come with him again. On Ashford Station, he tried to get chocolate out of the automatic machines without putting in a penny; and seeing some of the restaurant tea-cups on a ledge said: "Do you dare me to pinch some?" I said: "Please yourself", and he took one and wanted to bring it home with him.'

Alastair was also gambling. He invited Mr D. to pay his debtors with money from the Office. 'He produced the list showing amounts owed to him—4/6d. in respect of money-lending and 6/6d. for cigarettes. This he totalled at 10/6d. I took the list and told him the figures required digesting, as I had no authority to pay boys' debts. He said I was prejudiced. He came to me again when I was in bed and said: "Although I dislike you exceedingly, could you tell me ...?"—and asked for some technical information about his wireless set. I gave him the information, and he thanked me and went away.'

Alastair of course was not nearly as wretched as he had led his mother to suppose. He had a way of posting her emotional storms; by the time they reached her, he was sunbathing. He was cunning, sanctimonious, and often merry. In one photograph of that time he is wrestling with another boy, his face caked with mud; another photograph shows him looking like an assertive, mucky urchin. He had taken to games, which elsewhere had terrified him, and had begun to do lessons with Mr Knox.

Mr Knox was so rugged yet gracious and versatile an eccentric that he not only justifies but demands a digression.

Mr Lyward had first met him while searching for a second-in-command. On a friend's invitation, he had gone to a club near Pall Mall, and been introduced to a tall, thin, stooping gentleman with a red nose and a walrus moustache, who was wearing a high stiff collar. Mr Lyward immediately said to himself 'Impossible!', yet before the meeting was over, it had been decided that Mr Knox should come to Finchden. He remained on the staff until his death.

He gave his age as fifty-one, but was probably 60. He came of a brilliant family and had been a classical scholar at Balliol. For years he had lived in Paris, as foreign correspondent for a big newspaper. He spoke fluent French, and had the Légion d'Honneur and another French medal. He had jumped out of a window for a bet and broken both his arms below the elbow. He had written three books: one on electricity, one on engineering, one on *The Soil*, and arrived at Finchden with several dozen copies of *Newton—The Man*, foreword by Einstein, published by Mr Knox. He taught mathematics, science, French, history, English, Latin and Greek. He held formal classes, but most of his teaching was done as a running commentary on various kinds of practical work, on which he embarked as soon as he arrived.

His injury did not prevent him—sometimes alone, sometimes with the boys—building a suite of laboratories, some of which the Army left standing. He dug a well 18-feet deep at Guildables and, bending his shrivelled forearms perpendicular in front of him, carried piles of bricks and heavy blocks of cement, talking as he built and accompanying himself with quotations from Horace— whom he knew almost by heart—and with tremendous French and Elizabethan oaths. In one laboratory he made soap; the first experiments burnt the table, but later he turned out a pleasantly scented brand, some of which he sold. A skilled gardener, he planted a shrubbery of lavender and rosemary, out of which he distilled lavender water. Salesmen would be engaged in rich and stately conversation about cosmetics. Every few months packing cases arrived for Mr Knox, containing valuable equipment which he got cheap from a scientific friend. He also erected a printing press, and while at Finchden published a small anthology and a work on ratio and proportion called *The Bed of Procrustes*. During the war, unable to buy graph paper, he printed his own.

The boys called him 'The Old Boy'. They put Vim on his rice-pudding, but he did not notice. In the town he was known as the Professor. He smoked about eighty cigarettes a day, and sometimes had four going at a time. As soon as he had settled in, he discarded the formal dress in which Mr Lyward had first encountered him, and wore, while building, a white coat sprinkled with cigarette ash and trousers without turn-ups, held round his middle with a piece of string. He seldom bought clothes. When he did, he sent into the town the gardener's boy, who had come to Mr Lyward for treatment, with instructions to bring back half-a-dozen suits, from which Mr Knox chose one. He shaved off his moustache and substituted a beard, grizzled and stained with nicotine, which he either pruned like the late King George V or allowed to cascade to his breast bone. His fine hands were black with nicotine, his black nails like talons. When Sid—then a boy—asked why he did not cut them, Mr Knox picked a diminutive head of type off a glass-topped table used while printing, and enquired majestically: 'How could I do that with short nails?'

He had a wonderful twinkle in his eye, and false teeth which did not fit. When he wanted to put a cigarette to his mouth, his broken arms made necessary a superb circular movement; his teeth fell with a clack, and as he exhaled he hissed like an escaping jet. He slept little and ate little, but drank tea at all hours of the day and night, out of a mug encrusted outside with chemicals and printer's ink, and blackened inside with tea leaves like an ancient pipe. Mrs Lyward once brought him a new mug; the offer was received graciously but with pain, not successfully disguised.

He had the grandest of grand manners. When asked an unwelcome question, he pretended to be deaf. He could argue his way into or out of anything. His gestures were generous and vast. He took a liking to a dog of Mr Lyward's, gave it commands in several languages, alive and dead, and tossed it biscuits as a prize. 'Buy seven pounds of chocolate biscuits,' he ordered Sid. Sid bought them and Mr Knox fed them to the dog. 'Could I have one?' asked Sid. 'Of course,' said Mr Knox amazed: 'do *people* eat chocolate biscuits?'

Suddenly Mr Knox would give a boy a prize of one, ten or twenty cigarettes, if the boy remembered a French idiom or a scientific formula. During the war, when tobacco was hard to come by, he lost an apparently safe bet and had to give one boy a thousand cigarettes for remembering a quotation.

He had lost touch with his family, except for one sister. Once a well-dressed stranger came to Finchden. Mr Knox met him. 'May I speak to Mr Knox?' asked the stranger.

'I am he,' said Mr Knox, in his beautiful voice, rich and rare as the best claret. 'What can I do for you?'

'I'm your brother,' said the stranger.

Mr Knox seldom went away from Finchden, except to have his hair cut. When he did, standing well over six-foot, with his beard long or short, looking like a cross between Trader Horn, Father Christmas and a pillar of the Académie Francaise, members of the public thought they surely ought to know him. One Christmas Sid accompanied him. Mr Knox had taken pains with his appearance. His trousers, still tied up with string, were concealed under a long grey overcoat. His beard he wore outside. He had on a khaki shirt, a pink tie, and a pork-pie hat bought from one of the staff for sixpence. 'Who is that gentleman?' asked the railway porter.

'That's Mr Knox,' said Sid.

'Of course, of course.'

Mr Knox travelled first-class. He crouched in the window seat, brooding over the platform. It was war-time and all the carriages were full. A woman hurried along, complaining to the station master. She stopped, and pointed accusingly at Mr Knox. 'There!' she cried, 'People who haven't paid!'

'What are you doing in there?' demanded the station-master.

'I? Are you intimating that I have not paid? Mr Hopkins, (Sid), these people are incredulous. Be good enough to show them our tickets.'

A soldier laughed so much that he put his rifle through a window.

Mr Knox and Sid changed at Crewe. Mr Knox's brown shirt was hanging out. Watched by an austerity and uniformed crowd, he undid the string, tucked in the shirt and said to Sid: 'Now we'll have a spread.' War-time restrictions meant nothing to him. He took a taxi and they went to the best hotel—no food. They went to the second best—again no food. 'Never mind, young man,' said Mr Knox to the driver, 'take me anywhere we can get two dozen eggs!'

Even one egg was unprocurable. Time and change had passed him by. They stopped at some traffic lights. 'What are those?' asked Mr Knox.

He loved learning, and taught with enthusiasm and reverence. All his experiments were scrupulous and exact, all his instruments lovingly cared for. He double dug and weeded his patch of garden, laid down pipes and sprinklers, and collected cart-loads of manure.

He gave boys the feeling of history and the feeling of a language, and chuckled with delight when Sid once answered 'Mais oui' instead of only 'oui'.

A photograph shows Mr Knox at the desk of his self-built laboratory. Through the window is a glimpse of another building not yet finished. The mug of tea stands in front of him. The sun is shining on the gaunt, imperious face, the grizzled hair and beard, and he looks like Ulysses in old age. He died during the war before the return to Finchden. As he was dying, Sid would come to his room and read aloud in French Dumas' *Black Tulip* and *The Adventures of Arsène Lupin*, and Mr Knox would rouse himself from his coma to correct pronunciation. He told his sister that he had spent the best eleven years of his life at Finchden. Scruffy, civilized, lonely, brilliant, robust, he had found his haven there, and was loved, and those he taught have never forgotten him.

Mr Knox had a tolerant but not high opinion of Alastair Wilton.

'Alastair resembles every other boy who has come to Finchden Manor in that he presents problems which are entirely special to himself and demand immediate attention. In trying to give him the help he needs, the staff are very much handicapped by the difficulty he finds in believing that he stands in need of any help at all. ... He professes a high standard about sex, and is stern in castigating vice. At the same time he has gone out of his way to get other boys into debt by lending them money and cigarettes at usury, and inducing them to join him in a gambling game, which he plays for hour after hour of the day and night. He walks in to the laboratory where set teaching is in progress, and thinks nothing of disturbing it. He makes a noise at night and parades his money. ... All this does not condemn him ... but it will probably be a long time before he realizes that the very boys whom he affects to despise will be those to whose help he will owe his outlook. It is through some of those phases of life at Finchden Manor which he justifiably dislikes, that he will find it possible to set in order his own house.'

Alastair continued the furnishing of his room. 'Of course,' Mr Lyward wrote to Mrs Wilton, 'he tries to make me feel that this is all a sort of bargain he has struck with you and me. I gently waved aside the notion of bargaining—so gently, that he can still talk in that strain to other people, i.e. I have left him with the crutches he still needs.'

Alastair continued his conspiracy to divide and rule. He wangled holiday after holiday out of his mother for some time. He went home for a while, and in a chatty letter (still typewritten) to Mr Lyward said that he did not think he would come back yet. He tried to invoke his mother's support against Mr Lyward for a longer holiday; at the same time he decided while at home to like Finchden Manor and use it against her. He proceeded to 'analyse' his own family, in a way in which he was certainly not being analysed himself. Mrs Wilton took this seriously and was again upset.

February 27, 1937.
'Dear Mr Lyward,
Firstly I want to say how greatly improved we all found Alastair. He is *happier* in himself, more unselfish in small things. Will fetch and carry very kindly for me and his sister on many occasions. He admires you immensely *but* ... I would like to tell you some of his statements with which I found it impossible to agree. I imagine they are only half truths. (1) *We or he are not to blame for anything, nothing is his fault—merely his misfortune or else his mother's fault.* (2) *One need never feel any sense of shame for any failure.* (3) *It is no one's concern and matters nothing what one does with one's life or talents.* (4) *Psychology is the one and only way, an improved version of Christianity. It is impossible for anyone to achieve maturity by any other way. ...*'The letter went on for twelve pages. Mr Lyward replied in two lines: 'I do assure you that, as you said, you were merely seeing first effects or hearing half truths, and you need not take them to heart.'

In fact Alastair was gradually drawing away from his mother; she knew that the silver cord was being loosed. His letters home became less frequent. When he did write, he asked her and his sister never never to come to Finchden again, as a result, wrote Mrs Wilton 'of some rather tactless chaff on my part about the state of his room.' Mr Lyward again reassured her. In December, Alastair decided to stay at Finchden Manor for Christmas. It was the first Christmas he had ever spent away from home, and his mother was hurt and sad.

About this time, Alastair decided he would like 'to do some engineering'. Mr Knox included him in a class. Alastair's wish for learning at that moment was insincere; as with other boys, the time had not yet come. He tried an examination and failed. In his next reports he was described as 'showing a general joy in life. ... The rougher, more virile elements are beginning to demand incorporation into the whole ... and his aesthetic side is now quite pronounced.' He was 'for the most part happy and very alive, but now and again he gets a fit of depression. ... I have not actually discussed his depressions with him, but I consider them as important indications of a disturbance in the region of his instincts...'

Mrs Wilton wrote post-haste:

'Dear Mr Lyward,
In my ignorance of psychology, occasional fits of depression would not trouble me much. Are not all emotionally sensitive people prone to experience both more exquisite delight and a deeper sense of sorrow than are the thicker skinned type? I don't understand what you mean by the disturbances in the region of his instincts.'

Alastair was growing, that was about all, but Mrs Wilton suggested a visit, as she had not had a talk with Mr Lyward for some time. Alastair had already been there much longer than she had expected, and showed no wish to leave. She had done her utmost for a year and a half to continue her 'act of faith', yet despite her feeling of respect and friendliness for Mr Lyward, she could not get over her dislike of Finchden Manor and her distrust of the other boys. She was torn between her wish to keep Alastair to herself and her delight at his visible improvement.

One afternoon she arrived.

'Alastair seems very happy,' she said, seated in Mr Lyward's room, 'in spite of his companions.'

'Or perhaps because of his companions?' said Mr Lyward.

'Oh no. I refuse to believe that. How could anybody be happy with a lot of abnormal people?'

'But he is happy, isn't he?'

Mrs Wilton did not answer. Then she said: 'But I suppose you'd say no one was normal?'

She picked up a photograph of a not prepossessing-looking boy, which happened just to have arrived, and said with distaste: 'I suppose this is a finished product?'

Mr Lyward decided to bring about a crisis. As she continued to make disparaging insinuations about the other boys, he began to tap loudly on his desk, then brusquely interrupted her: 'I don't want to hear any more of this! Take Alastair away! Clear out! Take him away! And I don't expect you've ever heard that in a drawing room.'

Mrs Wilton suddenly wept. 'You know what's wrong,' she said: 'I'm jealous of you.' Troubles of her own childhood and youth came out and their release enabled her to explain why she had spoilt her son. She begged Mr Lyward to remain her friend. 'Will you keep Alastair?' she asked him.

'Of course I will.'

She went home. Next day:

'Dear Mr Lyward,

I would like to thank you very warmly for our talk yesterday. It helped very much to clear my mind of some of the difficulties you encounter in Alastair's development, and also has greatly deepened the confidence in which I leave him for a longer period in your care. I am so sorry that at times in the past I felt mistrustful and resentful towards yourself against my better judgment and reasoning. I think you do understand how difficult it's all been for me, and how my own pride has been hurt by Alastair's difficulties. How I would have rejoiced in the usual schoolboy successes in work or games! The greatest happiness that the future could hold would be the knowledge that my love was of some help to him. For it is the standing aside that is so bitter a lesson, and I've been trying during the past two years to learn its necessities.'

With his reply, Mr Lyward sent her the two long poems he had written at Glenalmond many years before.

'I send them not so much because they represent what I've been trying to say to you. But they may reveal to you a little that I am deeply moved by the facts of the spiritual life of which you are aware—not that I think you now look upon me as a destroyer of values. Your last letter makes me the more willing to let you see them. I dared not use them, or anything like them, to convince you earlier.'

And in another letter a few days later: 'I admire greatly the way you have yielded to certain facts. People like you have an innate strength which causes them to resist us forcibly—as you did at the start. The same strength enables them to share their boys' gradual release. Others, who accept us in a superficial sort of way, never say later that we have opened any windows for them.'

The rigidity of both Mrs Wilton and Alastair was now broken. The ice floes were melting, and as often happened during a movement of this kind when 'life's genial streams began to flow', there were revulsions and hesitations and blocks, which made it seem that nothing had changed, that nothing had been freed. The conflict of dawning relief and the old self-pity was harder for the elderly woman to bear than for the boy. A real person was stepping off the pedestal; sometimes she stepped back and became the marble ideal again. She wrote to Mr Lyward: 'I am developing slowly from the fundamental truths you have laid for me, and among them, as I see them, are these; that love which is jealous and possessive or looks for a return is worthless; and that the early fierce protective mother-love is, I suppose, largely an instinct for the preservation of the species, that must be outgrown.' When Alastair again decided not to come home for Christmas, she wrote: 'The last thing I could wish is that he should go against his feelings, though I do dearly wish that he had wanted to be with us, and that is what hurts.'

About this time Alastair became extremely truculent, which (Mr Lyward wrote to Alastair's doctor) 'gave us a great many chances of helping him, and me many chances of useful analysis. Alastair began to show much more hostility to his mother after he sensed that his mother was more with us, and we had to go very carefully in relationship to his hysterical tendencies. I would say that the hysteria is what prolongs matters so.'

Mrs Wilton found herself unable to pay for a holiday abroad, and Alastair resigned himself to not going. At about the same period Mr Lyward wrote 'For the first time I really felt it safe to speak to him "like a father", when to my dismay he got a letter from his sister offering him a few weeks in the South of France (for which their trustee was to pay). Rightly or wrongly, I felt I dared not say "no" at this particular juncture. It is not the first time that his sister has cut across his interests here.'

From near Antibes, Alastair wrote Mr Lyward his first really boyish and cheerful letter, chiefly on surf-riding. The priggishness was less marked and the typewriter had gone. He dreamed that he could not leave Finchden, and that a torrent was carrying him away from which he saved himself by clinging to a crumbling rock. On his return Mrs Wilton begged Mr Lyward to let her have Alastair at home for *at least* three weeks, so that she could hear all about France, and Alastair dreamed:

I went for a ride across a heath with my sister. When we got to the end of the heath, she went a different way, and I discovered I was riding two horses.

He went to his mother's, and was kind and considerate to her, but spoilt the holiday for her by being rude to his sister. 'He was very coarse and crude at her expense,' wrote Mrs Wilton. 'She tells me he drank too much while in France, and on one occasion was really offensively silly at *table d'hôte* in consequence. On one occasion here a very dear, older lady, for whom Alastair has a genuine liking and who is anything but narrow-minded, refused to dine with him, as a protest against his conduct. He does seem to take the line "Why should I bother about people I'm not likely to see much of?", though they are most kindly disposed towards him. ...'

'Dear Mrs Wilton, (wrote Mr Lyward)
...I should have expected a certain amount of what you wrote. Alastair's feeling of being inferior to his sister abroad and the feeling of being the little boy at home were the two most likely to be kept at bay by an "over-statement" in terms of crudity. ... It is very important that Alastair's extremely strong instincts should never again be merely bottled up to work their way along unsuspected channels. His fear of their strength has been for years the greatest of all his fears, and now that the lesser forms have been dealt with, he must inevitably come up against the real fear— "Whatever will happen if I let myself go?" ... What you see is the result of this conflict which is severely touched up by the presence of his sister, and of older people associated with the old days, when he felt small and could do nothing but boil up inside.'

Alastair dreamed of his dead father, of girls at the sea-side, riding horses, of rivers, and of his dislike of his sister. He dreamed of a prison guarded by nuns. Hitler occupied Prague. 'Alastair's fear of war (wrote Mr Lyward) was probably as great as that of any of the boys here.' He began to dream of being chased by Germans, of aeroplanes crashing in flames, and then of being chased by wolves.

He had more dreams of quarrels with his sister and an encouraging report.

'Alastair continues to show signs of working his way (irritably at times) through his humiliations in connection with his sister. This must be very painful, and for my part I am amazed by the underlying strength which enables him to go on with his contemporaries while these old feelings are being digested and dealt with inside. ... He is going through a terrifically he-man phase, spending most of his time in physical activity of one sort or another.'

Suddenly, Alastair wrote a letter, hitting out at his sister. 'From what I've seen of you,' he wrote, 'you might think you were the only person in the world who had suffered worries and unhappiness. In fact you're just the same as everyone else, and on the whole other people make less noise about it.'

Alastair told Mr Lyward that he had sent this letter. Mr Lyward reassured Mrs Wilton, but asked that the sister should not visit Finchden. 'She could so easily hold up Alastair's progress by interrupting the "working through" process.'

Dear Mr Lyward, (Mrs Wilton replied),
... that his complexity over his sister should be so deep-seated surprises us all, because it is absurd to consider her as out of the ordinary. She has failings, of course, and no doubt one failing is to be somewhat dominating. Is it likely that Alastair has inherited a jealous disposition from me? ... *We know that he has received deep and permanent help* from his stay with you, *but* I am puzzled that you should seriously consider a meeting with his sister could possibly endanger the work you are doing on his behalf.'

'Dear Mrs Wilton,' (replied Mr Lyward),
'... I do not just want you to agree with me blindly. What I hope always is that wherever your resistance is based purely upon instinct, vision (not pressure) will gradually reduce the resistance. I hope the same for myself. What I must do is to protect myself and the place, and individual boys, from anybody becoming too angry or

too weary to go on with a long drawn out case.... I wish you would feel more generous toward yourself regarding the jealousy. It will go quicker if you recognize it as the natural feeling of a child (not yet cleared) rather than think of it a something you *ought* not to feel. If you incorporate it, it becomes part of your strength; but if you do not, it remains something which from neglect goes on sapping from within.'

Four days later Mr Lyward held one of his 'sessions'. It was directed chiefly at another boy, but in the middle he turned on Alastair and told him to stop grinning. Next evening Alastair dreamed:

> I had gone mad and was rushing wildly about at home. I saw my mother and slapped her face. She didn't seem to mind, and then she and Mr Lyward told me to try and be quiet and put me to bed in the nursery.

It was now May, 1939. War was approaching, and Mrs Wilton wanted Alastair home. Her suggestions that he should leave Finchden became more insistent. But he did not want to go home and she was bitterly disappointed. Mr Lyward reassured her.

'Dear Mrs Wilton,

... I do not know if you had, as a girl, any experience of how difficult holidays with the family can be to adolescents. I have lost count of the number of adolescents who have had that experience and talked to me about it. In other words, Alastair is not being so very unique about this particular matter, only more frank, and a little more intense, owing to his fear of the confusion in his mind which would come about if he tried to hurry forward what I must call his reconciliation with those who (unwittingly or otherwise) have overpowered and humiliated him in the past. This reconciliation is on the way, but in so far as reconciliation constitutes a rebirth, it cannot be hurried ...

'... And may I be allowed to help you by warning you against feeling bitter at Alastair's attitude? There is no occasion for that. When we feel bitter about such attitudes of adolescents, as are universal, we are merely in the grip of unacknowledged self-pity which is looking for justification. It is hard sometimes to rejoice at the sight of the next generation really growing up, but at least we must not accuse them of a heartlessness which is not theirs.'

Mr Lyward did not think Alastair ready to leave Finchden. After explaining that the confusion in the boy's mind was not yet clear, he added an important paragraph: 'I hold that he would not have any serious difficulty in reaching an average public school academic standard in about a third of the usual time. Many boys by bringing their emotional troubles to their school work, create the difficulties which school-masters wrongly think of as residing (for those boys) in the subjects they study.'

These words summarize one of the principal aims and achievements of Mr Lyward's work. Many boys, before this letter and since, once cleared of their emotional trouble, settled down happily to work and passed examinations in which they had previously failed.

Another paragraph from a contemporary letter to the boy's trustee may here be quoted:

'About two years ago,' Mr Lyward wrote, 'two parents of prospective members of this community visited us in the same month or so. The first was a mother who had been sent by her husband to ask me to reduce my fees. In the course of conversation she suddenly said: "It has been a difficult year, you see, we have had to sell some of our hunters." The other was the wife of a merchant service captain who had just agreed to the reduction of his salary from £800 to £400 in order to keep his job. She said: "I will get rid of the house and live in rooms so that the boy can come to you."

It has been difficult since then to know what to reply to parents who may or may not be picking us out as the first or one of the first "luxuries" about which to economize. I feel also rather like the surgeon who met criticism of his account by altering it to: "For performing operation £25, for knowing how to perform operation £200".'

August came. A crisis had arrived in Alastair's development. He felt ready to go home, but for the moment Mr Lyward refused permission.

'I sympathize with you utterly,' he wrote to Mrs Wilton, 'in your desire to have Alastair home. But I feel that I must now speak in no uncertain way. He has once again reached the point where I can treat him firmly and say "You have just got to accept authority without question and without modifying everything to suit yourself." If this phase is now broken into, I shall probably have to do it over again. ... You have shown understanding, but I cannot refrain from telling you that there is always just that extra something that has to be surrendered. The something about which one says "Not that, please!!" ...'

At the same time, while on holiday, Mr Lyward sent Alastair a note, saying: '...I am so anxious that you should take advantage of this chance I have given you of accepting the decision of "somebody in authority" without question. In ordinary language, even if you don't like something, can you lump it cheerfully? This means a great deal to you. Please have a go at seeing what it's all about.'

War was declared, and at the beginning of October Alastair went home for three weeks. 'I want to tell you,' wrote Mrs Wilton, 'how lovely these weeks have been. He was so bright and considerate, and it did one good just to feel that he was around ...' *But*, 'there is still a little pang of jealousy, and I somehow feel I am just his little mother, whom he loves in a rather sweet protective way. I suppose I have lost for ever the power to be a friend on an equal footing ...'

'Dear Mrs Wilton,' (Mr Lyward answered),

'... I am sure you can hope to be treated as an "equal friend", if you will deal with the self-pity and gradually give up wanting to be "of influence". True influence can only come as a result of relationship, and only where the relationship is not desired *in order to exert influence* ... So long as one needs people as badly as you once needed Alastair, one is bound to try and hold them by being useful to them ...'

Alastair continued to dream about girls, of being carried out to sea, about his mother and his sister. In one dream he slapped his sister's face and told her exactly what he thought of her. He dreamed that an old boy returned to Finchden and said that Alastair had become more masculine, 'and I burst into tears ...' He dreamed that he had grown a beard.

In June, 1940 he went home again. His mother and sister, expecting him to return to Finchden at the end of the holiday, went away for a visit, leaving him alone. He rang up Finchden. Mr Lyward was away. Alastair wanted to know whether it would be all right for him to take a job as mechanic. 'I suggested,' noted the assistant who took the call, 'that he should write to Mr Lyward, and I said that there would be no harm in making some enquiries. I also advised him not to commit himself to anything until he had either heard from Mr Lyward or had had a talk with him.'

Thus began the last stage of Alastair's accoutrement for life, and perhaps the most interesting, since it was during this last stage, as with many other boys, that Mr Lyward had his hardest struggle with the parent concerning the real nature of his work. His own attitude was all the more difficult to vindicate, because the boy of his own accord now wished to leave. The parents' opposition to Finchden had evaporated. They acknowledged what Mr Lyward had done, and were grateful. It therefore seemed obvious that the time had come for Mr Lyward, his part played, to withdraw and leave the boy to choose his own path in the world. Against these solid arguments Mr Lyward had nothing but his own vision and diagnosis of the boy. As at the beginning, so at the end, he asked another 'act of faith'.

Mrs Wilton was naturally delighted when she heard of Alastair's project to go to work.

'Dear Mr Lyward,

You must know how I have been rejoicing in my heart. I am glad that Alastair feels himself ready to be independent ...'

Mr Lyward was still on holiday, and had not yet seen Alastair.

'Thank you for your letter,' (he replied). 'I did not trouble you about a meeting, because I can only judge the situation by seeing Alastair. He was not ready to go to work on a sound basis when I last saw him. And as the difference between being ready and apparently nearly ready is not a little, but a lot, in its effect and ramifications on his future life, I cannot offhand advise his going with something vital to go through after he leaves. He may, or may not, finish the last little bit after he leaves, whereas I *know* that when they have completely surrendered here they have saved themselves for *certain* (at the best) years of loneliness and bewilderment, and (at the worst) a further breakdown.

I am sorry. But I must keep on sticking by what I *know*. Alastair knows in his heart that I am right. And he knows that he will not be called upon to stay a day longer than is needed to crown our patient work and his own patience over these difficult years.

All the boys are back now, and Alastair owes it to himself to come back and see me, which shows how near he is to being free, even if I have to say that he has not quite made the final surrender and become as a little child.

With kindest regards to you, of whom I always think as yourself having made a very wonderful surrender where Alastair is concerned—one amply repaid I am sure, but made without certainty that it would be ...'

A week later Mr Lyward met Alastair in London, and wrote his account of the interview briefly in a report. 'I would have agreed to his going to work but for the quite obvious proofs he gave that he was not quite ready. It was three minutes after his statement "I intend to go whatever you say" that he suddenly said "I am coming back with you". It is the old business of accepting and therefore developing within himself "the father principle" without which he seeks life always as an "escape back to mothering".

Mr Lyward described the meeting at greater length in a letter to a doctor. Since it is of the highest importance in understanding Finchden Manor, and perhaps of interest to all who care to examine whether they have confronted life with fear or freedom, I give the relevant passages in full.

'...I went to London to see Alastair after he had telephoned that he wasn't returning. I would willingly have agreed to his trying himself out but the fact that he very soon revealed over lunch that he was not so much going out to a new adventure, as running from the final acceptance of that one element in life here which will clear him for life of the futility of rebellion.

It is extraordinary, even to us here, how he clings to the "right" to run his own life and be supported whenever things go wrong. His most revealing statement to me that day in London was: "Well, I thought if I went off—(i.e. left Finchden while nominally on a holiday)—and things didn't go right, you would out of your infinite kindness have me back." I do hope you will see what I saw in that. He is not quite free of what I called to him the "mother-child principle", which is equivalent to "whatever I do Mummy will be there", and is not yet strengthened by the "father-child principle" rooted in him. This latter is equivalent to "I am prepared to go and take the risks".

For quite a long time he hasn't been far off the change from the former to the latter. But the final inner change is evidently very hard for him to achieve. The difference, however, between having achieved it before leaving and leaving with the statement "Aren't I clever—so long as I'm secretly held up from behind", is enormous.

...I had already said to him over lunch in London, "Well, Alastair, I don't advise you to go on a runaway from Finchden basis, but I shan't stop you." So far as I knew, he was going, when he suddenly came to himself and said—"I will come back with you".'

The process of 'clearing' reached a climax four months later.

Finchden had moved into Shropshire. Alastair had been with Mr Lyward over four years. Mrs Wilton, who had not heard from

Mr Lyward since the meeting in London, wrote on Alastair's nineteenth birthday, 'You have effected such great and good changes in Alastair, that one does hope, despite possible weaknesses, which he must recognize and learn to guard against, and which even your teaching cannot wholly eradicate, that he is by now able and fitted to do something on his own. I have no doubt if it were not for this ghastly war, you would have advised Alastair to leave before.' She added that she had saved some petrol, and suggested coming to Shropshire for the week-end. Mr Lyward and Alastair both answered that she would be welcome.

She arrived, looking forward to the long country drive, and to seeing him, and bringing his sister with her.

The pleasant week-end became a crisis. Alastair had two rows, first with Mr Lyward in the streets of Ludlow, the second with his mother in a hotel, where he accused her of ruining his life, and behaved worse than ever before. She drove straight home and after resting for some days wrote to Mr Lyward. At the beginning of her letter she put two quotations: '*Holiness is an infinite compassion for others*', '*Happiness is a great love and much service*'.

'These are glorious truths,' she wrote, 'and I believed that your psychology was bringing Alastair towards them. I felt a great trust and a great hope. I am very bitterly sorry that that sad visit has destroyed my trust. I cannot see that your explanation, that he was suffering from the painful shock of discovering his utter lack of independence, could account for the return of symptoms of which there has been no sign for so long. I find it difficult to reconcile your statement that, after the scene you had described you had with Alastair in Ludlow, better relations than ever had been established between you. Neither Alastair nor I have written to each other. I don't suppose he has been hoping I would, as much as I had been hoping he would.'

Mr Lyward answered:

'... Before Alastair can be co-operative, he has got to stake out a claim for himself as a separate person, entitled to respect such as he has never had at home. The boldest and healthiest move he has ever made in this direction, to my knowledge, was the one which hurt you here recently. It was unpleasant because it was taking place years after it should have done, but couldn't. Through your pain and tears you might well have welcomed it as a sign of developing strength, without which he can never love you except in the self-seeking way a child does.

... Can you imagine anything more devastating than to be dominated and inwardly emasculated by two women and subsequently challenged by them to manifest the strength and *therefore* the generosity and chivalry of a contented male?

The real irony is that you tend to hold me responsible for the time it all takes, even after you have admitted that none of you was able to be co-operative for so long a period after Alastair came to us.

I know you have looked to yourself and the part you have played in the past. You will remember, as I vividly remember, about the time long ago now, when I told you to take Alastair away. Must I say that again now? And if I do will you say that it is a threat? Or will you realize that there must be a limit to the number of times I tell you what is in my power to do and what is not?

Eleven years of this work have provided me with enough evidence: (1) that I know what I am doing, (2) that I do it as fast as I can, (3) that there is no way of explaining to parents, who are trying to avoid the suffering of realizing the part they have played in the past, and the suffering connected with revising their values...'

Mrs Wilton did not write to Mr Lyward again for over two months, during which time she had several cheerful letters from Alastair. When she did write to Mr Lyward, it was to raise one final doubt—a doubt naturally in the minds of many parents in regard to any person whose position or character had given him influence over their sons.

'There are one or two aspects which disturb me, and the first is Alastair's intense dependence on yourself. It has taken me a long time to realize how dependent he was at one time, on me; and now how really dependent he is on you. Unless your teaching is going to develop Alastair himself and what there is of real individuality in him, you will surely have failed. His humour seems to me his truest self, and that he has always had. But his opinions, his very phraseology are echoes of yourself. I don't say it is not an interesting and agreeable self, but one feels too strongly that he feels so safe in being your reflection, that in giving in to your wishes and plans for him he is seeking refuge and shelter from an unpleasant world. That is surely not what you wish for him ultimately. Most people urge that the longer he stays with you, the more dependent he will become. If it were true, it would be very wrong for him to stay longer. Most of my friends beg me to urge Alastair to leave; but as they have not the advantage of knowing yourself, nor did they know, except in very few cases, what Alastair was like, their opinions cannot be wholly convincing. Two people only, whom I respect highly, have advised me still not to cut short the progress which seems to have set in again since Christmas ...'

Mr Lyward replied:

'... First and foremost dependence is—just dependence, neither good nor bad. What matters is not that a person "depends", but upon whom he depends and what is likely to come about eventually as a result. And again, will you forgive me if I say that you might by now have reached the view, that of all the people Alastair might depend on, I was (in virtue of my work and experience) the safest one—the one most certain to know a good deal (may I say, an exceptional amount) about "dependence" and its dangers. For this is what I claim to know,—this, and the futility of hoping that anybody like Alastair could ever become self-confident, without having first placed his full confidence in somebody of his own sex, who was above all (as a father should be) interested in using his dependence at a safe rate to free him of it.

Dependence is neither a good nor a bad thing. It is just inevitable. The special difficulty where Alastair is concerned, is that Alastair took so long to risk transferring his dependence from a woman to a man. I doubt whether it could have happened until he had broken away from you, as he did roughly and painfully last November.

I think it is now safe to say that he has at last complete confidence in me—not as a God (this was how as a child he trusted you), but as a person. The echoing about which you write is, however, a not too pleasant reminder that you have remained a God to him for too long (liable, therefore, to stand between him and God), and that he still finds it very hard to accept anything less. As he becomes more accustomed to sharing the responsibility for his life with me—this is how to use dependence to free him—he will not need to echo me. If he is echoing me now, it is because he needs to do so ...'

About two months later,

'Dear Mrs Wilton,' (Mr Lyward wrote),
'Alastair came to me about ten days ago with the statement that he wished to try himself out as a mechanic. I agreed to this ...'

And so Alastair Wilton left Finchden.

'I do most deeply thank you,' Mrs Wilton wrote in her last letter but one to Mr Lyward, 'for all your trouble and toil to help Alastair. I hope that in his healed adjustment of himself he will show his gratitude to you throughout his life. I still hope and look for the fulfilment of your early promise when you told me that although he would pass through a difficult phase with myself of apparent lack of affection, in the end the harmony of real love would be fully restored.'

The rest of the story is briefly told. For several months Alastair worked in a small factory not many miles from Mr Lyward. It worried him that he should have been exempted from military service. He thought of having himself 're-boarded' but the original exemption was confirmed. It was some while before he could bear to spend much time with his mother; his resentment against her was still strong. Yet he moved North, though not right into

Scotland. After some time he had saved enough to rent a garage. He married happily and had a child. His mother, far from being jealous, was delighted with his wife and the 'harmony of real love' for which she had hoped began to be restored.

Alastair worked hard. He had very little money, but made enough to buy his garage. In every sense he could now stand on his own feet. Such troubles as came his way he could now cope with by himself. He wrote to Mr Lyward every few months, and later paid Finchden a visit now and then. Sometimes he asked for advice, but the 'echo' had disappeared and he spoke in his own voice. He was elected to local councils and held a number of responsible positions. Amusing traces of hauteur remained, but he could laugh at himself and let others laugh at him. He had gained loyalty and depth, and developed the 'wide culture', of which Mrs Wilton had once spoken as coming from Mr Lyward and Mr Knox, although he no longer painted. (The canvases with which he had arrived at Finchden were never mentioned again and are still there.) Above all, self-pity had vanished.

Except for one more letter, Mrs Wilton's correspondence with Mr Lyward ceased. In 1951 Finchden Manor celebrated its twenty-first anniversary in London. The Fortune Theatre was taken over and the boys acted a play which Fitzy had produced. The audience consisted almost entirely of parents, doctors, social workers, teachers, probation officers, old boys, who had come to pay their tribute to Mr Lyward. Ten representatives of a County Council arrived to see one of their most difficult boys act, and four girls hired a taxi from Tenterden. Mr Lyward spoke from the stage after the play, Mrs Lyward spoke, the staff took their curtains, and one of the theatre attendants, who had never heard of Finchden before, burst into tears. Among the audience was Mrs Wilton.

That was the last time Mr Lyward saw her. In the same year she died. From things she said during her last illness Alastair believed that her friendship with Mr Lyward had given her a strength which enabled her to face death in peace. He afterwards found among her papers, and returned to Finchden, the two verse plays which

Mr Lyward had sent her after her visit fifteen years before. She had meant to post them back, but had kept them. A letter—one small sheet—written in 1946 had been attached to thank him for the plays '... you lent me, to help me in the unhappy days, which thanks to your goodness are over and passed. Alastair is a great joy to me now. Both my children are married, and when I am sometimes rather lonely and self-pitying, I summon to my help the help you opened my eyes to see. I am very well and happy. All my best wishes to you and yours, and your wonderful work ...'

CHAPTER TEN

FINCHDEN Manor had many stories with happy endings like the story of Alastair Wilton and his mother. I wish I had space for more. Perhaps one day Mr Lyward will tell them, and annotate and explain them, and so begin to tell his own story in his own words.

I wondered sometimes why I did not abandon my own book and leave the field to him. I wonder, since my heart had always seemed to be in imaginative work, how I had come to spend so many months on a documentary account of something in which, when I first made contact with it at Finchden, I was no more interested than are the majority of people. I could have selected such material as stimulated me at Finchden and woven it at leisure, regardless of fact, into a novel. I could very likely have unearthed many superficially more exciting stories from Borstals or approved schools, and written them in half the time.

I remained at Finchden, and spent so long on this book, because, from all I read and heard, the place seemed to be unlike any other in this or any country, and had a great deal, if only I could express it, to communicate. Possessing so little experience of education and psychiatry, I had no right to use the word 'unique', to which anyhow I feel an invincible aversion. It was used however by doctors and school-masters familiar not only with Finchden Manor, but with other people and places attempting the same kind of work. Why did they use this word?

We have seen that Mr Lyward was both teacher and healer, and made no divorce between preparation for subjects and preparation for life. The difficulties so many boys had elsewhere encountered in mastering subjects were not accepted as residing in the subjects, but were traced back to emotional tangles and obstacles in the boys. These tangles were gradually loosened, thanks to the creative respite afforded them at Finchden; thanks to a 'gift', which may have been personal to Mr Lyward, of rendering and keeping them disarmed; and thanks to a long process akin to weaning. The 'structure' within which they grew up was the structure within which a child grows up; in other words, meal-times and bed-time.

Other teachers have made the attempt to trace the 'backwardness', or 'laziness', or 'indifference' of boys (and girls) in their care back to a misunderstanding of needs in early childhood and a consequent arresting or narrowing of development. How many have turned this attempt into a thorough and continuous method, carried out, as it was at Finchden, over many years? How many who have not made such an attempt might be rewarded by considering it? How many teachers ever think of themselves as healers too? And might not those who appoint and employ teachers consider the need for such a dual role and for an environment which would make possible its exercise?

I know of course that more and more schools and educational authorities in recent years have been enabled or have wished to enrol psychiatrists, and that the report on maladjusted children recommends a great extension of this service. But Finchden Manor was not a school with psychiatry added. Once there, the boys were not analysed in the sense in which the word is generally used, although analysis in its original sense of 'loosening' did occur. 'The analysis,' Dr Selwyn had said, 'is lived, not done'. Fears, anxieties, and the treatment of fears and anxieties, were all absorbed and on the whole lost within a recaptured joy of living, and after a time boys fitted to pass examinations passed them. Part of the poetry was this recovery of a natural process, and of spontaneity, as if spring were to return to a year that seemed doomed to go without spring.

Did any other place permit so real, so fundamental, a re-living of a lost period as became possible there, or bring about, as a result, so entire and lasting a liberation?

From what doctors familiar with emotional disturbance had told me, I understood that, although most 'go back to the beginning', and some in such a way that the experience becomes a living experience for the patient, rather than a series of interviews in a consulting room, a whole community living such an experience almost without knowing it was extremely rare. But Finchden was not merely 'group therapy'. It was not 'community life' preached as an ideal. It combined the natural process of weaning all the time with indirect teaching and, at certain stages, for certain boys, with direct tuition in ordinary academic subjects. It was all the more astonishing that this re-birth and double development should have been attempted on such a scale, and should so frequently succeed, with unusually difficult boys of an average age of seventeen or more.

Finally, Finchden Manor had been in existence for quarter of a century, during which time some of the ideas it had helped to pioneer have come to be accepted and fairly widely practised. Others have been scarcely investigated. And has any other place combined so much that seems simple, and is alive and original, so successfully?

This conjunction of rarely found characteristics makes Finchden Manor a very remarkable place indeed; possibly this is what the doctors meant who told me that it was unique. Like many-sided people, it was liable to be misunderstood by visitors who specialized in only one of its sides, looked only for that one side, and expected that to be orthodox. Some educationalists, looking only for a school and for academic degrees in the staff, missed the therapeutic approach and did not even enquire into the staff's special and thorough training in psychotherapy. Some psychiatrists, looking only for the accustomed technique of the consulting-room, missed the healing that was achieved as a part of happy living, and did not even enquire into Mr Lyward's teaching methods.

Yet it is certain that teachers in ordinary schools, and people who have never been near a psychiatrist, would find something to provoke, stimulate and help them in the story of Finchden Manor and in its present life. It would not be the first time that a treatment devised to heal those who are sick brought help to those who had thought themselves whole. We know besides that the entire world is in some way sick; otherwise we should be less fearful of tyranny and war. Their seeds are sown not only in poverty and unhealthy living-conditions, but in the misunderstanding and mistaken treatment of little children, which will not necessarily be eradicated with the eradication of poverty and poor housing. After a child has reached adolescence, the ill done earlier (however unwittingly) has gone too deep to be removed except by special and prolonged attention; but not many places can offer the kind of respite, the disarming, the patient gradual weaning, which the boys received at Finchden.

Finchden provided cure. The structure of society, the pressure to get on, in all countries, is such that very soon, even in a child's life, there is no time for fundamental cure. The natural answer is prevention, before the sickness has taken hold; and Mr Lyward often said that it was at primary schools that some adaptation of his own work might become both essential and possible. But home was where the trouble began; and the people who could prevent it from developing at all were, of course, the parents.

When talking or writing to parents Mr Lyward often spoke of himself as 'mediating'. When a local educational authority paid the boys' fees, the triangle—boy, parent, Mr Lyward—became a quadrilateral. His work thus involved him permanently and intimately in two dramas. One developed out of the boy's relationship with father and mother, the other out of the relationship of the boy, as an individual with individual needs, to the needs and requirements of the State. This second drama also involved the autonomy of Mr Lyward's own work, the conditions under which it could or could not continue, and his own personality as a man of original vision not always amenable to rules. He and the bureaucracy (the word is meant in no derogatory sense) thus presented one another with the same problems, the same challenges, with which authority on the one hand and on the other artists—or it may be visionaries or inventors—have presented one another for centuries.

Most educational authorities did themselves great credit in

leaving Mr Lyward to himself; their attitude of understanding and restraint leads one to distrust conventional caricatures of the official mind. Now and then there was an exception. A young junior Inspector once called, who did not even take the trouble to enquire into Finchden's past record. His first question to Mr Lyward was: 'What is your name?' He spoke to none of the boys, nor did his questions to Mr Lyward ever get beyond the stereotyped formalities. Next morning after breakfast he telephoned that he had forgotten one thing: 'Have you a degree?'

So impertinent and trite an approach brings a whole host of men, who would not dream of behaving in this fashion, into undeserved discredit. It may well have been after such a visit that Mr Lyward said, speaking in 1948, at the Conference of the National Association for Mental Health: 'The problem of mental health is now ceasing to a certain extent to be one of health, and becoming one of education. But there is not much point in regarding it as an educational issue, if inspectors dealing with difficult children are going to look at the wrong things, instead of trying to find out, and knowing how to find out, whether, at the places they inspect, there is real love operating in a disinterested way.'

Against the formal attitude of a few uncomprehending and insensitive authorities may be set the opposite response of a Council who had written asking whether a certain boy, a few years after the war, might not be ready to be trained for a career and leave. Mr Lyward wrote back four pages for which 'report' is far too cold a word; they were a living story of the boy's changes and resistances and quiet growth. ... 'Since the boy turned his back on academic achievement, which is what happened, he presented a picture of someone groping in new territory, but not, I would say, completely lost or frightened. Certainly he had to be watched for depression or apathy or both, which he might as it were build into his play-acting. This last was a marked feature of his life when he came. After disappearing to some extent, it reappeared in a very marked manner indeed last summer ...

I decided not to interfere, apart from reintroducing him to an earlier part of his life by...' (some details follow). '... These touches the other boys took up, and by about the end of August his posturing was coming to an end, and since then he has returned to the circulation within the community which characterized his early days here, but at a deeper level. He is more relaxed and his humour is not tinged with bitterness. ... But he is still resistant, rather like a cat, who will do many things until it is asked to do them, when it asserts its independence by merely moving off. As long as this need exists, any attempt to involve him in the future seems to be premature, and therefore his general education here is still oblique rather than direct ...

I could never see anything coming of an attempt to patch up. I think risks had to be taken in helping him. But I also think that if he had been going to deteriorate he would be showing signs of doing so now, whereas I felt the other day that I had never seen him so quietly alive. ... It is not possible to write a report on him which doesn't relate to love and faith rather than plans...'

To this letter, which if given in full would illumine this infinitely gentle, infinitely patient, and to a few authorities and parents infinitely exasperating method, the Council in question wrote a warm reply, fully in agreement with Mr Lyward's wish that the boy should not be hurried. Hurry had so often been disastrous, but it was difficult for parents, as for authorities, and especially near the end of a boy's time, not to wish for hurry. 'How tired of it they must get,' Mr Lyward once said, thinking of parents, while we were going through Alastair Wilton's story. 'How long it takes ... on and on ... and on ...'

Many officials would have been glad to spend a few days at Finchden; so would many overburdened psychiatrists, and many probation officers, whose work (underpaid) each day ended as late as did that of Mr Lyward and his staff, and was often conducted in far less agreeable surroundings. One cannot help regretting a system which allowed so little time for staying at such a place to the officials who sent boys there. Now and then one or two might manage to come for a few hours. But on the whole the relationship between Finchden Manor and educational authorities, whether in County Councils or Whitehall, reminded me of the relationship between soldiers at the front and soldiers on the staff, or between diplomats in Embassies or foreign correspondents and their headquarters in London. People with different functions in the same field—and why should education be excepted?—benefit from changing places occasionally; their mutual attitudes are thereby saved from resembling two friendly but separated circles, closed except for a telephone wire.

In what direction, under what kind of auspices, Mr Lyward's work could, might, or ought to be extended, is not for me to discuss. I had been told of people who 'had the vocation, but lacked the training'. Beyond a doubt, as David had written in his notes, they must be 'the sort of people able to receive from the transmitter', if not the sort of people able immediately to transmit. A woman who had spent many years in child guidance thought that people possessing the sense of vocation who proposed working in the field of 'maladjustment' should spend several weeks at least at Finchden. Finchden would thus become a kind of training centre. It also struck me that any teacher in this field needed to combine, as Mr Lyward did combine, both academic teaching and psychiatric skill, and that those who possessed only one should be given opportunities to acquire the other; also, that some experience of life outside, the more diverse the better, was an advantage. One hopes that what has been achieved at Finchden, although—like most pioneering—risking the intrusions of those who try to over-systematize, will also inspire other people, who may alter, add to, and subtract from it in certain particulars, according to the inspiration of each one.

We have now seen something of the manner in which boys arrived at Finchden, and a little of what happened while they were there. At what point did they go? Alastair Wilton wanted to leave nine months before he finally left. His mother thought it high time even earlier. Only Mr Lyward knew that they were both watching a false dawn, and told them so. The stories of many boys show a similar conflict towards the end. Alastair Wilton's own realization that he was not yet ready made him decide to wait. Other boys could not wait. While I was at Finchden, several were approaching or passing through this final stage; one or two left before it was fulfilled, one or two before they were anywhere near it. 'There are those,' Mr Lyward wrote, 'whose departure is arranged by us; those taken away before we actually give the word; and those taken away against our advice.' At most schools boys pass a certain age and leave; at some they pass examinations and leave; at Sandhurst they pass out. What, at Finchden Manor, was the test of readiness? Not age, and not a written examination; and yet the boys did not leave haphazard. They themselves talked of 'making the grade', or of 'going with Mr Lyward's blessing', or, jokingly, of 'being cured'.

'Cure' of the particular trouble or 'offence' for which a boy had been sent to Finchden Manor was usually the least to be achieved. Some parents asked no more; to them Finchden Manor was only a kind of mental spa, a Harrogate of the emotions, at which their child was to do a quick course and depart. 'His habits must be cured at all costs,' wrote one father, 'I cannot let him stay with you more than a few months.' A mother decided that her son had taken the waters sufficiently and withdrew him. 'Last night I called all the family into the library,' she informed Mr Lyward, 'and told them that if any ordering about's to be done, it'll be done by me.' As she drove her son away she said, 'The first thing you'll do is have your hair cut'; in other words, he was going back to the circumstances which had caused him to be sent.

This assertion by parents that their sons were 'better' (often made before the boy had even arrived at Finchden) usually meant that the symptom of maladjustment—it might be pilfering, eczema, asthma, violence, etc.,—seemed to have disappeared. Content with an outward superficial adjustment, such fathers and mothers left the deeper causes scarcely touched, and the boy's liberation scarcely begun. They viewed Mr Lyward partly as a crammer of the brain, partly as a masseur of the emotions, who would first make sure the boy never got into trouble again and then push him through examinations, so that he could 'catch up' the time he had missed at an ordinary school.

It was not in those terms of 'cure and cram' that Mr Lyward thought of his work. The readiness to leave of Alastair Wilton did not only mean that he had stopped swallowing cards, or of a 'thief', that he had stopped stealing. The readiness to leave of someone 'unable to face schoolwork' or 'incapable of holding down a job' probably meant that he could now face schoolwork or take a job. But 'I'm not going through all this merely to pass exams,' Henry Carpenter told the Children's Officer who had sent him to Finchden Manor (a man who himself understood that examinations were not the only aim).

Mr Lyward wrote of a boy called Fred Sutton, who came to Finchden with a long list of minor crimes, and later did well, 'I do think that he is convinced at last that he counts. But he still will not be denied his own way in certain respects. Is he a weak character, who should not be expected to surrender to the total situation here? We find this difficult to answer. We are still inclined to hope that our life here will help the softened Fred Sutton, once so bitter and tight-lipped, to reach a realization of values clear enough to keep him out of all serious trouble, and away from the re-hardening effects of possible punishment.'

This report expresses a limited hope: that the boy will be able to 'keep out of serious trouble'; and a positive achievement: 'he is convinced at last that he counts'. The report also expresses what has not yet been achieved: 'he still will not be denied his own way in certain respects ... is he a weak character, who should not be expected to surrender to the total situation here?' The words imply a further stage. That particular boy might dubiously attain it. It had certainly been attained by others. Any boy who had passed through it was presumably considered 'ready to leave'.

What do those quoted phrases mean? Most of us are familiar

with 'certain respects' in which we will not be denied our own way, believing ourselves to be right and others wrong. One is also led to enquire why a boy should be expected to 'surrender to the total situation' at Finchden Manor, more than to 'the total situation' anywhere else. At first glance, it may seem extraordinarily presumptuous in one mortal man to declare, once boys have 'accepted a community' which happens to have grown up around him, that they are then ready to go out into the world.

Mr Lyward made no claim for his community other than that it was one. He did not assert that it was better or worse or more or less Christian than other communities. Surrender and acceptance could not imply surrender to any school or theory of his own, since he had founded no school and formulated no theory. What the words meant he put quite simply in a letter he once wrote, while on holiday, to a boy at Finchden:

> 'I hope you will welcome a letter from me even if it is only a small one. At the time I went away you were beginning to see things clearer. This is to say that I hope you are able to use that time as a kind of base from which to move on.
>
> There is no need for me to tell you that you have gifts. But it is important for you to discover that your real need at the moment is to measure yourself, as it were, with your contemporaries of all kinds (not primarily the clever ones by any means). This is the way to develop what I suppose must be called "guts". You see, you use up what guts you've got in rebelling or grumbling or "digging your toes in". Once you've started using them to mix and accept other people, (independent of their brains or attainments), *just because they're there*, all kinds of things would happen.
>
> I had the feeling that you were on the verge of seeing this, and that is why I have written. I've tried not to put it scientifically. But I know you will be on better terms with yourself, as soon as you do what I have tried to hint at above. Whoever or whatever (again to put it that way) robbed you

of your guts, only you can start acting in those ways which will reassure yourself that you've got them.'

In a postscript he wrote:

> 'This might perhaps be put "robbed of living your own life, so that you could live theirs"; but you must remember that it's no good sitting down and saying "now I'll live mine". That is best achieved by accepting the fact of other people around you and that we are all linked up; and not being "selective". Gradually, if you do that, you will find that you are living a life of your own (you can't do that in a vacuum). You need not confuse the above with "Being unselfish", etc. I'm merely suggesting that you accept a fact— the existence of others round you—and by "accept" I mean 'in practice". (The other thing would be mere acquiescence).'

Acceptance 'in practice' meant contact and commingling, rubbing of shoulders instead of turning a cold shoulder, friction not in the sense of dispute, but ordinary friction among other people. Amber, by friction, becomes electric; human beings become individuals by friction, not by remaining apart. 'You can't live a life of your own in a vacuum'. What the above letter recommended to one boy, the report of another showed to be already happening: 'He has in the past sought the unusual. Now he is beginning to become aware that the variety which lies in the usual is even more fascinating.' And elsewhere Mr Lyward wrote of boys 'coming to accept the common humanity each shares with his fellows and individuating out of that rather than by denial of it.'

Surrender—what did surrender mean? The gradual losing of an artificial self, which might have found expression 'in a boy's picture of himself ... or in one of those almost fanatic attachments ... or some connexion in the town.' Any of these attitudes was capable of keeping a part of him outside the community. Aloofness also found expression in certain attitudes towards the community itself, which on the surface gave certain boys a deceptive air of having 'made the acceptance' and begun to take part. Good mixers, for example: '... many good mixers are really aloof in the deepest sense, being under compulsion to mix all their waking hours.' Does one not know of many an adult, always in the midst of company, with which he (or she) never really mingles, but which he must continue to have about him, as a disguise and drug against his isolation? There were adolescents of this kind at Finchden Manor; 'they need sympathetic understanding, too,' wrote Mr Lyward, 'for ... they miss all that is missed by those, whose manifest aloofness matters only in so far as it tells us of the same deep-seated confusion.' Stand back for a moment in a crowded room. Who is aloof? Obviously, the man or woman in the window, unable or unwilling to take part; less obviously, the man or woman who is most surrounded, who talks most, makes the most jokes, is most apparently convivial. At the end of the evening, perhaps, these two will be left, and will be unable to exchange a word.

There is also a particular kind of helpful person, who, while appearing not merely to have "accepted the community", but to be its most devoted servant, has really not accepted it at all, but is using it as his foil. There were adolescents of this kind, too, at Finchden '... unhealthily generous towards its other members, trying to buy ... what cannot be bought ... feeling that they are wanted only for what they have or can do, and not for what they are.' A boy once arrived who, feeling inwardly humiliated by all his family, had consequently acquired a thirst for power. He brought this thirst with him to the new community, which he tried to dominate by being helpful, encouraged unwittingly by a probation officer who counselled him 'always to think what Mr Lyward would like you to do and be one move ahead'. Mr Lyward composed one of his imaginary cross-examinations round this story.

G. L.: Surely that was bad advice on the probation officer's part? But if (asked the imaginary questioner) the boy developed the habit of doing what society preferred, it would be good?

G.L.: Good for whom? This particular boy was quite capable of that particular trick, among others. ... He could dominate others quite easily by being helpful, couldn't he? He did, in fact, try this method and often anticipated me by at least one move—causing a great deal of consternation by so doing. Clearly we didn't do what he would have called the obvious thing. We didn't say 'Thank you'.

Q.: You let fly at him, I imagine?

G.L.: No—we took no notice, quite often.

Q.: But wouldn't it have given him self-confidence and assurance to feel that his help was acceptable and accepted?

G.L.: Have you ever watched a person like this giving his help? Is he clearly straightforward and honest? I'm not too sure that the effort to get a move or more ahead of me is straightforward. It's certainly calculating and—

Q.: One moment. I think I see one thing you are concerned to stop—calculating, planning, and the like.

G.L.: Agreed. But that must not be taken to imply that I am completely against all planning and calculating; certainly adults have to plan and calculate. But not concerning their near relations with others, nor in the daily ways of straightforwardness, honesty and helpfulness. This boy was calculating how to maintain power or (more accurately) how to maintain a precarious hold on life which he doesn't realize to be so precarious.

Q.: You want to loosen that hold?

G.L.: Yes. Slowly; no faster than he is unconsciously discovering a better way. This 'helpfulness' trick—a confidence trick if ever there was one—always breaks down here and leads to such a boy trying others, frequently stealing, or even bed-wetting.

Alastair Wilton, dominated at home by mother and sister, and bringing his own thirst for power to Finchden, tried for a long while to dominate the situations both there and at home by playing off one against another. Sometimes adults, men and women, who have been dominated in childhood and adolescence, seek in later life to dominate others, it may be by their beauty, or by their brains, or by their self-pity. Sometimes, surrendering themselves to some powerful group, they seek domination through the group. This is not a true surrender; it can often be the surrender of a coward, without inward strength, and deeply influenced by vengefulness. Several adolescents at Finchden, whom visitors might think to have surrendered to and accepted the community, were in fact trying either to own it or to be owned by it. In neither instance had they begun their deeper personal relationship with it.

The key to these two ciphers 'surrender' and 'acceptance' was, as I understood them, personal relationship. What the boys surrendered was a self too artificial to have personal relationship with anyone. What they accepted was a community of personal relationships, not 'the community' as an idea. 'I run a community,' Mr Lyward wrote early in the life of Finchden Manor, 'of which no one is expected to be a loyal understanding member. I have had the joy, in consequence, of continually watching a larger proportion of people co-operating, without stimulants, than in any community I have known, where "community spirit" is preached in and out of season as an ideal, to be achieved by all and sundry from the moment of entry, regardless of their capacity or their prior needs.'

Surrender took time. Acceptance took time. 'It is surely safe to assume that no adolescent is determined *never* to participate, but that all aloofness is an attempt to gain time. The more neurotically aloof adolescents are those, whose life to date has been one long cry of "give me time" ... their fear of the moment of contact dominates their whole lonely existence ... they have never had their external form of living properly informed by their spirit of spontaneity. They need to be helped not to worry about the group ... while they recapture the joy "of their own time".' Hence, respite. Hence, the patient willingness of the staff to be clung to. 'Release can only come for these boys if somebody will acknowledge ... their tendency to become identified with and possess everything and everybody they touch, somebody who thus will help them to move, little by little, towards the joy of free relationship with that one person. Relationship to a group may then follow.'

The change which occurred at Finchden was a change, in general and in particular, from habit to spontaneity, or unaffectedness, from unhuman perfectionism to imperfect humanity. The boys had been compelled, through mistaken treatment at school or at home, to assert themselves by defensive and one-sided or narrowed modes of behaviour, which were fast becoming habit, and if allowed to harden would pass for the expression of the 'true self'. At Finchden the accumulating crust gradually crumbled, the delicate defended heart was gently touched, until the boys began to find their natural way; until, in place of a lifeless protocol of obligations, there could grow a spontaneity in human relationships, the revelation that 'I count' passing into the revelation that other people count, and the feeling 'I am a person, not a pawn in the game of others' becoming the recognition in practice that other people too are persons, not pawns in my own game. The word 'family' is thus inadequate to describe Finchden, although many characteristics of a happy family were present there. The place achieved more than can be achieved in most homes. Communities of such a kind are, to some, necessary stages between the world and family into which each one of us is born, on one side, and, on the other, the family we beget and the world which, once grown-up, we influence.

In the early 'thirties, Mr Lyward used to take boys for short periods of treatment, after which they returned to school. Sometimes he arranged for boys to go on to some tutor, through whom he himself could remain in touch. One boy, terrified of his public school, had nonetheless gone back to it and Mr Lyward, by visits and correspondence, had helped him to remain there. It had not been long before he reached the conclusion that boys he treated should not return to school, but stay with him; and so the time they spent in his care and under his tuition had grown gradually longer, from a few months to a year, to two years, until in many instances it covered the whole period they would normally have spent elsewhere.

Of course, not all fulfilled the last stage of their development; not even those who were not withdrawn by their parents or who did not leave of their own accord. Mr Lyward might decide that Finchden Manor could do no more for one boy—at that moment; or that another would benefit from taking a job—at that moment. The boys jokingly said: 'I am cured!' Once, seriously, suddenly, dramatically, a boy declared, 'It's happened!' From that day colour came into his face and his relationship with Mr Knox, who was teaching him, grew warmer. Mr Lyward had taken over the expression. 'It' might 'happen' to one boy while at Finchden; to another, not until he left; of a third he said that 'it happened' as the boy went through the gates. It was often difficult for a boy—as for an adult—to change in front of the person who had made the change possible.

They left, as they had come, in all kinds of ways. Mr Lyward or one of the staff might take special pains to find a suitable job for one boy. Another had a stroke of luck. Some went to Labour Exchanges and found their own jobs. Mr Lyward might say: 'I suppose it's time for you to go—you'd better start looking in the papers.' One or two boys had to be 'eased out'.

Had Finchden Manor been nothing more than a cure or a crammer's, the boys' association might have ended when they left. Had the place been only a school, they might not have come back, or come back only on friendly and nostalgic visits. But since it had shown them the beginning of a way of life, their association continued naturally. Mr Lyward scarcely had to say 'Keep in touch'. Most boys took it for granted that they would. So many things, which had not been clear to them at Finchden, might become clear on a return visit. So many things he had not been able to do, so many words he had not been able to say, while they were still living there, became possible and appropriate after they had left.

One boy ran away to prove himself in the world, grew scared, returned for a month, and afterwards went successfully ahead. Another, withdrawn by his father, returned of his own accord.

Another, two years after leaving, came back and stayed for several months. Mr Lyward himself gave a job to another, married, with his wife expecting a baby, so that he could remain temporarily. Scores of boys asked for advice several years after they had left. One, who had run away, wanted to return twelve years later. Another, certified before he came to Finchden, carried on in the world with continued help from Mr Lyward and lately wrote to him of 'twenty years of struggle and friendship'. The way of life glimpsed at Finchden was an eternal way; boys came back as men, to have it lighted for them once again.

Arthur Ney left suddenly. For some time he had seemed easier. We had had no more long talks although one evening he declaimed for me the whole of *Lycidas*, without a fault, by moonlight on the football pitch. Not long afterwards, he came hurtling up and said that he must speak to Mr Lyward. Mr Lyward was in the drawing-room, playing Beethoven.

'Is it urgent?' I asked. 'Do you want me to disturb him?'

'Beethoven's indirect. I'm direct,' said the once circuitous and uncertain Arthur Ney.

I fetched Mr Lyward from the piano.

'I'm going to leave,' said Arthur Ney.

Mr Lyward took it lightly, and agreed. Ney produced a musical score he had found somewhere and asked the name of the composer. They went back to the piano, where Mr Lyward played the score, and I left them discussing whether Schubert, or Heller, or Pauer had composed it.

A week or two later Mr Ney arrived and, after a friendly conversation and a reminder from Mr Lyward to 'keep in touch', Arthur departed. He passed a difficult examination well. I saw him several times away from Finchden. He seemed lighter-hearted. The smile, the laugh, appeared without reluctance. He could take many things jokingly which once he had taken in hideous earnest. He still questioned life and himself, but far less feverishly, and without being rushed for an answer.

'What *was* Finchden Manor? *Was* there a secret? What *was* it?'

he began, then laughed and said, 'I suppose it'll be two or three years before I know what happened there.'
And so with others.

Sometimes a boy's departure coincided with an examination. Alastair Wilton had demanded to be prepared for an examination, long before he was equal to it, and had failed. This often happened. But when a particular kind of boy was ready, he could absorb knowledge easily and quickly.

I have in front of me a thick sheaf of notes which Mr Lyward used while preparing a boy called Stephen Morrison for the G.C.E.—chiefly for the advanced and scholarship papers in history and English literature. The notes cover several hundred pages, and had been supplemented by large but simple charts showing, as if on a family tree, the social and political development of the Western world, the flowering of language, the literary genealogy of our poets. Mr Lyward designed and drew about twenty such charts, for which Sid built a plywood case like a Corps Commander's map-case. The love and labour which went into these compilations remind one of a tapestry. The chart of European history is divided horizontally into four parts, 'Renaissance and Reformation', 'Bourbons and Hapsburgs', 'Enlightened Despotism', 'Liberal Movements and Nationalism'. The salient dates and personages of French history are written vertically down the left-hand side, and the dates and personages of other European countries parallel, the most important being circled and shaded in red. Names of influential writers are interwoven, so that the thought and events of the whole period and continent appear as part of an interrelated but not intricate pattern.

Mr Lyward's notes on the set books in English literature, written in that quick scholar's hand which so easily came to resemble music, defy summary. One sheaf is occupied with a comparison between Dryden's *All for Love* and Shakespeare's *Antony and Cleopatra*, another with Chaucer, another with Milton, and so on. One page recommends a modern critical work, with a note: 'If you understand this book and use it with your text, you can't want more on your Milton. When you've done that, turn over'; and, over, there follows a fresh sheaf outlining Milton's relationship to his predecessors. Another page presents a summary of a poem by John Donne, with a note to the boy: 'This is a prose analysis. Does prose analysis suggest the nature of the poem? It does not suggest the tenderness and real feeling. Actually the flimsiness of the argument accentuates the feeling'... and then, written boldly right across the page and underlined three times, 'But can *you* see (feel) that?', with an instruction crowded into the bottom corner, 'You will find the feeling only in the inflection and cadence, so read the poem aloud'.

Some of these notes were Mr Lyward's own, and some a re-created presentation of other people's thoughts. He seemed to me to be a great impresario of learning, a Diaghileff of education. He took European history, or the works of half-a-dozen great writers, and evening after evening staged them for one boy. I have a vivid picture in my mind of Mr Lyward teaching Stephen Morrison, although I never saw him at it. Here he is in his original role, 'the one who's been getting boys scholarships'; the tutor who, but for his other gift, would surely by now have been ensconced at a University. The shaded table-lamp, the books open and interleafed with notes, seem to be set in an ivory room at the top of a tower planted amid the swirl of life, whose noise came faintly through the panelled walls and leaded alcove window, and up the oak stairs, while tutor and pupil lost themselves in the music and battles of the fourteenth century. This particular human relationship can be one of the happiest and most moving in the whole of life. In a relationship so alive as Mr Lyward's, with both student and subject, the teacher was not one who merely imprinted, the boy was not just wax; but they seemed to have embarked together on a voyage, along which the examination existed merely as a cape, an incidental landmark, passed almost without awareness that it had been reached. How much more moving one feels education of this kind to be, when one recalls the boy's confused resentments and tense worries, which had had to be removed before the soil lay clear for sowing. Those five months of concentrated hard work had only been made possible by perhaps twenty-five, or it might be even fifty months of relaxation.

During the days of which the evenings were spent giving private tuition to Stephen Morrison, Mr Lyward was taking a class of about twenty boys in the big kitchen, the time of year being mid-winter, and the kitchen the warmest room in the house. Although these classes were chiefly concerned with French grammar, they verged and were so arranged as to verge upon at least a dozen other subjects, particularly algebra, phonetics, English literature, and the controversies of the Middle Ages. Sometimes they took an hour, sometimes two. They had no rigid continuity, years of experiments dating back a long way having shown Mr Lyward that something boys had been told on Monday they might have forgotten on Tuesday, but might have absorbed by Thursday; consequently he might not revert to it until Thursday, and then in a different light and from an unexpected approach. He seldom taught straight ahead, but with a carefully designed deviousness. He varied the frontal attack upon a point of information with enfiladings and outflankings and detours, so that it came to be seen in the round, from several angles, and not only, like a pylon, as a bare link along a formal chain.

Usually his 'digressions' had been minutely planned, although he sometimes departed from his own brief and digressed impromptu. None of the boys who had been at Finchden any length of time was surprised at his apparent irrelevancies, any more than they were surprised at his deliberate 'unfairnesses'. They came to accept and trust his treatment of a subject, as they had come to trust his treatment of themselves, having learnt from experience that in the end he led them somewhere. The journey held a fascination of its own. It is not in the least strange to find among Mr Lyward's notes an elementary translation into French, sandwiched between an algebraic equation and a few words on Tyndale's and Coverdale's translations of the Bible. When the classes in the kitchen were coming to an end, Mr Lyward, in order to discover what different boys remembered, gave them a craftily selected list of a hundred words and expressions they had discussed. The first nine are: connotation; mensae, of the table; relations; Comus; visual image; first person singular number future simple tense active indicative mood of the verb 'to have'; Dr Johnson; Ben Jonson; T. S. Eliot.

People may well ask what on earth this meant. The answer is that one boy might see the word mensae, for example, as nothing more than the genitive of a word meaning 'a table', another see beyond that to the meaning 'something that is measured'. The third might remember the Latin word 'mens' for 'the mind' or 'measure', and so recall that the role of the mind is to measure, not to dominate or possess. The word 'mensae' was thus directed particularly at an eighteen-year-old boy called Andrew Salter, a 'compulsive thinker' given to fantastic questions. It was not long afterwards that his compulsive thinking stopped. I saw him six months later as Aladdin in a pantomime the boys were putting on for a hundred local children. He was much happier and hardly bothering to think at all; when he started to think again, it would be as a more relaxed person, 'with head and heart reasonably at one', and produce better and quicker results.

The feeling at these classes was friendly, but not lackadaisical. A boy who did not understand might interrupt Mr Lyward, sometimes to be left behind deliberately or to have the whole class reduced to the speed of the slowest. Often Mr Lyward turned his own 'lecture' into a dialogue with a particular boy, or into a general discussion. He put written questions such as these: 'What is meant by "solving" an equation? Try to connect the word "solve" with another word you know'; 'Compose four lines in the style of "No more Latin, no more Greek", using the sound and the rhythm to express a mood or feeling', (30 minutes); 'Fill in the gaps in the following ... (among others) 'To use the word motor-car in a speech by an Elizabethan would be to perpetrate an ... But ... (who?) didn't worry about that.' He told the boys, 'You will either know how to fill in these gaps at once, or not know, in which event no amount of extra time will avail you.' He gave them three quarters of an hour to write 15-20 lines about—with two other subjects—the effect on themselves of a preliminary study of phonetics, particularly interesting among boys with several dialects '(... you can let it all take the form of a letter, if you like.)' His private notes on the boys in this class describe them severally as punctured; concerned and faint; wide open; earnest and frail; solid and held; slight and penetrating; rich and spendthrift; clever and precarious; thoroughbred; penny plain; canine and romantic.

He took words to pieces, passed the pieces round, then reassembled them and made them work, so that they became—as he had said in an interview quoted earlier—'words with power'. Sometimes he drew a diagram or picture to delineate a word's first meaning. All the time, whatever he was teaching, he illustrated, bringing the unfamiliar into touch with the familiar. Being particularly fond of constitutional history, he was not entirely sorry at having to attend an Assizes, at which a boy for whom he was pleading was bound over, but the judge also uttered a learned farewell to the last Grand Jury. 'There are a great many Tudor houses in Norfolk. That is perhaps a better way of starting a talk on Ket's Rebellion than to say, "Wealth and land had accumulated in a few hands." It startles by its apparent irrelevance. It belongs to the present. It refers to something that can be seen to-day by the two eyes in your head. It starts the less intellectual or more emotionally disturbed child trotting along with the others. It gives significance to the conclusion that the rebellion was social rather than political. It gives a good many wandering notions a local habitation. And if you refer to the memorial recently erected to the rebels on the four hundredth anniversary, you help your pupils to link their lives with to-day's people in Norfolk and with the other lovers of fair play of a bygone age. Both time and space are spanned.'

The boys in that kitchen class would have had little difficulty in composing one small essay Mr Lyward asked of them, on 'detective work in study'. He had turned each of them into a sleuth (as I have had to make myself, while writing this book). He had given them a host of clues; if they learnt to pick them up and follow them, the time approached for that more specialised tuition, with himself or Mr D. or some other member of the staff, which enabled Stephen Morrison to pass the G.C.E. in five months, at advanced and scholarship level, in two subjects he had never touched before.

The boys were thus involved in a kind of treasure-hunt. Stephen's private tuition and the kitchen classes were set pieces. But in fact education, 'nourishing', continued casually and conversationally all the time, as would happen at those discussions of which I had already given several examples. Another began during a visit by a woman friend of the Lywards, at the bottom of the boys' staircase. Another started with the National Debt, and somehow came to the difficulty of deciding what was good for people. Mr Lyward quoted:

> Ah Love! could thou and I with Fate conspire
> To grasp this sorry Scheme of Things entire,
> Would not we shatter it to bits—and then
> Re-mould it nearer to the Heart's Desire!

The boys all thought this mushy; they wouldn't be taken in by that kind of philosophy, they said. Soon they were partly talking about and partly listening to the conception of an abstract good; and so they were brought to Plato, to idealists, and to God. A boy remarked that before he came to Finchden he had never believed in God, but now took it for granted that God existed. Another, Thomas, said that all Doubting Thomas's doubts had been wished on to himself. All this went on after breakfast, with a boy outside trumpeting Purcell's Voluntary, which had been used a few nights before to accompany the entrance of the King and Queen in *Hamlet*. 'You look happy,' I told a boy, as the group broke up. 'Are you in love?'

'Oh—with life,' he answered.

And later, two boys were talking about a farmhouse above the marshes and wooded slopes, on the side of Finchden hidden from the London road. 'It hasn't got any windows overlooking that view,' I heard one of them say, 'The people who built it must have been dead.'

In such an atmosphere, among so many opening hearts and minds beginning quietly to become receptive, nothing seemed impossible. One evening Mr Lyward had spent an hour or two in his own part of the house, giving two boys a music lesson. They went back to the dining-room for supper, where he followed them, meaning to finish his remarks about scales. He noticed a boy, John Farmer, a recent arrival, round whom a kind of stalemate had developed. John could do nothing but mooch about, reiterating that he was going to leave. Mr Lyward decided that this situation could not be allowed to continue, and shouted at the boy, deliberately appearing to have lost his temper. He went on to shake up the others in the room. Two boys who should have been washing up were not there; a custom had evidently grown up that boys who did other people's chores one evening need not do their own the next. He wanted to know why. A discussion began, and continued while he chivvied them, sending two to clean the kitchen, another to sweep the dining-room, and joining another in the scullery who volunteered to wash the plates, 'if you'll do the pots and pans, sir.' Another, who had lately won a valuable University scholarship, was kidded into doing the washing by another 'while I do the drying', which meant 'while I do nothing'. Soon a dozen boys were involved round Mr Lyward. He took them into his confidence and discussed aloud what could be done to help John Farmer to take part in their community life.

'I've never seen you in a temper before,' observed a tiny boy who had just arrived.

'You all shirk the hard work of chores,' Mr Lyward told them. 'It's instinctive. But here you are actually enjoying them.'

'I've noticed it's always enjoyable when you're doing a job and we're helping,' said one boy.

'Well, I'm going to start the history of French literature with you,' Mr Lyward told him, and quoted Ronsard's 'Dieu est en nous et par nous fait miracle'. At that moment a boy who had been out on a 'holiday', and far from certain to return, slipped into the room. No one paid particular attention. Mr Lyward noticed him, went on talking about John Farmer, and added quietly: 'After all, miracles do happen.' One boy murmured or muttered: 'Especially here.'

On numberless occasions such as this one felt the easy and humorous coherence of a group with whom an aside could be a revelation. The unenshrined tradition consisted in a heartfelt understanding among nearly all the boys, that they, Mr Lyward and the staff were in some inexpressible way involved with one another for good. Few—perhaps four or five boys—felt this consciously, unless someone coming from outside misinterpreted the spirit of the place, or moralized, in which event all seemed to become alive to it. A sensation-seeking journalist once arrived to interview Mr Lyward, who took him seriously and spent a great deal of time trying to explain Finchden. Little of what he had said appeared in the article the journalist later published, which was full instead of inaccurate stories calculated to excite or shock. The boys were disgusted and thought the journalist more in need of special attention than themselves.

Their trust made Mr Lyward's great variety of methods possible. He could 'improvise' a few minutes' parrying with one boy, in order to make something clear to the community, or spar with the whole community, in order to help one boy. On these occasions, too, the boys' detective instinct was provoked. Where was he leading? What was he going to say next, and to whom? The younger boys were rather bewildered, but the relaxed and friendly feeling was probably new to them and since everyone else seemed to listen, most of them listened. A few boys were bored by his circuitousness. The older waited quietly; somewhere round a corner of allegory or digression would appear some moral issue, deepened, concentrated to the point where it shone as a fact.

Headmasters at other places, wishing to issue an admonition or inculcate a value, often lecture the whole school publicly or, privately, a particular boy. At those 'sessions', which Mr Lyward summoned from time to time with the same object, he suggested rather than lectured. If he had decided to attack a particular boy, he normally did it by way of poignard-like questions. The boy thrust back vigorously, merely exposing his defences and weak spots. Mr Lyward might manoeuvre into a position where he could administer a *coup-de-grace*, or laugh and allow himself—not often— to be worsted, or drop both their weapons and refer the whole issue to discussion. There were so many possibilities that no 'session', just as no boy, seems in retrospect to have been 'typical', except that all ended, for the majority, gaily, and in all Mr Lyward made great play with visual images. If ever people by indirections found directions out, the boys at Finchden did. Mr Lyward would have told the parable of the Good Samaritan as though the accident had just happened on the Tenterden road. When I first went to Finchden I did not glimpse the parable at all and took almost everything he said literally.

We have seen him with individuals and with groups. Now let us see them all together.

One evening Mr Lyward called all the boys into the hall. They sat waiting for him in a semicircle, on the stage, round the walls, on the floor, on window-ledges. He came in, wearing his Trilby and a woollen scarf, and took a chair in the middle.

'Who knows algebra, I wonder?' he asked vaguely. He had just been doing algebra with one boy; it had suggested the kind of game he was now playing, aimed at discovering whether they could think in symbols. 'Henry, do you know algebra?'

'No, sir.'

'Oh, I'm sure you do. What would you say is one more than Z?'

'One more than Z?'

Long silence.

'If you know that, Henry, you know the whole of algebra.' This was said with that kind of *double entendre* to which I have already referred; as if he knew and they knew he was talking rubbish, and yet there was something serious behind.

'Why Z? Why not another letter?' asked a boy.

'Don't spoil it. Come on, Henry.'

Henry was coaxed into agreeing that one more than Z was Z+1.

'Now why did I say Z?' Mr Lyward asked.

A boy answered: 'Because if you'd said A, someone might have said that one more than A was B.'

'And ...?'

'Well—B's different.' This was good for that particular boy.'

'All right. If you know that, you know all algebra.'

Most of the boys received this calmly. Some looked puzzled. Two or three shrugged their shoulders, as if to say 'mad'. (Some boys had told Mr Lyward that when they first met him they thought he was mad. They had been used to authority always being only authority. Later they thought the people they had been with before were mad.)

'I'm afraid this session is going to be about money,' said Mr Lyward curtly. 'We don't often have sessions about money, do we?' Silence. 'I thought coming back in the car this evening that we'd have to. I'm going to talk about hop-pickers first. Some time ago two or three of you went hop-picking. They earned quite a lot of money, and put it in the office as arranged. But the last two apple-pickers—your money isn't in the office. How much of it do you have left—Alan?'

'I don't know.'

'You don't *know*?' Mr Lyward looked amazed. 'You must know. You've got it, haven't you?'

'Some of it.'

'How much?'

'I don't know exactly.'

'You must have quite a lot.' It turned out that Alan had about £6 left.

'And you, Paul?' Paul was a boy, like Alastair Wilton at one stage, all for 'divide and rule'.

'I haven't got any.'

'You haven't got *any*?' Mr Lyward looked astounded.

'No.'

'Where is it, then?'

'In the bank.'

'In the bank! The office is the bank. What do you mean by the bank?'

'It's in my father's bank.'

'*In your father's bank*! Who told you to put it there?'

'No one told me. I sent it home. It's my money.'

'Is it your money?'

'I earned it—'

'It was agreed that when any of you went hop-picking or apple-picking, you should put the money into the office.'

'I don't agree. I made the money and it's mine.'

'The whole question of money is becoming rather urgent,' said Mr Lyward. 'I'll tell you why. People (actually the police) have been inquiring about some unfortunate accidents to Mr Cope's chickens. Mr Cope is our neighbour. It seems that one of our dogs is under suspicion. If convicted he—or rather she—will have to pay. Has she any money to pay, Riff?' to the boy who owned the dog.

'I tied her up. She can't have done it.'

'Is she tied up now?'

'Yes.'

'Are all our animals tied up? Eric, is your tortoise tied up?'

'No. She's asleep.'

'How do you know she can't get out when she wakes up?'

'Because she's in my suitcase.'

'It seems the tortoise is acquitted. Still, it looks as if Riff's dog is going to be arrested for destroying Mr Cope's chickens. She'll have to appear in Court. She'll have to get up on her hind-legs and say: "I can't help it, I've been led a dog's life." Is that an excuse? And who'll defend her?'

'I'll defend her,' said Riff.

'Suppose she's guilty?' (She was). 'She can't pay. *We'll* have to pay. We—who is *we*?' Long pause. 'Do you *really* think you had a right to put that money in your father's bank, Paul?'

'Yes.'

'And Archie Combe—you've just had ten shillings from the office for your fare home.'

'Yes.'

'On top of the ten shillings your mother sent you?'

'Yes,' laughing slightly awkwardly.

'It was bad luck your mother wrote and mentioned it,' said Mr Lyward gaily.

'Yes.'

'And you still ask for ten shillings from the office.?'

'The other was my own money.'

'There!' exclaimed Mr Lyward, slapping his knee. 'That's one we know well, isn't it? Isn't it amazing? "Oh, but I can't spend that on it! *That's* my birthday money." But the money from the office *isn't* different. There's always this special thing that's my own—something that's got nothing to do with us here at Finchden Manor. Why is it your own money?'

'Because my mother gave it to me.'

'And so it's all right for Paul to put his ... ten pounds? ... fifteen pounds? ... twenty pounds? ...'

'Eleven pounds,' said Paul.

'His eleven pounds in his father's bank?'

'I don't know,' said Archie.

'Paul does. You don't think he's hoping for parental support? Parents. I'll have to sit up for this.' Mr Lyward sat up. 'Do you *want* your parents to be involved?' He surveyed the boys over his spectacles. 'Perhaps I ought to involve them and you in the chickens. When the barn was burnt I was asked to pay for that. I don't know why the boy who burnt the barn didn't wait till the chickens were in it. We could have had it all together.'

Mr Lyward opened a book. 'I'll read you something about money. It's from Spenser's *Faerie Queen*':

> God of the world and worldlings I me call,
> Great Mammon, greatest god below the sky,

> That of my plenty poure out unto all,
> And unto none my graces do envye,
> Riches, renowne, and principality,
> Honour, estate, and all this worldes good ...

'Do you like this metre—the way it goes?'

'Couldn't care less,' Paul answered, but only Paul. The others were enjoying.

Mr Lyward continued, 'Mammon had a daughter', and went on quoting,

> 'There as in glistring glory she did sitt,
> She held a great gold chaine ylincked well,
> Whose upper end to highest heven was knit,
> And lower part did reach to lowest Hell;
> And all that press did round about her swell
> To catchen hold of that long chaine, whereby
> To climbe aloft, and others to excell:
> That was ...

What was Mammon's daughter's name, do you suppose?'

'Ambition,' said Riff.

'That was Ambition,' Mr Lyward finished the quotation.
'It seems to me you, Paul, and you, Alan, have married her already. Do you really want to have large sums of money floating about this place? Do you, Jimmy?'

'Yes, sir.'

'You'd get into the position of the boy who was here once who used to lend it out at interest.' Mr Lyward closed the book. 'Who thinks money can really supply you with all you want?'

'Nine-tenths,' said one boy.

'Four-tenths.'

'Two-tenths,' said a boy particularly keen on money.

'All I know,' said a boy called David Bradley, 'is that I find it difficult to live on four bob a week.'

'Do boys never do anything for nothing? When I was a boy ...' Mr Lyward slipped this in deliberately. It was an old joke and he expected interruption.

Sure enough it came. 'Ah!' said a boy. 'Geoff Miller would have walked out.' Geoff Miller had once sent Mr Lyward a note "forbidding" him to use certain expressions including "When I was a boy".

'Would *you* go hop-picking for nothing?' asked David Bradley. 'I'd say that anyone who did that was out of his mind.'

Mr Lyward looked round them all. 'People sometimes say "Why not get them all to do some gardening and pay them for it?" I've always refused. It always seemed to me that something would be lost. Do you agree?'

Almost everyone said 'Yes', and obviously sincerely.

'Of course, Mr Lyward murmured, 'there was the incident of Francis's tent. Remember it caught fire—by an act of internal combustion? Who paid then?'

'*We* did.'

'You all most gracefully agreed to a suggestion I made at that time (boos). How many of you think I'm going to ask you to pay the thirty-two pounds for the chickens? That's what I think we owe.'

Half the boys held up their hands.

'Hands up those who think I'm not.'

Almost all the rest held up theirs. Mr Lyward paused and said, 'Well, I'm not. When is the dance to be, Owen?'

'It's up to you, sir.'

'Of course, you do realize we might have to have the dance without food and without music, if there isn't any money to pay for it?'

Long silence.

'The hop-pickers are having their money kept for them. '*But*' (as it were, underlined in red) 'the apple-pickers' money might even have been used to increase your four-shillings a week. That was another possibility I had in mind. I had been thinking of something of that sort.' Again this was said half-teasingly, since the apple-pickers knew their money was not going to be made community money; and yet there was a serious point.

Another long silence.

'I'll contribute one pound towards the dance,' said Paul.

'Who thinks that a good idea?' asked Mr Lyward.

'I don't,' said a boy. 'We'd never hear the last of it.'

'Of course, there's Archie Combe's ten shillings. How many of you think I'm going to ask him for it back?'

Half the hands went up.

'I don't know,' said one boy.

'Nor do I yet,' said Mr Lyward. He got up. 'Well, anyhow, the situation's exactly the same as when I came in. We haven't decided anything. You all know perfectly well that I wouldn't let you have a dance here without food or some new records. But you *do* see that all we've been talking about is related?'

General assent.

'Henry, what is one more than Z?'

'Z + 1.'

'Good.'

Mr Lyward walked away. A group surrounded him at once, Owen wanting to know about the dance, Riff protesting the innocence of his dog, and Paul offering to surrender all the money in his father's bank to Mr D., an offer which was passed by.

Flynn and Nigs Walker continued to remain outside the community.

I had with Nigs one of those long talks to which I had listened so curiously when first I arrived, but now avoided. I had to get him to go to bed, and he refused to go. He would not talk at all at first, then said he would sleep where he chose.

'Why shouldn't I?' he declared. 'Anyhow, I'm enjoying myself. I like playing at cat and mouse.'

'Do you really think you're a cat?' I asked.

'Perhaps I'm just a mouse pretending to be a cat. Anyhow, I'm enjoying myself. The world's full of destruction,' Nigs said. 'Why shouldn't I be destructive?'

'Of yourself?'

'Well, that might be interesting. I'd like to destroy the world and build a space-ship and find a planet to start another world.'

'Well, that might be creative.'

'Oh, I've got a creative side, too.'

'All the same, this is the world you've got to live in.'

'Unfortunately. You say destruction came to an end with the war. Well, it hasn't. It's building up all the time, A-bombs, H-bombs, etc.'

He talked about his home, and said: 'There are nothing but rows at home whenever I go there.' He said he felt 'frustrated'. 'Flynn is, too, about horses, other people about other things. I think Flynn would do very well looking after horses. They understand him, he can feel them, just as I feel glass. I get irritated by little things all the time. Two months ago I used to be in things more, now I'm not, because people spoil it. Jim, for example. If you give a party or try to arrange something, he's sure to push his way in. And I get irritated with people trying to help. When I'm playing chess, they come up and say "You ought to have moved here or there", and it irritates me.'

'Can't you dismiss it, or let it go over your head?'

'No, it's all the time.' He said that he resented people trying to help him. He had to have some enemy, something to resent. He was prepared, he said, to listen to helpful advice, but later didn't want to follow it, because it might deprive him of his enemy and grounds for resentment.

'Some people are really horrible, he exclaimed. 'Did you know about my birds-nest? There were some tits who'd built a nest in a wall, and someone came and cemented it up. So I uncemented it, and they walled it up again. It wasn't even in an important part of the wall.'

He talked of the boys he liked, and said of one: 'People pity him too much and don't bring him into things enough. He'd like to play chess or L'Attaque, but he doesn't like to ask and people don't ask him. They're self-conscious with him, trying not to talk about things that might offend him. It's the same with Richard. He's a bit of a philosopher, is Richard. You know he was amazed at the monkey. He thought a monkey was a sort of monster, like a barrel. He feels colour. He knows what green is. He calls it verdant. When we asked him what colour the mantelpiece here was, he said it was an oak-like colour. But people pity him too much, trying to avoid saying "blind" and saying "loss of sight" instead.' (This was worlds away from the truth about all but one or two boys, who transferred their own self-pity to Richard.) 'I'll tell you something I'd like to destroy,' Nigs said. 'In fact, almost the first thing. Snakes, and all the animals that bring disease, and all the people too. I'd give them six months' psychological treatment, and then if they weren't cured I'd have them killed. It'd give me great pleasure. But I couldn't bear to destroy things myself. I'd just like to give the orders. I don't even like to see flowers when they've been picked, and I can't pick them. I'd rather they were left growing, I hate to see them dying in a vase. I feel like talking quite poetically about flowers sometimes.'

I said, although I had no commission to say it, 'I wish you could see some of the things you've been saying in relation to yourself. You've said quite a lot of intelligent things, but they all seem to be just ideas.'

'I wish I could see myself, too,' Nigs answered. His silences grew longer. Finally, though I had not mentioned it for at least half-an-hour, he said, 'Well, I'll go to bed, I won't keep you up any longer. And thanks for the talk, it relieves the tension,' and went to bed.

One day Nigs presented Mr Lyward with an ultimatum. Either he or another boy who had returned and was 'getting on his nerves' must go. Mr Lyward decided very sadly that the one to leave must be Nigs. Nigs could not go to bed his last night. He stayed in front of the staff room fire, polishing his shoes, while Neville washed his clothes. Next morning he was driven to the bus-stop and set out to present his premature challenge to the world. The domestic circumstances with which he found himself faced in

London the same evening would have daunted most boys. In effect he was completely alone, with hardly a soul to support him except the friends at Finchden whom he had left, and a devoted welfare officer with forty other boys in his charge. Nigs felt loneliness at once and acutely, and made the one reversed telephone call which Mr Lyward had promised him. I saw him many times in London. He got a job as a laundry-boy and looked happy hanging on at the back of the van; it reminded me of the days when he gaily taught Mr Lyward the St Bernard's Waltz and dressed up as a crusader with a biscuit-tin for helmet. He came often to our house, seldom without bringing a present, and seemed quite content to sit with a New Yorker album or a picture-book about antiques. Several people in London befriended him, and he was found a job with considerable opportunities, such as his high intelligence, though perhaps not his emotional state, deserved. Suddenly, a few months after he had left Finchden, something went wrong.

He has not written to Mr Lyward since. He once told me that his time at Finchden Manor had prevented him from becoming entirely cynical and bitter. I like to think that he meant this, and has remembered it, and will one day be in touch again.

Flynn left Finchden Manor more dramatically than Nigs Walker, after a 'session' far less peaceful than the one I have described earlier in this chapter.

Two nights before it took place he had kept the lamp in his and Geoff Miller's shack burning till midnight, in order to read a magazine about horses. Neville had seen the light, come out and taken the lamp away. This had angered Flynn, who had gone into the house and banged on Neville's door, insisting on seeing him. Neville had told him to go away. Flynn was thus in a thoroughly bad mood.

This time the 'session', which Mr Lyward called without any particular reference to Flynn, took place in the staff room. Mr Lyward sat deep in an armchair, with the boys crowded round the walls and on the floor. He began in his usual leisurely fashion, elaborating an allegory about people who preferred the condiments of a meal to the meal itself, which Flynn, who was standing just behind me, accompanied with impatient comments under his breath. When Mr Lyward mentioned pickles and sauces Flynn, who was feeling far from allegorical or poetic, grunted, "We never get them". Mr Lyward spoke next about the boys' growing habit of asking permission to go into Tenterden on Mondays (that day was a Monday). Why? he asked. Was it so necessary for them to get away from Finchden immediately the new week began? Why were they so impatient?

"Do you consider Sunday as a different day from all the rest of the week?" Mr Lyward asked.

"Yes," said some; others, "No". Some thought Monday a special day, because it was then the new film began.

"Is it so necessary for you to see the new film at once?" Mr Lyward asked.

This discussion about days of the week went on for some time. Flynn continued his angry mutterings. I have said that he had called Finchden 'a peaceful place', but at this 'session' he felt, as he later told me, that Mr Lyward was 'tightening up on it, forbidding more and more things, and when that happened the peacefulness was lost and I began to feel more and more confined'. I thought I could see the point round which Mr Lyward was taking his preliminary ramble. On Sunday the neighbourhood seemed dead; no distractions, above all, no cinema. If therefore the boys all demanded permission to go out the moment Monday dawned, did it not appear that they could not manage without those distractions? Were they the kind of boys who used home as a hotel? Did they use Finchden merely as a hotel, for its accessories, and were they indifferent to its sustenance and spirit? Hence the allegory of the condiments.

The telephone rang. Mr Lyward went into his room to answer. When he returned a boy had lit a cigarette.

"Who told you you could smoke?" Mr Lyward demanded angrily, by now aware of hidden possibilities in this session, and saying, "Here goes!" to himself. 'Put it out!'

The boy put it out. Mr Lyward went on talking about cinemas.

'Films are a drug,' a boy said virtuously.

'I suppose you sometimes do have to have drugs for sick people,' said Mr Lyward. He started to quote some lines of poetry:

> 'They pass me by like shadows, crowds on crowds,
> Pale ghosts of men, who hover to and fro,
> Hugging their bodies round them like thin shrouds,
> In which their souls were buried long ago.'

He had forgotten the next lines, said so, and continued:

> 'Whose ever-open maw by such is fed
> Gibber at living men and idly rave,
> "We only truly live, and ye are dead"
> Poor souls! the anointed eye can surely trace
> A dead soul's epitaph in every face.'

The calm tone in which this quotation was delivered particularly angered Flynn, although he told me later that he liked the words. His mutterings became louder and more frequent. Mr Lyward and one or two boys began to discuss what was meant by 'killing time', which led Mr Lyward to talk about the kind of boy who was attracted outside, who went often to the cinema, who sat alone, went for walks alone. 'Yes, you ——', Flynn was rumbling, 'I want to go for a walk now. ... I want to go to the pictures now. ...'

'Has anyone anything to say?' Mr Lyward asked, as if casually.

'Yes, I've got plenty,' Flynn said under his breath.

I heard him and asked in an aside, 'Why don't you say it?' and it was then that he exploded.

'What else is there to do except kill time!' he flung at Mr Lyward. 'What the —— hell have we got to do here! What do you expect us to do except grub up fag-ends and collect enough —— empty bottles to get enough money to buy another fag!' He was trembling all over. Geoff Miller, also in a tense excited state, was crushing his hand with a kind of dead man's grip, and without knowing it was crushing his foot too. He could only keep his balance by remaining unnaturally rigid. And all the time Geoff Miller was urging him on in whispers, 'Go on! Give it him!'

All Flynn's frustrations came pouring out, all his pent-up arguments. He felt completely confident for a moment, more confident than he had ever felt. 'If we have any one main thing we can do, we have it taken away from us,' he shouted. 'Wireless—horses—whatever it is! So we've got nothing left except to sit around and go to the pictures. There's no week here, no week-end! The only day that counts is Friday, because that's when we're paid! The day we come here's the beginning of the week and the day we leave's the end and that's all! Weeks are like seconds, they don't count! Nobody remembers the seconds of an hour that's past, but I'll make bloody sure you remember this second for the rest of your life!'

'Why did you come here?' demanded Mr Lyward, rounding on him deliberately.

'Because I've been kicked here and kicked there and now I've been kicked to —— Finchden!'

'Why did you come—?'

'Because I was —— well made to come—'

'You didn't have to come here—'

'I didn't want to come—'

The telephone rang again and Mr Lyward spoke without leaving the room. This telephone call was Flynn's undoing. Before, he had felt in command. Everything had poured out without thought. After the call was finished he tried to collect the threads and lost them. Trying to gain points, thinking before he spoke, he became inarticulate and in a minute or two really hysterical. Amid the rage of words and tears I heard all his hates—names of head-masters, names of doctors, names of psychiatrists—and then Mr Lyward cutting in, attacking him in a hard, cold, deliberate voice. When he spoke of Flynn's 'guttersnipe existence', it seemed for a moment that Flynn might become physically violent. Perhaps he didn't hear.

'You're told you can go when you like,' he shouted, 'and then you're kept here, just by words and talk and being told you're not ready to go, until you —— well don't know what to think about yourself.' He went on for a minute or two, then, when he had no more to let go, shoved his way to the door and left.

There was a long silence.

Mr Lyward sent Neville to follow Flynn. Two or three boys could not throw off the tension Flynn had left behind and had identified themselves so emotionally with him that they had to say something in his support.

'Where is all this leading to, sir?' one of them exclaimed.

'Nowhere,' retorted Mr Lyward, 'unless it shows you something. Do you think that boy's ready to leave? Did he sound like it just now?'

'All the same,' said another boy, 'Some people do want to go and try things out for themselves.'

Mr Lyward turned on him. 'What effort have you made?' he demanded. 'You've been given permission to look for a job for yourself. What have you done about it?'

In fact this boy had done nothing.

Mr Lyward gently and slowly recovered the threads of allegory. He knew exactly what he had done, and that the vibrations would be felt for some time by himself and others. He needed and contrived to end the 'session' lightly on laughter and a dying fall, and most of the boys dispersed quietly.

Flynn packed his rucksack and waited to see Mr Lyward in order to get money for his departure. He refused to speak to Neville, went round to the entrance to Mr Lyward's part of the house and arrived just in time for Neville, who had dodged round another way, to put his foot in the door. Flynn refused to wait and left. Neville followed him to Tenterden; not for the first time. They tossed who should pay for a cup of coffee. Neville lost. No wonder; it was a double-headed penny. But somehow Neville managed to coax Flynn back to Finchden, where he came to see me. He resumed his accusations against Mr Lyward and the whole place in a calmer tone of voice. After he had been talking for a few minutes, I interrupted him and went to tell Mr Lyward that he was with me. Mr Lyward consented to see Flynn for ten minutes in the staffroom.

They talked like old friends not for ten minutes, but for an hour. Flynn started by saying: 'I want to leave whether it's bad for me, or not.'

Mr Lyward answered that if Flynn wanted to do that, he could always feel that he had Finchden behind him, as a place to which he could return not, of course, as a resident, but as a friend; the staff and he himself would always be ready to listen and help with advice. He made it abundantly clear that he thought Flynn in no way ready to leave; but if he did leave, it would be with everyone's best wishes 'though not (smiling) with my blessing'. Flynn became quite relaxed. He apologized for his outburst, and was soon giving an account of the time when he and Geoff Miller had run away and Fitzy had had to fetch them back from Hampshire. When he described the two of them asleep in a ditch with a white flag flying, Mr Lyward laughed and said: 'I wish I'd come to fetch you,'—all this in the room in which Flynn had been swearing at Mr Lyward only two hours earlier.

Finally Flynn asked how much money he could have. Mr Lyward asked how much he had been given on his last hike.

'Five pounds.'

'How long was that for?'

'Ten days.'

'How long are you going for, this time?'

'Well, I shall try to find a fellow who's starting a ranch in Suffolk. I may need a week.'

'What proportion of five pounds does that make?'

'Oh, come on, let me have the whole five pounds.'

Mr Lyward laughed. 'Oh, all right, have it,' he said.

So Flynn went off in search of a job early next morning, with five pounds from the office, a ticket to London he had bought to run away, and three pounds he had extorted out of another boy which he had not mentioned. If he had mentioned the three, he would not have got the five.

He rang up a day or two later with an insolent and silly message for Geoff Miller, which he was not allowed to pass on, and a bland announcement that he would be back three days later, not having found the ranch in Suffolk. A letter followed from the adoptive mother. Flynn had told her that Mr Lyward thought him 'ready to leave', and she had believed him. 'I quite agree with you,' the lady wrote, 'that the boy is now ready to try his luck.'

'Aren't they amazing?' said Mr Lyward.

Flynn asked for another extension, and finally returned, having failed to get a job. However, he had made an appointment with an aged circus-master, who was going to give him a trial as a trick rider.

'But this is where I'm really going,' he declared, pointing at a travel advertisement labelled 'South America'.

After one more reconnaissance he returned for the last time as a boy at Finchden to collect his belongings and acquisitions, and to say good-bye. I was with Mr Lyward when he came in. They talked in a friendly laughing way for a while. Then Mr Lyward said: 'There's something I knew about you when you first came here. I couldn't say it to you then, and I haven't been able to say it the whole time you've been here. Now I can.'

He took a sheet of paper and drew a large figure, like a small child's drawing, holding out two pin-like arms. Underneath he wrote 'Giver'. Further along he drew a large square package, inscribed 'Gift'; further along still, a much smaller figure, inscribed 'You', holding out its arms to the larger figure. 'What you have always been asking for is the gift,' Mr Lyward said. 'What you have really wanted is the giver.'

For a moment Flynn said nothing. He and Mr Lyward bore a strange resemblance to one another at that moment, Mr Lyward seated, his face down on his collar-bone, Flynn standing, his face dug into the collar of a blue polo sweater. Then Flynn reached out a hand, folded the paper, put it into his pocket, shook hands and went out.

I drove him to the station. He said he had never expected to leave

Finchden in so friendly a way. He had expected to be chucked out, he said, 'as I was everywhere else', and he named boys, who—as he thought—had cordially disliked him, but had come up to wish him luck.

'Have you got that bit of paper?' I asked.

He tapped his breastpocket. 'I'll keep it all my life,' he said.

Peter Storey, Nigs Walker, and Flynn were the only three boys who lived more than six months at Finchden and left 'on their own judgment', entirely against Mr Lyward's advice, during the time that I was there. Only about a dozen others, who had remained more than six months, had left in this fashion, during the whole twenty-five years of its existence, nearly all of them during or after the war. It is interesting to know what became of them.

One of them was a Norwegian of great charm. He arrived in April 1940, and stayed nearly a year. He gave the staff parcels to post during the days before he decamped, which afterwards turned out to have contained Mrs Lyward's jewellery. He wanted to help free Norway and joined the Norwegian Navy. After the war he wrote to Mr Lyward apologizing for his brusqueness and misappropriations, and asked himself to stay. He brought presents of huge packages of tobacco and cube sugar, stayed a week-end, was charming as ever, and departed with all the spare parts of Mr Lyward's wireless. Several years later he wrote Mr Lyward a most friendly letter, announcing that he was now a reporter on a foreign paper and asking for an article on education. Mr Lyward did not send one, and the boy has not been heard of since.

Two of these boys got into trouble soon afterwards, and Mr Lyward was able to help both.

Another is still dodging from job to job, and depends immensely on the help given him by a former member of the staff.

One was having great trouble at home, and had not settled. Another, William, can hardly be described as having been a 'part' of Finchden. Five months after his arrival, Mr Lyward was doubtful if he could be kept. The boy's mother implored him, and William remained. He had run away and come back eleven times before going finally. A year later, the mother begged Mr Lyward to do something on behalf of William's brother, whom he had never seen. Mr Lyward wrote a long letter to the authorities with whom the brother was in trouble. Four years later, William was receiving in-patient treatment at a mental hospital.

Eric Maitland asked to visit Mr Lyward eighteen months after he had left, about 'something very important'. The fact was that he was due to go to prison. He went in for a short spell, and then asked to be returned to Finchden. The prison doctor advised against. Eric insisted, saying that afterwards he would be able to stand on his own feet. Mr Lyward accepted him for a week. Three years later, the boy wrote that he was happy and in a good job. He was next heard of after another three years, cheerful, determined, and about to take a job offered him in Canada.

George was a foreigner, a victim from a land of victims. He had had a terrible childhood. His indigent parents, victims as much as he, had tried to get rid of him and shipped him off without any documents by which his name and origin might be discovered. He insisted on leaving Finchden after eighteen months, when he was sixteen. George wrote long letters to Mr Lyward about his life in a factory, which he soon left. He wandered through the hostels of London without country, home, money, or even an overcoat. 'How many people understand friendship?' he wrote. 'Most people think it is just something when a person and you go to the pictures. I learned many things from Finchden, and matured quicker than most people because of what you've done for me. I am deeply grateful. It's true I never admitted it, but now I have. You should tell your boys that they are very lucky; they shouldn't lose the advantages they've got.' The boy went on to describe the doss-houses he had slept in. One night, unable to find rooms, he had slept in a station lavatory, until a policeman found him and turned him out. 'Could you please describe Finchden to me as it is now?' he asked. 'Somehow I can't imagine it, although I can imagine almost everything else.' Mr Lyward answered, and the lonely boy wrote back: 'Your letter makes a lot of difference to my day.' Not many months later he went to prison, awaiting deportation.

One boy—and one alone—Jed Mullins, seems so far to have left Finchden Manor, as it seemed to him, of his own accord and made an unmistakeable success at once. Yet it appears likely that the leaves he spent there afterwards were necessary to him. During the war he went into Bomber Command, and talked at Finchden about his operational experiences, which had disturbed him deeply. More than ten years afterwards, happy, doing well, married and with a child, he was still in touch.

These stories have four striking characteristics in common:—

(1) Nearly all these boys had had no home life to speak of; such home life as they had, was difficult. The parents of only two or three were living together, precariously, and one had left his parents to become what I can only describe as maladopted. The parents of some were disastrous to them.

(2) Nearly all came from financially a fairly poor background, and were paid for out of public funds.

(3) All went to Finchden either during or after the war.

(4) Nearly all needed help, and several got into serious trouble.

Mr Lyward once said that truancy had become more of a problem everywhere since the war. Before the war most boys came to stay, whatever other difficulties they caused. Flynn once said: 'I am a nomad'. Mr Lyward seized the word and used it the same evening half-jokingly to a Probation Officer. 'There is now a nomad population'.

These boys who left on their own were an extremely small minority. The overwhelming majority never even thought of walking out. It does stand out, however, that a larger number of boys took their lives into their own hands after the war than before. The reason may be that Mr Lyward now had a different kind of boy. Many now came to him from a much poorer class. They felt the pressure to get on much more acutely than the well-to-do, especially if they had also had difficult homes, or none.

Although there were boys who had suffered from both homelessness and poverty, and had refused to stay elsewhere, yet stayed at Finchden, one is nonetheless drawn to the conclusion that a certain kind of boy, who has neither the security of a happy home nor money, will tend to run away. He may move on afterwards from job to job—as did several who walked out of Finchden—before finding his place in the world. Such boys need the help of mature and disinterested friendship during youth more deeply than do most people. Either Mr Lyward or some other member of the staff gave them help after they had gone; help not in money, but in merely 'being there'. Finchden came to mean a great deal to them, after they had left it for the world.

I will end this chapter by examining briefly the stories of some eighteen boys who remained at Finchden more than six months and left against Mr Lyward's advice, not—like those just mentioned—because they wanted to leave, but because their parents removed them. About one, it is too early to tell. There is no recent news of two or three. About half-a-dozen seem to have done well; the doctor of one thanked Mr Lyward for 'doing the bulldozing'. One boy insisted on returning to Finchden. Three have been to prison, of whom one used to return to Finchden of his own accord for advice and friendship. The parents of the second were described as completely without understanding; the boy stayed at Finchden just before his case came on. The relatives of the third slandered Finchden as long as he was there, and forced him to tell Mr Lyward that he wanted to leave, which was not true; after he had left, they would not let him speak of it, saying 'all that's dead and gone'. Many years afterwards, in another country, he gave as a reference the name of Mr Lyward, the only man who had befriended him and whom he respected. He returned years later to make up his own mind about Finchden, and decided that all that his relatives had told him had been false. It was too late for him to avoid a prison sentence, but a member of the staff was able to stand by him in Court—twelve years after the boy had left.

Of the remaining three boys, Mr Lyward described one as 'developing well' when his father decided to remove him, and added: 'This is an outstanding instance of a parent's lack of understanding wrecking his son's life.' The second boy was also removed by his father. Some time later, living alone in lodgings, this boy wrote to Mr Lyward, 'If you haven't put me out of your books, might I just come down, because I am sure that you could help me? Remember, the last day I saw you, you told me to find someone to go out with? Well, I have, but my parents said the other day, "I hope you haven't started going out with anyone yet?" I didn't say anything, but it reminded me. My father was always anxious to hurry things on, and afraid of the financial and emotional cost to him. There was a certain spot near Finchden I could never pass, because it was there he went for me when he first brought me.'

The last of these boys was one who had always suffered deeply from the worryings of his family. He felt torn between loyalty to them and his own inclinations. They removed him because they needed him in the family business. He wrote often to Mr Lyward 'longing to be back'. Two years after he had left he returned on a visit, and when the time came to go, could not bring himself to say good-bye. He wrote a few days later: 'I believe that what really got me down was to revisit a life that had been nearest and dearest to my heart. Everything I saw seemed to rub salt into the wound received when my parents demanded my return home. I began to doubt my wisdom in coming to see my dear friends again.

This boy visited no more.

CHAPTER ELEVEN

WHAT became of other members of the Finchden community and family? The question is better put this way, than by asking: 'What were Mr Lyward's results? How large a percentage of "successes"? How many "failures"?' These are words most psychiatrists prefer to avoid, words that beg enormous questions; in particular the question by what 'standards' a success or failure is to be judged. By some 'standards' William Randolph Hearst and Henry Ford were each a success; so in 1938 was Mussolini. By some 'standards' at all times Christ was a failure.

A truly loving family thinks of 'results' not only in terms of ordinary success or failure, but in terms of the spirit with which its sons have used success or confronted failure. Such a family, understanding the innate strength or weakness of its members, relates their achievement to the capacity of each and to the difficulties each has been forced to surmount. One could discuss the boys' after lives in terms of 'maladjustment' and 'cure' in the ordinary sense; indeed, a list follows giving the immediate reasons why many of them came, together with a note of their subsequent careers. Such a catalogue, although necessary, ignores Finchden's deeper effect. The prisons from which the boys were delivered were inner prisons, and the keys which released them keys not made with hands. 'Adjustment' therefore must be referred, like 'maladjustment', to a condition within themselves, and not merely to a relationship between them and the world of money and prestige. This qualitative measure of achievement must be deferred for the moment, while we look at some of the boys' after lives in terms of what they did.

The stories have not yet been discussed of about one hundred and seventy boys who, although they lived at Finchden Manor more than six months, actually come into none of the groups mentioned in earlier chapters; they were neither too sick nor too disturbing to keep; they did not leave 'of their own judgment'; they were not withdrawn against Mr Lyward's advice. Some forty of this total number are at Finchden Manor now. About one hundred and thirty thus remain to be considered. A catalogue follows of about twenty 'results'. (In some instances, for obvious reasons, the boys' later careers have been disguised, but the true proportions are kept, and I have tried to bring disguise as close as possible to fact; for example, a distinguished career in one Service or profession will have been given its equivalent in another.) The list is taken at random.

MAX BALDWIN, described as 'beyond control, stealing, lying, truancy, completely up against his family', found a job on the land, changed it on his own initiative, and has settled down happily.

ALAN PIPER, of whom his psychiatrist wrote: 'I cannot warn you too strongly of the depths of his depravity ...,' expelled from two schools, 'pathological liar, anti-social, stealing and destruction of property', commanded a light cruiser during the war, was decorated, and after being seconded to a Government Department, became head of a big business.

RUPERT ANDERSON, 'aggressive and rebellious', visited Finchden at intervals spread over a year and a half. Mr Lyward engaged a special tutor, whom the boy used to bite and kick. Rupert went back to school, became head boy, and got a Blue and a good degree at a University.

STUART ROPER, 'a precocious exhibitionist, a thief, who set a church on fire', passed several difficult examinations, and has done well in journalism, giving particular attention to the problems of those who are now as delinquent as once he was.

HAMISH CONGREVE, 'unable to fit in at school and completely self-willed, dominated by his mother', is happily married and has charge of a successful business.

MERVYN BRUCE, 'sex misdemeanours, infantile, and completely disheartened', came to Finchden Manor for eighteen months after 'a miserable school record of laziness, inertia and inability'. Mr

Lyward prepared him for the Merchant Service examination. He failed at the first two attempts, succeeded at the third, and passed to R.N.V.R., then to R.N., by sheer persistence. He specialized in gunnery and torpedoes.

PAUL SINCLAIR, 'slack, indecent exposure, sexual offences', passed a difficult examination, survived an exceptional ordeal in the war; and is now in charge of a Government Department.

JAMES MERIVALE, 'his breakdown looks ominously like schizophrenia', became a Captain in the Army. He married, and his present work is dedicated and not far short of heroic.

FRED SUTTON, 'a liar, with twenty-one criminal offences, for house-breaking, larceny and roguery', remained at Finchden Manor three years. He found a responsible job, moved of his own accord to another, is married, and appears to be on the road to success.

DUSTY RHODES, 'a thief and possible psychopath, with a severe anxiety neurosis of long standing', took a decent job, married, and has so far done well.

ARTHUR DREW, was 'a thief, brought up away from his broken family by tyrannical relations, with a feeling he was not wanted'. He stayed at Finchden nearly five years, passed difficult examinations brilliantly, took two professional degrees, and is now head of a department in an exceptionally demanding and valuable occupation.

SAM HALE, 'indecent exposure, aggressiveness, bullying', became skilled and well-paid in his job. He came to Finchden Manor from a 'completely feckless family'. He remained a particular friend of Sid's, and has begun to study at night schools, against the time when he will no longer be fit for his present job.

REX YOUNG, 'anti-social behaviour, a rebel, up against his mother', was a vigorous, flamboyant character. He went to an art school after leaving Finchden, joined the R.N., was commissioned in submarines during the war and decorated. He was lost at sea.

REGGIE FOX, came from a broken home. 'Generally a nuisance and completely unreal'. He married, and is in business.

ANGUS SANDYS, was described as 'frail physically and mentally, extremely backward'. He went on a farm and later took a small but responsible job. 'He did very well on the whole.' Also described as mentally backward was

PETER BROWN, He also took to farming, then went into the Army, and returned afterwards to farming. 'Happy and doing well'

JEREMY BLAIR, sent as 'very confused and sexually delinquent', was an adopted child with other special problems. Jeremy passed a number of examinations; did well in the war, and is now Managing Director of a big shipping firm.

PATRICK SUTHERLAND, 'fast developing an obsessional state about himself, his mind, and his work; terribly over-conscientious and afraid of authority', relaxed and recovered sufficiently at Finchden for eighteen months, to pass into the University. After his first term he came back to Finchden and would not return to the University. The University accepted Mr Lyward's statement that he would return, which, a month later, he did. He took a good degree, was decorated in the war, won a big prize in engineering and became second in charge of a department.

PHILLIP ORWELL, 'confirmed liar and sex offender', passed a difficult examination and went on to a highly responsible job. 'If only he had not been so brusque with the Prime Minister', said one of his superiors, 'he would be head of the department.' The brusqueness may be regretted, but when he came to Finchden he was not the person who was ever likely to be in touch with a Prime Minister.

PETER NORMAN, now, twelve years after leaving Finchden, is married with two children and is farming on his own account. He had been sent to Mr Lyward as 'suicidal and unable to keep any job'.

Here is another catalogue of labels attached to boys when they came to Finchden: 'heavily in debt'; 'unable to settle down to a job, confused and feeling persecuted'; 'sexually delinquent and grossly inattentive to studies'; 'a thief'; 'depressed, with wrecking tendencies'; 'manic-depressive'; 'schizophrenic'; 'rebellious, unable to accept school discipline'; 'hysterical, emotionally infantile, egocentric, sexually confused, almost entirely incapable of controlling his behaviour, more neurotic than psychotic'; 'a thief, expelled from school'; 'transferred or expelled from fourteen schools'; 'unable to fit in at school, a truant, full of irrational fears'; 'a liar, with no money sense'; 'hysterical and refusing to eat'; 'suffering from persecution mania'; 'a thief'; 'unable to fit in, a compulsive thinker and bed-wetter'; 'schizoid, a shoplifter, and suffering from persecution mania'; 'profoundly disturbed, and detested by his parents'; 'immature and educationally backward'; 'schizoid, truant, and a thief'; 'hysterical, and a burglar of his own home'; 'truant from school in order to look for his mother, and later put on probation after prostitution on London streets'; 'hysterical, physically violent to his friends, a destroyer of property'; 'a thoroughgoing rebel'; 'backward, difficult, unable to face life'; 'a thief'; 'a liar, thief, and bedwetter'; 'a thief and mentally backward'; 'hostile to all aspects of school life'; 'dangerously anti-social and expelled from two well-known schools in England and America'; 'violent, resentful, possessed with a chronic feeling of guilt'.

So far had these labels been forgotten that both Mr Lyward and his staff said, when I produced this list, "Who on earth were they all?" Once at Finchden the boys did not seem like that, and it may be thought encouraging that those to whom such descriptions were applied afterwards became (not in the same order as the labels): Commissioned, then tea-planting; civil servant, and later an expert on the 'maladjusted'; officer; salesman, helped refugee organization at great personal risk, later an administrator; passed examination top and is doing well; Navy, later an accountant; Navy, later tea-planting in India; aircraft inspector during war, later returned to industrial firm; high Colonial official; fighter pilot, later in aircraft industry; clerk in shipping firm; Woolwich, then R.A.; apprenticed to aircraft firm, farmed in Africa, returned to business combine in this country; teaching; farming; artist, and adviser to well-known firm; apprentice in building trade; apprenticed to electrical firm; farming; teaching; farming; farming; farming, later salesman; farming, later in hotel business; chartered surveyor; director of shipping business; business, developed serious physical illness, now doing secretarial work; runs his own business; owns a market garden; Army; group-captain in R.A.F., now runs large business.

The study of at least thirty-five more stories would yield similar pictures of adjustment to life. These bleak lists indicate merely that boys whom no ordinary school had been able to manage, after being sent to Finchden on doctors' and other recommendations, proved able to manage their lives. Many are now happily married. A few hold positions with important and exacting responsibility. But one should never assume that the boy who later commanded a light cruiser was a 'more remarkable cure' than one originally described as 'crushed, backward, possibly schizophrenic' who managed to hold down some small job. Had a former member of Finchden become an Archbishop, he might still have been a less striking 'success', and his story far less moving, than the stories of those boys described when they came as 'not very promising', and reported later, as 'having found a job and stuck to it', or 'managing all right', or 'carrying on'. Alastair Wilton once dreamed of a horse that had only three legs 'yet seemed to get along all right'. Some boys are born 'with only three legs', and no one can give them a fourth; yet after such boys had left Finchden, they 'got along all right'. Many boys did not go into the kind of jobs their parents might have chosen, the members Mr Lyward's staff possibly among them; yet it cannot be questioned that the latter are 'doing well'.

Four boys remained at Finchden Manor for a number of years, but have never been able to take any place in the world. All four are now in some kind of rest home or rehabilitation centre, from which they correspond with Mr Lyward. They were kept at Finchden at their parents' request, since, as was said of one, 'there seemed nowhere else he could go, once Finchden had made him happier'.

It may be thought premature to speak about ten boys who left Finchden while I was there. But all found jobs in which they have done well, and there seems to be every chance of a steady future.

A small number of old boys have lost touch with Finchden. Some were doing well when last heard of; about four were described as 'not very satisfactory'. One boy, suffering also from severe head injuries, remained at Finchden for a long time, had a 'relapse' soon after leaving, and served a short prison sentence. He appears to have since recovered and the latest news is encouraging. The lives of two other boys have not been successful.

Mr Lyward's 'results', viewed statistically, come to this. Over two hundred and ninety people have lived at Guildables and Finchden Manor as patients. This includes about a score of young men whom Mr Lyward helped, but whose stories have not been considered. About fifteen boys came in the early thirties for brief treatment and were able to return to school. In all about twenty more boys were mentally ill, and had to be sent away for hospital treatment, and a further seven boys caused too much disturbance to be kept. Nine ran away almost at once, and a dozen or so left 'on their own judgment', after staying over a year. Some thirty-five were withdrawn by parents or others, half of them after a few days or weeks, the other half after more than six months. Some of these, and nearly all who left on their own judgment, came back for advice.

Nearly all the remainder have settled down, some in distinguished careers, many in jobs which would have appeared fantastic when they came. Out of forty or fifty, about whom Mr Lyward ventured a firm hope, only one got into trouble at once. In this instance, particular pressure had been brought to bear on the boy to leave, and Mr Lyward for once had gone against his own judgment. Only one of those who left of his own accord caused surprise by making good immediately. All seems well so far with the boys who left recently, and it is probable that the boys now at Finchden will follow the general pattern set in the past. It seems therefore that Mr Lyward has helped more than two hundred boys and young men towards a happier and fuller life, and, of these, has saved scores from the ruin of themselves and others.

Lists are lifeless. To some boys, Mr Lyward gave literally the will to live. In childhood, Peter Herrick had a particularly frightening time at home, and had gone to a preparatory school where the head-master told him that if he masturbated he would die. He came to Finchden for a month, during the war, but stayed longer. After nine months he ran away, but returned and apologized. As he was an athlete he determined to volunteer for particularly dangerous work. Seeing that there was no stopping him, Mr Lyward made use of the kind of treatment he had seldom used since early days, and gave him thirty-two interviews, evening after evening. The boy left for the war, and soon afterwards received terrible wounds which made necessary nearly twenty operations. He told a friend that but for those interviews and his time at Finchden, he would never have wanted to go on living. Finchden, said another boy, had enabled him to survive three years as a prisoner of the Japanese.

Tony Hacket, now in a good job, told me that had it not been for Finchden Manor, he would have spent the rest of his life in prison. Len Fletcher, now a paratrooper, and happy in his way— and particularly contemptuous of teddy-boys—said: 'I always thought before I went to Finchden that I was bound to be a gang leader'. David Norris arrived at Finchden, having been found in possession of a cosh.

'What do you most want?' Mr Lyward asked him.

'A home,' said the boy. 'And I'd have had one if my mum hadn't gone off with the bloody lodger.'

'What would you think of a place where you would be given stern love?' Mr Lyward asked.

'I've never heard of that kind,' the boy answered. 'Sounds as if it might be all right.'

He stayed for eighteen months, did well in the Air Force, and has taken a good civilian job.

Lists do not show how boys who arrived violent, bitter, or morose, because they were undersized, or deformed in some way, or illegitimate, left not only unlikely to revenge themselves upon the world, but strengthened by being enabled to forget or become bigger than their misfortunes. A boy 'of un-coordinated speech and movements, full of self-pity', lost the self-pity, returned home, took up farming, and was described cheerfully by his mother (married to an Air Vice-Marshal) as 'the most adjusted member of the family'. Another, born with a physical injury, used to work himself into appalling frenzies and attack the staff. He took a good job afterwards, and was looking for another 'in which', as he said, 'I can be of more use to people.'

In several instances a boy, though not cured of his personal doubts, has learnt to control them and moved on to a creative life. One, after writing to Mr Lyward of 'the miracle you performed with me', explained in these terms: 'You began the operation of stripping my outer skins. Life has removed most of the others. I feel singularly naked, but I am beginning to enjoy life.'

Many boys acquired the indispensable power to relax and to stand back from themselves. One of the first boys Mr Lyward ever took, after adventures over half the world, married, had children, and settled down happily in England. He once wrote: 'My family all sniff rather at psychology, since it shows up people's faults so plainly. My parents thought I was still a rebel, or a good little boy. There were rows, because I said I wasn't fond of my home. Naturally I said that, because at home I was treated as a know-nothing baby, and at Finchden as an ordinary person. In my spare time now, years later, I often have an 'interview' with myself to straighten things out. I think we all want to keep pace with ourselves, and not just let things slide. If anything unexpected crops up, we aren't always ready to cope naturally, and so we are in danger of attacking it like a rebel, or running away again.'

I was glad to meet Bruno Marcus, now a man of thirty-five, formerly a boy at Finchden. After the war he had been cheated in business and lost everything. Because, he said, of what Finchden had done for him, he had been able to start business again, and was now prospering, with his wife and three children. He talked comically of the ordinary difficulties—taxation, overdrafts, cost of living. 'I worry and can't sleep,' he said. 'If I want to get to sleep, I either take two pheno-barbitones, or think of some particular scene at Finchden, and then I go straight off.' When he made this contrast between an artificial and a natural way to peace, he seemed to me to sum up in a few words exactly what Finchden meant to many of its former members. The boys went into the world as human beings, not doped, and not as machines. Sid once dreamed: 'I was being chased round the corner by an immense robot. I ran out on to the road, climbed into the milk lorry, and drove it past Finchden. I then turned it round and drove it slap into the robot. I jumped clear, but the lorry and the robot collided, leaving a mass of metal on the road.'

Above almost all else in importance, Finchden outflanked self-pity. All their previous lives had disposed the boys to pity themselves. They had been nagged or neglected or misunderstood, they had not been given a fair start, and so on indefinitely, with a reiterated litany of complaints. One boy could write later to Mr Lyward like this. (He was working in a factory and had bicycled a hundred-and-twenty miles to visit Finchden). 'Your talk made me feel rather silly. As a result, I can now laugh at myself better than ever, and how else can one gain real happiness? I had begun to feel too clever, owing no doubt to my constant contact with people who have had little or no chance to develop their thinking faculties.' Another boy, in letters many pages long, wrote from a distant station during the war of 'what Finchden has enabled me to bear and adapt myself to'. In childhood he had witnessed many scenes of violence and brutality between his parents, and been described when he came as of 'manic-depressive make-up'. Many years after leaving, he wrote: 'Thank you for helping me to obtain an optimistic view on life. If it wasn't for that and a sense of humour, I should be right down and yelling 'Nobody loves me!' How stupid that sounds now. And to think that at one time I actually believed it! It is a tremendous help to be able to talk about the worst happening in a humorous way, and at the same time hope for something better'.

To some, even as grown men, Finchden meant a relaxation. One boy, now a busy executive, wrote: 'Each time I leave after a visit to you, I feel that the deadening effect of rushing hither and thither has been removed, as if a hand had been stroking my forehead'. To others it meant a stimulus: 'You open up so many new fields of thought, and you startle one out of comfortable everyday life.'

Many boys felt that they had never entirely left, or that Finchden still accompanied them. 'It amazes me, the way one can again become part of the community on opening the gates,' wrote one, 'though in fact I am part of Finchden anywhere'; and another, from a battlefield, 'You are with me and within me.'

The story of Finchden Manor is overwhelmingly one of happy endings, or rather of happy beginnings, since there the boys were given that chance to start again which life so seldom affords in later years. One thinks of all those other boys, who never went to Finchden, and are now in prison or needlessly unhappy. Over and over again I read in the newspapers the childhood story of some adolescent who was evidently beginning a life of crime; and the details read exactly like the story of some boy who had gone to Finchden, and there been saved, and found himself.

One thinks too of those parents who withdrew their sons against Mr Lyward's advice, and of those others, who continued to confuse their sons, perhaps unwittingly, during the time they were at Finchden or when they came home on holidays. A boy's inability, before he arrived, to pass examinations was nearly always largely due to pressure put on him at home. Several boys who remained unable to pass examinations really continued to be subject to those pressures. There were, for instance, a few boys whose parents, while permitting them to remain at Finchden—sometimes at public expense—spoke slightingly of the place whenever the boy came home, thereby hindering his development and reducing his mind to muddle. A few parents remained unable to acknowledge, despite doctors' evidence, that their son was 'disturbed' and that they themselves were partly responsible. When the boy did not turn out as they wanted, they blamed Mr Lyward. This happened about half-a-dozen times. Their attitude might either impose a continued strain on the boy after he had left Finchden, or cause him to break with them completely; in the latter event such a reconciliation, as came about between Alastair Wilton and his mother, never came about, and these parents lost their sons' love for ever.

Anxieties, national and international, have increased the anxieties of all parents concerning the future of their children. Fathers and mothers, once secure in their riches, have been worried and begun in consequence to put pressure on their sons. Advanced education has come well within the reach of the less wealthy, so that they too, naturally hoping great things, attempt pressure on their sons, with the result that in all social strata a certain kind of boy, often of a high intelligence, has collapsed or got into trouble and been 'deemed maladjusted'.

It has been said before, yet needs to be repeated, that many parents, in their effort to protect their children, forget that it is impossible to inject into the young the experience which they themselves have acquired by living and by making the inevitable mistakes of youth. Endeavouring to enforce rules and regulations, they have denied natural freedom and adventure of living to the child, who, becoming in turn secretive and closed in, has denied the parents access to his heart, whereby they have lost all chance of helping him. Barriers within families have grown all the more difficult to break down where one or both parents has suffered from some inner disturbance—such as jealousy, or dissatisfaction in marriage—which together with anxiety about lack of means has been unloaded on to the child.

The over-emotional, or too coldly practical approach of parents had repelled many of the boys at Finchden, and made them strangers within their own families. It appears that parents, who urge a certain kind of boy too far and too fast, end by defeating their object. The experience of Finchden suggests that ideals and standards are best left 'as stars to mariners', rather than laid down like tramlines. Now, as in the past, parents who exhort their children to lead the same kind of life that they themselves have led, however successful, risk revolt from sons of strong character and despair from the weak. It seems that many parents have not had the emotional tranquillity to reach that understanding of their child's needs, which would give far deeper and more lasting help, than the mere indulgence or refusal of his wants; and that those parents are wise who avoid, as the staff at Finchden avoided, a phrase like 'You've done it *again*!' which tends to make an action appear a habit.

Finchden shows the strength of a treatment rooted in life, and demonstrates the might of disinterested love. Mr Lyward had recreated a lost family, welcoming into it boys whose roots were shrivelled by striking them afresh, and nourishing their natural growth. He disowned none, and never withdrew needed help when the boys had become men. This recreated family, although never able to equal the warmth and strength of the natural family, has none the less illumined the way of love for many parents, and may illumine it for many others, whose love is in danger of becoming parched or distorted by tiredness, possessiveness, or self-interest. It was partly because Mr Lyward could supply the insight which had been lacking in the boys' own families, that he succeeded as he did. This strange power of seeing with the eyes of others is an attribute of love. 'At the first glance they have changed eyes,' said Prospero, watching the encounter of Ferdinand and Miranda. Mr Lyward and his staff offered the boys this love, patiently visualizing, beyond their outward wants, the true nature of their needs.

Is it surprising, then, that Finchden was often able to help parents, or to read of Mr and Mrs Lyward's deep friendships and lifelong associations with the families of boys who had lived and been liberated there? The mother of a boy called Ed Hargreaves had been far more hostile than Mrs Wilton. Years after he had left, at the christening of his first child, she came across to Mr Lyward and said: 'I owe you a thousand thanks.' Norman Gilling had never shown any kind of relationship with his parents. After he finally returned home, his mother wrote: 'It's a kind of dream come true story'. An Austrian Jewish boy came to Finchden, and later rejoined his parents, who had fled from the Nazis to Oslo, and from Oslo to America. From Hawaii the mother invited Mr Lyward to send his own son to live with them, as long as the war lasted. One boy's father took Mr Lyward's place at Finchden for a fortnight. The sister of one boy became a 'patient'; the mother of another; the wife of a third; the entire family of two or three. Paul

Montagu, wild in the worldliest of ways, brought his troubles back to Finchden. His mother, who had given him an allowance, against Mr Lyward's advice, without telling Mr Lyward, wrote: 'You are the only living person who knows what to do with him and how to do it.' After Rex Young was lost at sea, his mother wrote to Mr Lyward: 'You were the only person in the world who really did him any good at all, the one person who understood him and to whom he owed everything.'

Many boys brought their wives and girls to see Mr Lyward; in one or two instances where the marriage had begun to go wrong, they came to him for advice. Many wrote on becoming engaged. One boy spoke of the 'happy culmination, with your aid, of a 27-year battle with myself'; another: 'I am learning things about people and life at an alarming and sometimes painful rate. I shall never forget that I owe it largely to you that I was in a position to take my chance when it came'; a third, just before the birth of his child: 'It has not been possible coherently to express my thanks for the great services you have done me in the past, until now. I have not felt justified in writing to you, since as far as the outside world was able to see, I was not living a life yielding any decent fruit. I have now taken a big job, and am able to look everyone in the face. I realize the more I go on, that without what I learnt at Finchden, I should never have been able to have done this. Our child will soon be born; up to now such a thing would have been the last straw, and beyond us. We can now go serenely ahead.'

'New beginning' is an old phrase. The civilization into which my generation was born had come to so hideous a climax that the time seemed over-ripe to many to tear out its roots and start instead with something different. Many turned to mass solutions. Since we had grown up in a period of mass unemployment and mass war, this is not surprising.

But solutions in themselves, like gifts, are nothing. It is people who have to apply them. The new beginning at Finchden was a new beginning of people. It was before the age of seven that things started to go nearly but not irrevocably wrong with the boys who went there; and the committee of maladjusted children observes that it is during the first cycle of seven years that 'the support and approval of adults (understanding would have been a better word) are the most potent influences on a child's development... and the eighth and ninth years constitute one of the peak periods for reference to child guidance clinics.'

How much disturbance in children and adolescents is to be traced solely to external things? No one is to be taken seriously, who denies that overcrowding and bad housing may have a bad effect on children. Surprise has been expressed that so much adolescent crime should have come lately from 'respectable' homes.

Yet it was from such homes in Germany, swamped by a tidal wave of inflation which, so far, is only felt as a high tide in this country, that so many of the Nazi youth came. The Nazi movement was, in one aspect, the militarisation of maladjusted adolescents by maniac adults, and maladjustment partly a result of an external economic ruin. An economic and social structure which can exclude the possibility of such a ruin will also exclude one cause of maladjustment, and of the frightful consequences which ensue when it grows widespread; but only one.

For it has always been as foolish to assume that people will become happier and more peaceful through an improvement only in their environment, as to assume that environment has nothing to do with disturbance of heart and mind at all. One does not always find that improvements in environment improve people, or that a less extravagant environment spoils them. Changes in environment alter many, but not everybody, either for better or for worse. In external respects, the change of environment at Finchden Manor made some boys more and others less comfortable than they had been at home and school. The real and necessary change, common to all, was in the atmosphere and spirit they found there. This indeed was a transformation, and brought about a transformation in their hearts.

In particular, as we have briefly seen, that gulf between their heads and hearts was closed, those feelings whose development had been arrested were re-awakened and slowly became spontaneous again, as they had seldom been since childhood. Boys in peril of growing up ever more narrow, ever more stunted and one-sided, were able gradually to go forward 'with head and heart reasonably at one'

This is a great achievement and contribution to the world. Never has it been easier than now for young people, whose feelings have lacked understanding and been denied natural response, to find a camouflage. One has to consider influences far beyond and far more insidious than, for example, the much talked-of cinema and comic; many of these, though certainly not all, show stories it is natural and not harmful for a boy to watch. Mr Lyward once said that he would far rather see his boys reading Westerns they enjoyed, than books on sex and psychology they did not understand, and I never noticed any of the latter at Finchden the whole time I was there. Far more important than particular cinemas and comics are the general extension of knowledge, and of the means of communication. Daily they furnish more and more equipment to the mind, from which people deprived in other ways can construct an effective but one-sided self. Much of this material is devoured half-baked by people who could not digest it anyhow. Yet even the man with the most brilliant mind I know, renowned internationally, is not mature, not wise. I should not care to entrust a child to him, and miss continually in such men the humility of Einstein, who declined the Presidency of Israel on the grounds that he had not enough experience of human beings.

We know that we are desperately in need of experts, and that without a vast extension of technological education our survival as an independent nation will be threatened. Yet if our new technologists are to be only technologists, what will their children be? Our deepest inadequacies will not have been removed if, having once landed on the moon, we remain as far as ever from ourselves and one another.

Mr Lyward was no enemy to technological education, nor to specialists. But he saw their dangers, and within the boundaries of Finchden met them, helping the boys to develop a full whole personality, within which any special skill acquired later—and acquired without strain—would only be a part.

To homeless boys he gave the warmth of home, and more; to the friendless, the trustfulness of friendship, and more; to the despaired of, a future, and more; to the self-pitying, clarity, humour, courage, and more. Many were able to create within themselves more than merely that peace, that respite from anxiety, which thousands of people, even in this age, have never lost, whether in crowds, or alone, or in their homes at evening—

> "After sleep has come
> To limbs that had run wild"...

—peace, that begins as a clearing away, and ends as a falling away, of all external pressures. I believe that for many who have lived at Finchden this peace has been creative. A man called Ingram Fisher once told me what his time there had meant to him. He borrowed Jung's image of the mountain. Whatever storms range beneath its summit, the mountain stands unmoved. The image is grand but inadequate, implying too passive a serenity. I prefer an image of water to an image of rock. Sometimes, in wild country, one comes across a torrent pouring into—as it first seems—a lake; the lake turns out to be a reservoir behind a dam, whose harnessed power brings light and warmth to a far-off city. Since none of the Finchden boys had been a genius, none had had that much power. Their lives were streams, not torrents; but several streams, the streams, at the best, of a full/whole personality, spread like the fingers of Henry Carpenter's hand, and harnessed, bringing light and warmth into their immediate surroundings.

I have long had in mind one last analogy with Finchden

from my own profession—writing. Whenever, in an imaginative work, I have to write some passage which I know is going to be difficult, I start by removing from my table all that has accumulated during the past days or weeks. Sometimes I collect this débris into neat piles, sometimes push everything on to the floor: books, annotations, all kinds of imaginings, letters, bills paid and unpaid, newspapers. I sit in front of a cleared space, or lie down. I empty myself of all prejudice, all judgments, all preconceived ideas, all defences of my own, and let anything and everything come freely in. Occasionally, within that cleared space within myself, something dawns, something is born. I become more vividly aware of my true self, as the boys at Finchden became aware of theirs. My own identity begins to merge in the identities of those I am seeking to create. Visualizing their deep needs, I am able to express their superficial active wants. Lovers or beloved, I suffer with them, am happy with them, pretend with them, and am sincere with them.

It is not difficult to surrender one's defences against love, vicariously, in this way, through an imaginary character, or, through an imaginary character, to love vicariously, not looking for return. It is not easy in real life. It was not easy for the boys at Finchden. Grown men and women, whose defences have hardened with the years, find surrender even more painful. Yet once surrender has been made, we admit the beginnings of an inward strength no outward force can shake, and from this seed begin to grow.

The poetry at Finchden was not only in the acceptance of love, but in the growing, until the day acceptance turns to giving, to family, or society, or both, and giving bring fulfilment. Those in whom this seed of love had been most deeply sown would increase the inheritance of happiness, and themselves, not having feared to grow throughout their lives, would face the end of life as an adventure.

> The soul's dark cottage, battered and decayed,
> Lets in new light through chinks that time hath made.
> Stronger through weakness, wiser men become,

As they draw near to their eternal home.
Leaving the old, both worlds at once they view,
Who stand upon the threshold of the new.

One evening, I left Finchden to begin my book. As I drove away, mist was rising from the marshes, islanding Tenterden Church tower. The house looked tranquil and immune. The boys were going to bed. The windows blazed with light, and I heard Riff's gramophone.

Narrow, built-up, the road to London resembled the beaten track which, for many, meant life. Out of sight, on the other side of the house, lay the marshes and wooded slopes which seemed as ever to be awaiting an explorer.

Whatever I might write was certain to be incomplete. Material remained for half-a-dozen books. These limitations I had to accept, if I were ever to begin, or ever make an end. I thought of all the young lives saved; of that small group for whom nothing could be done, yet who still continued, from hospital or prison, to write and ask for news; of those other insecure adolescents, of whose sentence or arrest I should probably read in the evening newspaper, yet who were neither more nor less dangerous than many who had lived at Finchden. The difficulties of parents came to mind; and the State, and the eternal problem how to reconcile the vision of an individual with the rulings of authority.

I thought of the staff at Finchden, renouncing opportunities they made possible for the boys. I wished I could write vividly of Mrs Lyward, who gave the strength that is not seen to a work in which she took no visible part.

I thought of Mr Lyward. In most places the day's work had ended long ago, and most people had returned to homes pleasantly distant from factory or office. But even at this late hour a boy would probably insist on seeing him. Interviews had filled the day, but reports still had to be made out, replies sent to troubled parents and to those all-powerful nobles, Surrey, Kent, Northumberland. To-morrow would bring a visit from some new young educational officer, who had taken the place of an old friend.

All would have to be explained afresh, without tiredness or impatience.

I wondered if Mr Lyward would ever find time to give his story to the world himself; or if his work would be extended and passed on by other means, or was destined to continue as before, inspired by love like the work of others, and like theirs honoured but little known. How great a healer is not only time but life, how patient and radiant a miracle! He had reminded me, and proved, in the world of speed and enmities, that this remains so; stern, forbearing, courteous, light of touch; one of life's beloved teachers; one of the life-givers.

THE END

Finchden
circa 1970's

EPILOGUE

Mr. Lyward died in 1973, and at the end of the next year Finchden Manor closed. Times had moved on. Lyward's radical and improvisational methods only survived into the era of centralised control and risk-aversion because, while he was alive, well-connected professionals who knew his worth ensured that Finchden was allowed its autonomy. Also there is no doubt that Finchden's existence was deeply intertwined with Lyward's personality and singular vision. No other individual or group would have had the unique abilities required to sustain it. Yet, although Finchden Manor may have vanished, the enduring echoes of the work done there most certainly remain.

The "square pegs" he had so carefully nurtured formed a strong and vibrant community. In their lives and the communities they touched, his lessons continued to resonate. Some achieved public recognition, such as musicians Alexis Korner, Robert John Godfrey, Francis Lickerish, Tom Robinson and Danny Kustow, the author Sydney Hopkins and art critic Matthew Collings. As well as these public figures, many others quietly excelled in diverse fields, or simply had fulfilling relationships and family lives, their resilience and individuality fostered by their time at Finchden.

The world has changed significantly since Lyward's time, evolving in complexity. Yet, in classrooms where rigid systems falter, in therapy sessions where theories prove insufficient, and in homes where connection seems elusive, Lyward's ideas seem more and more relevant.

He said his life's work began when, in front of a classroom for the first time, the thought came to him almost like a blow : 'These are people - we are all people together in a room – that is the most important thing about this situation.'

Lyward was fond of quoting the apostle Paul in trying to capture the essence of Finchden Manor : 'We are members one of another'. The fundamental human need for authentic connection that transcends surface behaviour, for an understanding that reaches into the heart of an individual's experience, and for a profound recognition of the inherent worth of every person – these are enduring truths.

circa 1955-1956